Notes On
The Book Of Deuteronomy
Volume I

by

Charles Henry Mackintosh

Double 9
BOOKS

Notes On
The Book Of Deuteronomy
Volume I
by Charles Henry Mackintosh

ISBN: 978-93-64283-49-6

Published by

DOUBLE 9 BOOKS

2/13-B, Ansari Road
Daryaganj, New Delhi – 110002
info@double9books.com
www.double9books.com
Tel. 011-40042856

ABOUT THE AUTHOR

Charles Henry Mackintosh (1820-1896) was a prominent 19th-century Christian preacher, writer, and evangelist, known for his extensive biblical expositions and commentaries. Born in Ireland, Mackintosh became a key figure in the Plymouth Brethren movement, a Christian group that emphasized the authority of Scripture, simplicity of church gatherings, and the priesthood of all believers. Early Life and Conversion, Mackintosh was born into a religiously mixed family; his father was a Roman Catholic, and his mother was a Protestant. This background influenced his deep interest in religious matters. He converted to Christianity at a young age and became deeply involved in evangelical activities. ministry and Writing, Mackintosh's ministry was characterized by his clear, expository preaching and his ability to make complex biblical truths accessible to ordinary people. He was a prolific writer, and his works were widely read and highly regarded within evangelical circles. His most famous work, "Notes on the Pentateuch," is a comprehensive commentary on the first five books of the Bible (Genesis, Exodus, Leviticus, Numbers, and Deuteronomy). These notes are noted for their practical application and spiritual insights. Influence and Legacy, Mackintosh's writings continue to influence Christians, particularly within the Brethren movement and among those who value in-depth Bible study. His ability to combine theological depth with practical application has made his works enduringly popular.

His teachings emphasized the sufficiency of Christ, the importance of the believer's walk with God, and the practical implications of biblical doctrine. Mackintosh's legacy lives on through his numerous writings, which continue to inspire and instruct believers worldwide.

CONTENTS

PREFACE

The value and importance of the Word of God cannot be over-estimated at the present moment. Its integrity and authority are being assailed from almost every quarter and in every form of attack. "If the foundations be destroyed, what can the righteous do?" (Ps. xi. 3.)

Infidel thoughts and principles are not limited to a few literary and speculative minds, as they were fifty years ago, but are now asserted by many who ought to be the true guardians of Christianity and the defenders of the Bible as a revelation from God.

In this way the multitude of the simple and unsuspecting are deceived. If the style of address be pleasing, few care to compare what they have been hearing with the holy Scriptures. The conscience not being aroused, they take no further trouble.

But what of the state of immortal souls, under such a ministry, in view of eternity? On whom does the weight of responsibility rest? Fine-spun theories will never awaken a soul asleep in sin: the lost sinner must be brought face to face with the plain Word of God and the solemn realities of eternity. His voice must be heard. All is absolute, positive, and definite here, whatever infidelity may say. "The Word of the Lord endureth forever."

The burden of the following pages, I am thankful to find, is well calculated to meet and counteract the looseness and indefiniteness of the prevailing teaching of the present day.

And this, I may also say, is the burden of the book of Deuteronomy. The Jewish lawgiver presses with great earnestness the Word of Jehovah on the heart of Israel. It is not a book of ceremonials, but the reminding of the people of their obligation to keep the commandments, the statutes, and the judgments of the Lord.

This is the first moral duty of man in every age—implicit obedience and submission to the revealed will of God. Moses speaks to the children of Israel as a father, and appeals to them in the most tender and loving way. "Hearken, O Israel," he says, "unto the statutes and unto the judgments which I teach you ... ye shall not add unto the word which I command you, neither shall ye diminish aught from it, that ye may keep the commandments of the Lord your God which I command you." And again, he says, "Thou shalt bind them for a sign upon thine hand, and they shall be as frontlets between thine eyes. And thou shalt write them upon the posts of thy house, and on thy gates."

The welfare of the people individually and nationally depended on their faithfully observing these oft-repeated laws. To neglect them was to bring upon themselves the displeasure and chastening of the God of Israel.

But more need not be said here on these subjects. The reader will find in the following pages the most ample unfolding and practical application of these divine exhortations and warnings. But the writer has not confined himself to what Deuteronomy teaches, but has enlarged on what it suggests. In this way we have brought before us the grand cardinal truths of Christianity: a wide circle of truth is embraced, and much that applies to the individual Christian, the family, the household, and the Church of God will be found in the accompanying book.

It now goes forth with the earnest desire that the Lord may be graciously pleased to use it for the glory of His own name, the help of His people, and the eternal blessing of many precious souls.

A. M.

London, November, 1880.

INTRODUCTION

The character of the book on which we now enter is quite as distinct as that of any of the four preceding sections of the Pentateuch. Were we to judge from the title of the book, we might suppose that it is a mere repetition of what we find in previous books. This would be a very grave mistake. There is no such thing as mere repetition in the Word of God. Indeed, God never repeats Himself, either in His Word or in His works. Wherever we trace our God, whether on the page of holy Scripture or in the vast fields of creation, we see divine fullness, infinite variety, marked design; and just in proportion to our spirituality of mind will be our ability to discern and appreciate these things. Here, as in all beside, we need the eye anointed with heavenly eye-salve. What a poor idea must the man entertain of inspiration who could imagine for a moment that the fifth book of Moses is a barren repetition of what is to be found in Exodus, Leviticus, and Numbers! Why, even in human composition we should not expect to find such a flagrant imperfection, much less in the perfect revelation which God has so graciously given us in His holy Word. The fact is, there is not, from cover to cover of the inspired volume, a single superfluous sentence, not one redundant clause, not one statement without its own distinct meaning—its own direct application. If we do not see this, we have yet to learn the depth, force, and meaning of the words, "All scripture is given by inspiration of God."

Precious words! Would they were more thoroughly understood in this our day! It is of the utmost possible importance that the Lord's people should be rooted, grounded, and settled in the grand truth of the plenary inspiration of holy Scripture. It is to be feared that laxity as to this most weighty subject is spreading in the professing church to an appalling extent. In many quarters it has become fashionable to pour contempt upon the idea of plenary inspiration. It is looked upon as the veriest childishness and ignorance. It is regarded by many as a great proof of profound scholarship, breadth of mind, and original thinking to be able, by free criticism, to find out flaws in the precious volume of God. Men presume to sit in judgment upon the Bible as though it were a mere human composition. They undertake to pronounce upon what is and what is not worthy of God. In fact, they do virtually sit in judgment upon God Himself. The present result is, as might be expected, utter darkness and confusion, both for those learned doctors themselves and for all who are so foolish as to listen to them. And as for the future, who can conceive the eternal destiny of all those who shall have to answer before the judgment-seat of Christ for the sin of blaspheming the Word of God, and leading hundreds astray by their infidel teaching?

We shall not, however, occupy time in dwelling upon the sinful folly of infidels and skeptics (even though called Christians), or their puny efforts to cast dishonor upon that peerless volume which our gracious God has caused to be written for our learning. They will some day or other find out their fatal mistake. God grant it may not be too late! And as for us, let it be our deep joy and consolation to meditate upon the Word of God, that so we may ever be discovering some fresh treasure in that exhaustless mine — some new moral glories in that heavenly revelation!

The book of Deuteronomy holds a very distinct place in the inspired canon. Its opening lines are sufficient to prove this.—"These be the words which Moses spake unto all Israel on this side Jordan in the wilderness, in the plain over against the Red Sea, between Paran, and Tophel, and Laban, and Hazeroth, and Dizahab."

Thus much as to the place in which the lawgiver delivered the contents of this marvelous book. The people had come up to the eastern bank of the Jordan, and were about to enter upon the land of promise. Their desert wanderings were nearly ended, as we learn from the third verse, in which the point of time is as distinctly marked as is the geographical position in verse 1.—"It came to pass in the fortieth year, in the eleventh month, on the first day of the month, that Moses spake unto the children of Israel, according unto all that the Lord had given him in commandment unto them."

Thus, not only have we both time and place set forth with divine precision and minuteness, but we also learn, from the words just quoted, that the communications made to the people in the plains of Moab were very far indeed from being a repetition of what has come before us in our studies on the books of Exodus, Leviticus, and Numbers. Of this we have further and very distinct proof in a passage in chapter xxix. of the book on which we are now entering.—"These are the words of the covenant which the Lord commanded Moses to make with the children of Israel in the land of Moab, *beside the covenant which He made with them in Horeb.*"

Let the reader note particularly these words. They speak of two covenants—one at Horeb and one in Moab; and the latter, so far from being a mere repetition of the former, is as distinct from it as any two things can be. Of this we shall have the fullest and clearest evidence in our study of the profound book which now lies open before us.

True, the Greek title of the book, signifying the law a second time, might seem to give rise to the idea of its being a mere recapitulation of what has gone before; but we may rest assured it is not so. Indeed, it would be a very grave error to think so. The book has its own specific place. Its scope and object are as distinct as possible. The grand lesson which it inculcates, from first to last, is *obedience*; and that, too, not in the mere letter, but in the spirit of love and fear—an obedience grounded upon a known and enjoyed relationship—an obedience quickened by the sense of moral obligations of the weightiest and most influential character.

The aged lawgiver—the faithful, beloved, and honored servant of the Lord was about to take leave of the congregation. He was going to heaven and they were about to cross the Jordan, and hence his closing discourses are solemn and affecting in the very highest degree. He reviews the whole of their wilderness history, and that, too, in a manner most touching and impressive. He recounts the scenes and circumstances of their forty eventful years of desert life, in a style eminently calculated to touch the deepest moral springs of the heart. We hang over these most precious discourses with wonder and delight. They possess an incomparable charm, arising from the circumstances under which they were delivered, as well as from their own divinely powerful contents. They speak to us no less effectively than to those for whom they were specially intended. Many of the appeals and exhortations come home to us with a power of application as if they had been uttered but yesterday.

And is it not thus with all Scripture? Are we not continually struck with its marvelous power of adaptation to our own very state, and to the day in which our lot is cast? It speaks to us with a point and freshness as if it were written expressly for us—written this very day. There is nothing like Scripture. Take any human writing of the same date as the book of Deuteronomy; if you could lay your hand on some volume written three thousand years ago, what would you find? A curious relic of antiquity— something to be placed in the British Museum, side by side with an Egyptian mummy, having no application whatever to us or to our time—a musty document—a piece of obsolete writing, practically useless to us, referring only to a state of society and to a condition of things long since passed away and buried in oblivion.

The Bible, on the contrary, is the book for to-day. It is God's own book— His perfect revelation. It is His own very voice speaking to each one of us. It is a book for every age, for every clime, for every class, for every condition—

high and low, rich and poor, learned and ignorant, old and young. It speaks in a language so simple that a child can understand it, and yet so profound that the most gigantic intellect cannot exhaust it. Moreover, it speaks right home to the heart; it touches the deepest springs of our moral being; it goes down to the hidden roots of thought and feeling in the soul; it judges us thoroughly. In a word, it is, as the inspired apostle tells us, "quick and powerful, and sharper than any two-edged sword, piercing even to the dividing asunder of soul and spirit, and of the joints and marrow, and is a discerner of the thoughts and intents of the heart." (Heb. iv. 12.)

And then mark the marvelous comprehensiveness of its range. It deals as accurately and as forcibly with the habits and customs, the manners and maxims of the nineteenth century of the Christian era as with those of the very earliest ages of human existence. It displays a perfect acquaintance with man in every stage of his history. The London of to-day and the Tyre of three thousand years ago are mirrored, with like precision and faithfulness, on the sacred page. Human life, in every stage of its development, is portrayed by a master-hand in that wonderful volume which our God has graciously penned for our learning.

What a privilege to possess such a book!—to have in our hands a divine revelation!—to have access to a book, every line of which is given by inspiration of God!—to have a divinely given history of the past, the present, and the future! Who can estimate aright such a privilege as this?

But then, this book judges man—judges his ways—judges his heart. It tells him the truth about himself. Hence man does not like God's book. An unconverted man would vastly prefer a newspaper or a sensational novel to the Bible. He would rather read the report of a trial in one of our criminal courts than a chapter in the New Testament.

Hence, too, the constant effort to pick holes in God's blessed book. Infidels in every age and of every class have labored hard to find out flaws and contradictions in holy Scripture. The determined enemies of the Word of God are to be found, not only in the ranks of the vulgar, the coarse, and the demoralized, but amongst the educated, the refined, and the cultivated. Just as it was in the days of the apostles, "certain lewd fellows of the baser sort," and "devout and honorable women"—two classes so far removed from each other socially and morally—found one point in which they could heartily agree, namely, the utter rejection of the Word of God and of those who faithfully preached it. (Comp. Acts xiii. 50 with xvii. 5.) So we ever find that men who differ in almost every thing else, agree in their determined opposition to the Bible. Other books are let alone. Men care not to point out defects in Virgil, in Horace, in Homer, or Herodotus; but the Bible they cannot endure, because it exposes them and tells them the truth about themselves and the world to which they belong.

And was it not exactly the same with the living Word—the Son of God—the Lord Jesus Christ when He was here among men? Men hated Him because He told them the truth. His ministry, His words, His ways—His whole life was a standing testimony against the world; hence their bitter and persistent opposition. Other men were allowed to pass on, but He was watched and waylaid at every turn of His path. The great leaders and guides of the people "sought to entangle Him in His talk," to find occasion against Him, in order that they might deliver Him to the power and authority of the governor. Thus it was during His marvelous life; and at the close, when the blessed One was nailed to the cross between two malefactors, these latter were let alone; there were no insults heaped upon them—the chief priests and elders did not wag their heads at them. No; all the insults, all the mockery, all the coarse and heartless vulgarity—all was heaped upon the divine Occupant of the centre cross.

Now, it is well we should thoroughly understand the real source of all the opposition to the Word of God—whether it be the living Word or the written Word. It will enable us to estimate it at its real worth. The devil hates the Word of God—hates it with a perfect hatred; and hence he employs learned infidels to write books to prove that the Bible is not the Word of God, that it cannot be, inasmuch as there are mistakes and discrepancies in it; and not only so, but in the Old Testament we find laws and institutions, habits and practices, unworthy of a gracious and benevolent Being.

To all this style of argument we have one brief and pointed reply. Of all these learned infidels we simply say, They know nothing whatever about the matter. They may be very learned, very clever, very deep and original thinkers, well made up in general literature, very competent to give an opinion on any subject within the domain of natural and moral philosophy, very able to discuss any scientific question; moreover, they may be very amiable in private life—truly estimable characters—kind, benevolent, philanthropic, beloved in private and respected in public,—all this they may be, but being unconverted, and not having the Spirit of God, they are wholly unfit to form, much less to give, a judgment on the subject of holy Scripture. If any one wholly ignorant of astronomy were to presume to sit in judgment on the principles of the Copernican system, these very men of whom we speak would at once pronounce him utterly incompetent to speak, and unworthy to be heard on such a subject. In short, no one has any right whatever to offer an opinion on a matter with which he is unacquainted. This is an admitted principle on all hands; and therefore its application in the case now before us cannot justly be called in question.

Now, the inspired apostle tells us, in his first epistle to the Corinthians, that "the natural man receiveth not the things of the Spirit of God; for they are foolishness unto him; *neither can he know them*, because they are spiritually discerned." This is conclusive. He speaks of man in his natural state, be he ever so learned, ever so cultivated. He is not speaking of any special class of men, but simply of man in his unconverted state—man destitute of the Spirit of God. Some may imagine that the apostle refers to man in a state of barbarism, or savage ignorance. By no means; it is simply man in nature, be he a learned philosopher or an ignorant clown. "He cannot know the things of the Spirit of God." How, then, can he form or give a judgment as to the Word of God? How can he take it upon him to say what is or what is not worthy of God to write? And if he is audacious enough to do so (as, alas! he is), who will be foolish enough to listen to him? His arguments are baseless, his theories worthless, his books only fit for the wastepaper basket; and all this, be it observed, on the universally admitted principle above stated, that no one has any title to be heard on a subject of which he is wholly ignorant.

In this way we dispose of the whole tribe of infidel writers. Who would think of listening to a blind man on the subject of light and shade? And yet such a man has much more claim to be heard than an unconverted man on the subject of inspiration. Human learning, however extensive and varied—human wisdom, however profound, cannot qualify a man to form a judgment upon the Word of God. No doubt a scholar may examine and collate MSS. simply as a matter of criticism; he may be able to form a judgment as to the question of authority for any particular reading of a passage; but this is a different matter altogether from an infidel writer undertaking to pronounce judgment upon the revelation which God has, in His infinite goodness, given to us. We maintain that no man can do this. It is only by the Spirit, who Himself inspired the holy Scriptures, that those Scriptures can be understood and appreciated. The Word of God must be received upon its own authority. If man can judge it or reason upon it, it is not the Word of God at all. Has God given us a revelation, or has He not? If He has, it must be absolutely perfect in every respect; and being such, it must be entirely beyond the range of human judgment. Man is no more competent to judge Scripture than he is to judge God. The Scriptures judge man; not man the Scriptures.

This makes all the difference. Nothing can be more miserably contemptible than the books which infidels write against the Bible. Every page, every paragraph, every sentence, only goes to illustrate the truth of the apostle's statement, that "the natural man receiveth not the things of the Spirit of God; ... *neither can he know them*, because they are spiritually discerned." Their gross ignorance of the subject with which they undertake to deal is only equaled by their self-confidence. Of their irreverence we say nothing; for who would think of looking for reverence in the writings of infidels? We might perhaps look for a little modesty were it not that we are fully aware of the bitter *animus* which lies at the root of all such writings, and renders them utterly unworthy of a moment's consideration. Other books may have a dispassionate examination; but the precious book of God is approached with the foregone conclusion that it is not a divine revelation, because, forsooth, infidels tell us that God could not give us a written revelation of His mind.

How strange! Men can give us a revelation of their thoughts (and infidels have done so pretty plainly), but God cannot! What folly! What presumption! Why, we may lawfully inquire, could not God reveal His mind to His creatures? Why should it be thought a thing incredible? For no reason whatever, but because infidels would have it so. The wish is, in this case assuredly, father to the thought. The question raised by the old serpent in the garden of Eden nearly six thousand years ago, has been passed on from age to age by all sorts of skeptics, rationalists, and infidels, namely, "Hath God said?" We reply, with intense delight, Yes; blessed be His holy name, He has spoken—spoken to us. He has revealed His mind; He has given us the holy Scriptures. "*All scripture is given by inspiration of God*, and is profitable for doctrine, for reproof, for correction, for instruction in righteousness; that the man of God may be perfect [αρτιος], thoroughly furnished unto all good works." And again, "Whatsoever things were written aforetime were written for our learning, that we through patience and comfort of the Scriptures might have hope." (2 Tim. iii. 16, 17; Rom. xv. 4.)

The Lord be praised for such words! They assure us that all Scripture is given of God, and that all Scripture is given to us. Precious link between the soul and God! What tongue can tell the value of such a link? God has spoken—spoken to us. His Word is a rock against which all the waves of infidel thought dash themselves in contemptible impotency, leaving it in its own divine strength and eternal stability. Nothing can touch the Word of God. Not all the powers of earth and hell, men and devils combined can ever move the Word of God. There it stands, in its own moral glory, spite of all the assaults of the enemy, from age to age. "Forever, O Lord, Thy Word is settled in heaven." "Thou hast magnified Thy Word above all Thy name." What remains for us? Just this: "Thy Word have I hid in my heart, that I might not sin against Thee." Here lies the deep secret of peace. The heart is linked to the throne—yea, to the very heart of God by means of His most precious Word, and is thus put in possession of a peace which the world can neither give nor take away. What can all the theories, the reasonings, and the arguments of infidels effect? Just nothing. They are esteemed as the dust of the summer threshing-floor. To one who has really learnt, through grace, to confide in the Word of God—to rest on the authority of holy Scripture, all the infidel books that ever were written are utterly worthless, pointless, powerless; they display the ignorance and terrible presumption of the writers; but as to Scripture, they leave it just where it ever has been and ever will be—"settled in heaven," as immovable as the throne of God.[2] The assaults of infidels cannot touch the throne of God, neither can they touch His Word; and, blessed be His name, neither can they touch the peace that flows through the heart that rests on that imperishable foundation. "Great peace have they that love Thy law, and nothing shall offend them." "The Word of our God shall stand forever." "All flesh is as grass, and all the glory of man as the flower of grass. The grass withereth, and the flower thereof falleth away; but the Word of the Lord endureth forever. And this is the Word which by the gospel is preached unto you." (1 Pet. i. 24, 25.)

Here we have the same precious golden link again. The Word which has reached us in the form of glad tidings is the Word of the Lord which endureth forever; and hence our salvation and our peace are as stable as the Word on which they are founded. If *all* flesh is as grass, and *all* the glory of man as the flower of grass, then what are the arguments of infidels worth? They are as worthless as withered grass or a faded flower; and the men who put them forth and those who are moved by them will find them to be so, sooner or later. Oh, the sinful folly of arguing against the Word of God—arguing against the only thing in all this world that can give rest and consolation to the poor, weary human heart—arguing against that which brings the glad tidings of salvation to poor lost sinners—brings them fresh from the heart of God!

But we may perhaps here be met by the question so often raised, and which has troubled many and led them to fly for refuge to what is called "the authority of the church." The question is this: "How are we to know that the book which we call the Bible is the Word of God?" Our answer to this question is a very simple one—it is this: The One who has graciously given us the blessed book can give us also the certainty that the book is from Him. The same Spirit who inspired the various writers of the holy Scriptures can make us know that those Scriptures are the very voice of God speaking to us. It is only by the Spirit that any one can discern this. As we have already seen, "the natural man receiveth not the things of the Spirit of God; ... neither can he know them, because they are spiritually discerned." If the Holy Spirit does not make us know, and give us the certainty that the Bible is the Word of God, no man or body of men can possibly do it; and on the other hand, if He does give us the blessed certainty, we do not need the testimony of man.

We freely admit that on this great question a shadow of uncertainty would be positive torture and misery; but who can give us certainty? God alone. If all the men upon earth were to agree in their testimony to the authority of holy Scripture—if all the councils that ever sat, all the doctors that ever taught, all the fathers that ever wrote, were in favor of the dogma of plenary inspiration—if the universal church, if every denomination in christendom were to assent to the truth that the Bible is, in very deed, the Word of God—in a word, if we had all the human authority that could possibly be had in reference to the integrity of the Word of God, it would be utterly insufficient as a ground of certainty; and if our faith were founded on that authority, it would be perfectly worthless. God alone can give us the certainty that He has spoken in His Word; and blessed be His name, when He gives it, all the arguments, all the cavilings, all the quibblings, all the questionings of infidels, ancient and modern, are as the foam on the water, the smoke from the chimney-top, or the dust on the floor. The true believer rejects them as so much worthless rubbish, and rests in holy tranquillity in that peerless revelation which our God has graciously given us.

It is of the very last possible importance for the reader to be thoroughly clear and settled as to this grave question, if he would be raised above the influence of infidelity on the one hand and superstition on the other. Infidelity undertakes to tell us that God has not given us a book-revelation of His mind—could not give it: Superstition undertakes to tell us that even though God has given us a revelation, yet we cannot be assured of it without man's authority, nor understand it without man's interpretation. Now it is well to see that by both alike we are deprived of the precious boon of holy Scripture. And this is precisely what the devil aims at. He wants to rob us of the Word of God; and he can do this quite as effectually by the apparent self-distrust that humbly and reverently looks to wise and learned men for authority, as by an audacious infidelity that boldly rejects all authority, human or divine.

Take a case. A father writes a letter to his son at Canton—a letter full of the affection and tenderness of a father's heart. He tells him of his plans and arrangements, tells him of every thing that he thinks would interest the heart of a son—every thing that the love of a father's heart could suggest. The son calls at the post-office in Canton to inquire if there is a letter from his father. He is told by one official that there is no letter, that his father has not written and could not write—could not communicate his mind by such a medium at all, that it is only folly to think of such a thing. Another official comes forward, and says, Yes; there is a letter here for you, but you cannot possibly understand it; it is quite useless to you, indeed it can only do you positive mischief inasmuch as you are quite unable to read it aright. You must leave the letter in our hands, and we will explain to you such portions of it as we consider suitable for you. The former of these two officials represents Infidelity; the latter, Superstition. By both alike would the son be deprived of the longed-for letter—the precious communication from his father's heart. But what, we may inquire, would be his answer to these unworthy officials? A very brief and pointed one we may rest assured. He would say to the first, I know my father can communicate his mind to me by letter, and that he has done so. He would say to the second, I know my father can make me understand his mind far better than you can. He would say to both, and that, too, with bold and firm decision. Give me up at once my father's letter; it is addressed to me, and no man has any right to withhold it from me.

Thus, too, should the simple-hearted Christian meet the *insolence* of Infidelity and the *ignorance* of Superstition—the two special agencies of the devil, in this our day, in setting aside the precious Word of God. "My Father has communicated His mind, and He can make me understand the communication."—"All Scripture is given *by inspiration of God;*" and, "Whatsoever things were written aforetime were written *for our learning.*" Magnificent answer to every enemy of God's precious and peerless revelation, be he rationalist or ritualist!

We do not attempt to offer any apology to the reader for this lengthened introduction to the book of Deuteronomy. Indeed we are only too thankful for an opportunity of bearing our feeble testimony to the grand truth of the divine inspiration of the holy Scriptures. We feel it to be our sacred duty, as most surely it is our high privilege, to press upon all to whom we have access, the immense importance—yea, the absolute necessity of the most uncompromising decision on this point. We must faithfully maintain, at all cost, the divine authority, and therefore the absolute supremacy and all-sufficiency, of the Word of God at all times, in all places, for all purposes. We must hold to it that the Scriptures, having been given of God, are complete, in the very highest and fullest sense of the word; that they do not need any human authority to accredit them, or any human voice to make them available: they speak for themselves, and carry their own credentials with them. All we have to do is to believe and obey, not to reason or discuss. God has spoken it: it is ours to hearken, and yield an unreserved and reverent obedience.

This is one grand leading point throughout the book of Deuteronomy, as we shall see in the progress of our meditations; and never was there a moment, in the history of the Church of God, in which it was more needful to urge home on the human conscience the necessity of implicit obedience to the Word of God. It is, alas! but little felt. Professing Christians, for the most part, seem to consider that they have a right to think for themselves—to follow their own reason, their own judgment, or their own conscience. They do not believe that the Bible is a divine and universal guide-book. They think there are very many things in which we are left to choose for ourselves; hence the almost numberless sects, parties, creeds, and schools of thought. If human opinion be allowed at all, then, as a matter of course, one man has as good a right to think as another; and thus it has come to pass that the professing church has become a proverb and a by-word for division.

And what is the sovereign remedy for this widespread disease? Here it is: *Absolute and complete subjection to the authority of holy Scripture*. It is not men going to Scripture to get *their* opinions and *their* views confirmed; but going to Scripture to get the mind of God as to every thing, and bowing down their whole moral being to divine authority. This is the one pressing need of the day in which our lot is cast—reverent subjection, in all things, to the supreme authority of the Word of God. No doubt, there will be variety in our measure of intelligence, in our apprehension and appreciation of Scripture; but what we specially urge upon all Christians is that condition of soul, that attitude of heart expressed in those precious words of the psalmist, "Thy Word have I hid in mine heart, that I might not sin against Thee." This, we may rest assured, is grateful to the heart of God. "To this man will I look, even to him that is poor and of a contrite spirit, and trembleth at My Word."

Here lies the true secret of moral security. Our knowledge of Scripture may be very limited; but if our reverence for it be profound, we shall be preserved from a thousand errors—a thousand snares. And then there will be steady growth. We shall grow in the knowledge of God, of Christ, and of the written Word; we shall delight to draw from those living and exhaustless depths of holy Scripture, and to range through those green pastures which infinite grace has so freely thrown open to the flock of Christ. Thus shall the divine life be nourished and strengthened; the Word of God will become more and more precious to our souls, and we shall be lead, by the powerful ministry of the Holy Ghost, into the depth, fullness, majesty, and moral glory of holy Scripture. We shall be delivered completely from the withering influences of all mere systems of theology, high, low, or moderate—a most blessed deliverance! We shall be able to tell the advocates of all the schools of divinity under the sun that whatever elements of truth they may have in their systems we have in divine perfectness in the Word of God; not twisted and tortured to make them fit into a system, but in their right place in the wide circle of divine revelation which has its eternal centre in the blessed Person of our Lord and Saviour Jesus Christ.

CHAPTER I

"These be the words which Moses spake unto all Israel on this side Jordan in the wilderness, in the plain over against the Red Sea, between Paran, and Tophel, and Laban, and Hazeroth, and Dizahab. (There are eleven days' journey from Horeb, by the way of Mount Seir, unto Kadeshbarnea.)"

The inspired writer is careful to give us, in the most precise manner, all the bearings of the place in which the words of this book were spoken in the ears of the people. Israel had not yet crossed the Jordan; they were just beside it, and over against the Red Sea where the mighty power of God had been so gloriously displayed nearly forty years before. The whole position is described with a minuteness which shows how thoroughly God entered into every thing that concerned His people. He was interested in all their movements and in all their ways. He kept a faithful record of all their encampments. Their was not a single circumstance connected with them, however trifling, beneath His gracious notice. He attended to every thing. His eye rested continually on that assembly as a whole, and on each member in particular. By day and by night He watched over them. Every stage of their journey was under His immediate and most gracious superintendence. There was nothing, however small, beneath His notice; nothing, however great, beyond His power.

Thus it was with Israel in the wilderness of old, and thus it is with the Church now—the Church as a whole, and each member in particular. A Father's eye rests upon us continually, His everlasting arms are around and underneath us day and night. "He withdraweth not His eyes from the righteous." He counts the hairs of our heads, and enters, with infinite goodness, into every thing that concerns us. He has charged Himself with all our wants and all our cares. He would have us to cast our every care on Him, in the sweet assurance that He careth for us. He most graciously invites us to roll our every burden over on Him, be it great or small.

All this is truly wonderful. It is full of deepest consolation. It is eminently calculated to tranquilize the heart, come what may. The question is, Do we believe it? are our hearts governed by the faith of it? Do we really believe that the almighty Creator and Upholder of all things, who bears up the pillars of the universe, has graciously undertaken to do for us all the journey through? Do we thoroughly believe that "the Possessor of heaven and earth" is our Father? and that He has charged Himself with all our wants from first to last? Is our whole moral being under the commanding power of those words of the inspired apostle, "He that spared not His own Son, but delivered Him up for us all, how shall He not with Him also freely give us all things?" Alas! it is to be feared that we know but little of the power of these grand yet simple truths. We talk about them, we discuss them, we profess them, we give a nominal assent to them; but with all this, we prove, in our daily life—in the actual details of our personal history, how feebly we enter into them. If we truly believed that our God has charged Himself with all our necessities—if we were finding all our springs in Him—if He were a perfect covering for our eyes and a resting-place for our hearts, could we possibly be looking to poor creature-streams, which so speedily dry up and disappoint our hearts? We do not and cannot believe it. It is one thing to hold the theory of the life of faith, and another thing altogether to live that life. We constantly deceive ourselves with the notion that we are living by faith, when in reality we are leaning on some human prop, which sooner or later is sure to give way.

Reader, is it not so? Are we not constantly prone to forsake the Fountain of living waters, and hew out for ourselves broken cisterns, which can hold no water? And yet we speak of living by faith! We profess to be looking only to the living God for the supply of our need, whatever that need may be, when, in point of fact, we are sitting beside some creature-stream and looking for something there. Need we wonder if we are disappointed? How could it possibly be otherwise? Our God will not have us dependent upon aught or any one but Himself. He has, in manifold places in His Word, given us His judgment as to the true character and sure result of all creature-confidence. Take the following most solemn passage from the prophet Jeremiah: "Cursed be the man that trusteth in man, and maketh flesh his arm, and whose heart departeth from the Lord. For he shall be like the heath in the desert, and shall not see when good cometh; but shall inhabit the parched places in the wilderness, in a salt land and not inhabited." And then mark the contrast—"Blessed is the man that trusteth in the Lord, and whose hope the Lord is: for he shall be as a tree planted by the waters, and that spreadeth out her roots by the river, and shall not see when heat cometh, but her leaf shall be green; and shall not be careful in the year of drought, neither shall cease from yielding fruit." (Jer. xvii. 5-8.)

Here we have, in language divinely forcible, clear, and beautiful, both sides of this most weighty subject put before us. Creature-confidence brings a certain curse; it can only issue in barrenness and desolation. God, in very faithfulness, will cause every human stream to dry up—every human prop to give way, in order that we may learn the utter folly of turning away from Him. What figure could be more striking or impressive than those used in the above passage?—"A heath in the desert," "parched places in the wilderness," "a salt land not inhabited." Such are the figures used by the Holy Ghost to illustrate all mere human dependence—all confidence in man.

But on the other hand, what can be more lovely or more refreshing than the figures used to set forth the deep blessedness of simple trust in the Lord?—"A tree planted by the waters," "spreading out her roots by the rivers," the leaf ever green, the fruit never ceasing. Perfectly beautiful! Thus it is with the man who trusteth in the Lord, and whose hope the Lord is. He is nourished by those eternal springs that flow from the heart of God. He drinks at the Fountain, life-giving and free. He finds all his resources in the living God. There may be "heat," but he does not see it; "the year of drought" may come, but he is not careful. Ten thousand creature-streams may dry up, but he does not perceive it, because he is not dependent upon them; he abides hard by the ever-gushing Fountain. He can never want any good thing. He lives by faith.

And here, while speaking of the life of faith—that most blessed life, let us clearly understand what it is, and carefully see that we are living it. We sometimes hear this life spoken of in a way by no means intelligent. It is not unfrequently applied to the mere matter of trusting God for food and raiment. Certain persons who happen to have no visible source of temporal supplies—no settled income—no property of any kind, are singled out and spoken of as "living by faith," as if that marvelous and glorious life had no higher sphere or wider range than temporal things—the mere supply of our bodily wants.

Now, we cannot too strongly protest against this most unworthy view of the life of faith. It limits its sphere and lowers its range in a manner perfectly intolerable to any one who understands aught of its most holy and precious mysteries. Can we for a moment admit that a Christian who happens to have a settled income of any kind is to be deprived of the privilege of living by faith? Or, further, can we permit that life to be limited and lowered to the mere matter of trusting God for the supply of our bodily wants? Does it soar no higher than food and raiment? Does it give no more elevated thought of God than that He will not let us starve or go naked?

Far away, and away forever, be the unworthy thought! The life of faith must not be so treated. We cannot allow such a gross dishonor to be offered to it, or such a grievous wrong done to those who are called to live it. What, we would ask, is the meaning of those few but weighty words, "The just shall live by faith"? They occur, first of all, in Habakkuk ii. They are quoted by the apostle in Romans i, where he is, with a master-hand, laying the solid foundations of Christianity. He quotes them again in Galatians iii, where he is, with intense anxiety, recalling those bewitched assemblies to those solid foundations which they, in their folly, were abandoning. Finally, he quotes them again in chapter x. of his epistle to the Hebrews, where he is warning his brethren against the danger of casting away their confidence and giving up the race.

From all this we may assuredly gather the immense importance and practical value of the brief but far-reaching sentence, "The just shall live by faith." But to whom does it apply? Is it only for a few of the Lord's servants, here and there, who happen to have no settled income? We utterly reject the thought. It applies to every one of the Lord's people. It is the high and happy privilege of all who come under the title—that blessed title, "The just." We consider it a very grave error to limit it in any way. The moral effect of such limitation is most injurious. It gives undue prominence to one department of the life of faith which, if any distinction be allowable, we should judge to be the very lowest. But in reality, there should be no distinction: the life of faith is one. Faith is the grand principle of the divine life from first to last. By faith we are justified, and by faith we live; by faith we stand, and by faith we walk. From the starting-post to the goal of the Christian course it is all by faith.

Hence, therefore, it is a serious mistake to single out certain persons who trust the Lord for temporal supplies, and speak of them as living by faith, as if they alone did so. And not only so, but such persons are held up to the gaze of the Church of God as something wonderful; and the great mass of Christians are led to think that the privilege of living by faith lies entirely beyond their range. In short, they are led into a complete mistake as to the real character and sphere of the life of faith, and thus they suffer materially in the inner life.

Let the Christian reader, then, distinctly understand that it is his happy privilege, whoever he be or whatever be his position, to live a life of faith, in all the depth and fullness of that word. He may, according to his measure, take up the language of the blessed apostle, and say, "The life that I live in the flesh, I live by the faith of the Son of God, who loved me, and gave Himself for me." Let nothing rob him of this high and holy privilege which belongs to every member of the household of faith. Alas! we fail. Our faith is weak, when it ought to be strong, bold, and vigorous. Our God delights in a bold faith. If we study the gospels, we shall see that nothing so refreshed and delighted the heart of Christ as a fine bold faith—a faith that understood

Him and drew largely upon Him. Look, for example, at the Syrophenician in Mark vii, and the centurion in Luke vii.

True, He could meet a weak faith—the very weakest. He could meet an "If Thou *wilt*" with a gracious "I will"—an "If Thou *canst*" with "If thou canst believe, all things are possible." The faintest look, the feeblest touch, was sure to meet with a gracious response; but the Saviour's heart was gratified and His spirit refreshed when He could say, "O woman, great is thy faith; be it unto thee even as thou wilt;" and again, "I have not found so great faith, no, not in Israel."

Let us remember this. We may rest assured it is the very same to-day as when our blessed Lord was here amongst men. He loves to be trusted, to be used, to be drawn upon. We can never go too far in counting on the love of His heart or the strength of His hand. There is nothing too small, nothing too great for Him; He has all power in heaven and on earth; He is head over all things to His Church; He holds the universe together; He upholds all things by the word of His power. Philosophers talk of the forces and laws of nature: the Christian thinks with delight of Christ, His hand, His Word, His mighty power. By Him all things were created, and by Him all things consist.

And then His love! What rest, what comfort, what joy, to know and remember that the almighty Creator and Upholder of the universe is the everlasting Lover of our souls! that He loves us perfectly; that His eye is ever upon us, His heart ever toward us; that He has charged Himself with all our wants, whatever these wants may be—whether physical, mental, or spiritual! There is not a single thing within the entire range of our necessities that is not treasured up for us in Christ. He is Heaven's treasury—God's storehouse, and all this for us.

Why, then, should we ever turn to another? Why should we ever, directly or indirectly, make known our wants to a poor fellow-mortal? Why not go straight to Jesus? Do we want sympathy? Who can sympathize with us like our most merciful High-Priest, who is touched with the feeling of our infirmities? Do we want help of any kind? Who can help us like our almighty Friend, the Possessor of unsearchable riches? Do we want counsel or guidance? Who can give it like the blessed One who is the very wisdom of God, and who is made of God unto us wisdom? Oh, let us not wound His loving heart, and dishonor His glorious name by turning away from Him. Let us jealously watch against the tendency so natural to us to cherish human hopes, creature-confidences, and earthly expectations. Let us abide hard by the Fountain, and we shall never have to complain of the streams.

In a word, let us seek to live by faith, and thus glorify God in our day and generation.

We shall now proceed with our chapter; and in so doing, we would call the reader's attention to verse 2. It is certainly a very remarkable parenthesis. "(There are eleven days' journey from Horeb, by the way of Mount Seir, unto Kadesh-barnea.)" Eleven days! and yet it took them forty years! How was this? Alas! we need not travel far for the answer. It is only too like ourselves. How slowly we get over the ground! What windings and turnings! How often we have to go back and travel over the same ground again and again! We are slow travelers, because we are slow learners. It may be we feel disposed to marvel how Israel could have taken forty years to accomplish a journey of eleven days; but we may, with much greater reason, marvel at ourselves. We, like them, are kept back by our unbelief and slowness of heart; but there is far less excuse for us than for them, inasmuch as our privileges are so very much higher.

Some of us have much reason to be ashamed of the time we spend over our lessons. The words of the blessed apostle do but too forcibly apply to us — "For when for the time ye ought to be teachers, ye have need that one teach you again which be the first principles of the oracles of God; and are become such as have need of milk, and not of strong meat." Our God is a faithful and wise as well as a gracious and patient Teacher. He will not permit us to pass cursorily over our lessons. Sometimes, perhaps, we think we have mastered a lesson, and we attempt to move on to another; but our wise Teacher knows better, and He sees the need of deeper ploughing. He will not have us mere theorists or smatterers: He will keep us, if need be, year after year at our scales until we learn to sing.

Now, while it is very humbling to us to be so slow in learning, it is very gracious of Him to take such pains with us, in order to make us sure. We have to bless Him for His mode of teaching as for all beside — for the wonderful patience with which He sits down with us over the same lesson again and again, in order that we may learn it thoroughly.[3]

"And it came to pass in the fortieth year, in the eleventh month, on the first day of the month, that Moses spake unto the children of Israel, according unto all that the Lord had given him in commandment unto them." (Ver. 3.) These few words contain a volume of weighty instruction for every servant of God — for all who are called to minister in the Word and doctrine. Moses gave the people just what he himself had received from God — nothing more, nothing less. He brought them into direct contact with the living Word of Jehovah. This is the grand principle of ministry at all times. Nothing else is of any real value. The Word of God is the only thing that will stand. There is divine power and authority in it. All mere human teaching, however interesting—however attractive at the time, will pass away and leave the soul without any foundation to rest upon.

Hence it should be the earnest, jealous care of all who minister in the assembly of God, to preach the Word in all its purity, in all its simplicity; to give it to the people as they get it from God; to bring them face to face with the veritable language of holy Scripture. Thus will their ministry tell, with living power, on the hearts and consciences of their hearers. It will link the soul with God Himself, by means of the Word, and impart a depth and solidity which no human teaching can ever produce.

Look at the blessed apostle Paul. Hear him express himself on this weighty subject.—"And I, brethren, when I came to you, came not with excellency of speech or of wisdom, declaring unto you the testimony of God. For I determined not to know any thing among you, save Jesus Christ, and Him crucified. And I was with you in weakness, and in fear, and in much trembling. And my speech and my preaching was not with enticing words of man's wisdom, but in demonstration of the Spirit and of power." What was the object of all this fear and trembling? "That your faith should not stand in the wisdom of men, but in the power of God." (1 Cor. ii. 1-5.)

This true-hearted faithful servant of Christ sought only to bring the souls of his hearers into direct personal contact with God Himself. He sought not to link them with Paul. "Who then is Paul, and who is Apollos, but ministers *by whom ye believed?*" All false ministry has for its object the attaching of souls to itself. Thus the minister is exalted, God is shut out, and the soul left without any divine foundation to rest upon. True ministry, on the contrary, as seen in Paul and Moses, has for its blessed object the attaching of the soul to God. Thus the minister gets his true place—simply an instrument, God is exalted, and the soul established on a sure foundation which can never be moved.

But let us hear a little more from our apostle on this most weighty subject. "Moreover, brethren, I declare unto you the gospel which I preached unto you, which also ye have received, and wherein ye stand; by which also ye are saved, if ye keep in memory what I preached unto you, unless ye have believed in vain. *For I delivered unto you first of all that which I also received"* — nothing more, nothing less, nothing different—"how that Christ died for our sins *according to the Scriptures;* and that He was buried, and that He rose again the third day *according to the Scriptures."*

This is uncommonly fine. It demands the serious consideration of all who would be true and effective ministers of Christ. The apostle was careful to allow the pure stream to flow down from its living source—the heart of

God, into the souls of the Corinthians. He felt that nothing else was of any value. If he had sought to link them on to himself, he would have sadly dishonored his Master, done them a grievous wrong, and he himself would most assuredly suffer loss in the day of Christ.

But no; Paul knew better. He would not, for worlds, lead any to build upon himself. Hear what he says to his much-loved Thessalonians.—"For this cause also thank we God without ceasing, because, when *ye received the Word of God* which ye heard of us, ye received it *not as the word of men*, but *as it is in truth, the Word of God*, which effectually worketh also in you that believe." (1 Thess. ii. 13.)

We feel solemnly responsible to commend this grave and important point to the serious consideration of the Church of God. If all the professed ministers of Christ were to follow the example of Moses and Paul, in reference to the matter now before us, we should witness a very different condition of things in the professing church. But the plain and serious fact is, that the Church of God, like Israel of old, has wholly departed from the authority of His Word. Go where you will, and you find things done and taught which have no foundation in Scripture. Things are not only tolerated but sanctioned and stoutly defended which are in direct opposition to the mind of Christ. If you ask for the divine authority for this, that, and the other institution or practice, you will be told that Christ has not given us directions as to matters of church government; that in all questions of ecclesiastical polity, clerical orders, and liturgical services, He has left us free to act according to our consciences, judgment, or religious feelings; that it is simply absurd to demand a "Thus saith the Lord" for all the details connected with our religious institutions: there is a broad margin left to be filled up according to our national customs and our peculiar habits of thought. It is considered that professing Christians are left perfectly free to form themselves into so-called churches, to choose their own form of government, to make their own arrangements, and to appoint their own office-bearers.

Now the question which the Christian reader has to consider is, "Are these things so?" Can it be that our Lord Christ has left His Church without guidance as to matters so interesting and momentous? Can it be possible that the Church of God is worse off, in the matter of instruction and authority, than Israel? In our studies on the books of Exodus, Leviticus, and Numbers, we have seen (for who could help seeing?) the marvelous pains which Jehovah took to instruct His people as to the most minute particulars connected with their public worship and private life. As to the tabernacle, the temple, the priesthood, the ritual, the various feasts and sacrifices, the periodical solemnities, the months, the days, the very hours, all was ordered and settled with divine precision. Nothing was left to mere human arrangement. Man's wisdom, his judgment, his reason, his conscience, had nothing whatever to do in the matter. Had it been left to man, how should we ever have had that admirable, profound, and far-reaching typical system which the inspired pen of Moses has set before us? If Israel had been allowed to do what (as some would fain persuade us) the Church is allowed, what confusion, what strife, what division, what endless sects and parties, would have been the inevitable result!

But it was not so. The Word of God settled every thing. "As the Lord commanded Moses." This grand and influential sentence was appended to every thing that Israel had to do, and to every thing they were not to do. Their national institutions and their domestic habits—their public and their private life, all came under the commanding authority of "Thus saith the Lord." There was no occasion for any member of the congregation to say, I cannot see this, or, I cannot go with that, or, I cannot agree with the other. Such language could only be regarded as the fruit of self-will. He might just as well say, I cannot agree with Jehovah. And why? Simply because the Word of God had spoken as to every thing, and that, too, with a clearness and simplicity which left no room whatever for human discussion. Throughout the whole of the Mosaic economy there was not the breadth of a hair of margin left in which to insert the opinion or the judgment of man. It pertained not to man to add the weight of a feather to that vast system of types and shadows which had been planned by the divine mind, and set forth in language so plain and pointed, that all Israel had to do was to *obey*— not to argue, not to reason, not to discuss, but to obey.

Alas! alas! they failed, as we know. They did their own will; they took their own way; they did "every man that which was right in his own eyes." They departed from the Word of God, and followed the imaginations and devices of their own evil heart, and brought upon themselves the wrath and indignation of offended Deity, under which they suffer till this day, and shall yet suffer unexampled tribulation.

But all this leaves untouched the point on which we are just now dwelling. Israel had the oracles of God, and these oracles were divinely sufficient for their guidance in every thing. There was no room left for the commandments and doctrines of men. The Word of the Lord provided for every possible exigence, and that Word was so plain as to render human comment needless.

Is the Church of God worse off, as regards guidance and authority, than Israel of old? Are Christians left to think and arrange for themselves in the worship and service of God? Are there any questions left open for human discussion? Is the Word of God sufficient, or is it not? Has it left any thing unprovided for? Let us hearken diligently to the following powerful testimony: "All Scripture is given by inspiration of God, and is profitable for doctrine, for reproof, for correction, for instruction in righteousness; that the man of God may be *perfect* [αρτιος] *throughly furnished unto all good works.*" (2 Tim. iii.)

This is perfectly conclusive. Holy Scripture contains all that the man of God can possibly require to make him perfect, to equip him thoroughly for every thing that can be called a "good work." And if this be true as to the man of God individually, it is equally true as to the Church of God collectively. Scripture is all-sufficient—for each, for all. Thank God that it is so! What a signal mercy to have a divine guide-book! Were it not so, what should we do? whither should we turn? what would become of us? If we were left to human tradition and human arrangement in the things of God, what hopeless confusion! what clashing of opinions! what conflicting judgments! And all this of necessity, inasmuch as one man would have quite as good a right as another to put forth his opinion and to suggest his plan.

We shall perhaps be told that, notwithstanding our possession of the holy Scripture, we have, nevertheless, sects, parties, creeds, and schools of thought almost innumerable. But why is this? Simply because we refuse to submit our whole moral being to the authority of holy Scripture. This is the real secret of the matter—the true source of all those sects and parties which are the shame and sorrow of the Church of God.

It is vain for men to tell us that these things are good in themselves—that they are the legitimate fruit of that free exercise of thought and private judgment which form the very boast and glory of Protestant Christianity. We do not and cannot believe for a moment that such a plea will stand before the judgment-seat of Christ. We believe, on the contrary, that this very boasted freedom of thought and independence of judgment are in direct opposition to that spirit of profound and reverent obedience which is due to our adorable Lord and Master. What right has a servant to exercise his private judgment in the face of his master's plainly expressed will? None whatever. The duty of a servant is simply to obey—not to reason or to question, but to do what he is told. He fails, as a servant, just in so far as he exercises his own private judgment. The most lovely moral trait in a servant's character is implicit, unquestioning, and unqualified obedience. The one grand business of a servant is to do his master's will.

All this will be fully admitted in human affairs; but in the things of God, men think themselves entitled to exercise their private judgment. It is a fatal mistake. God has given us His Word; and that Word is so plain, that wayfaring men, though fools, need not err therein. Hence, therefore, if we were all guided by that Word,—if we were all to bow down in a spirit of unquestioning obedience to its divine authority, there could not be conflicting opinions and opposing sects. It is quite impossible that the voice of holy Scripture can teach opposing doctrines. It cannot possibly teach one man Episcopacy; another, Presbyterianism; and another, Independency. It cannot possibly furnish a foundation for opposing schools of thought. It would be a positive insult offered to the divine volume to attempt to attribute to it all the sad confusion of the professing church. Every pious mind must recoil, with just horror, from such an impious thought. Scripture cannot contradict itself; and therefore if two men or ten thousand men are exclusively taught by Scripture, they will think alike.

Hear what the blessed apostle says to the church at Corinth—says to us, "Now I beseech you, brethren, *by the name of our Lord Jesus Christ*" (mark the mighty moral force of this appeal) "that ye all *speak the same thing*, and that there be no divisions among you; but that ye be perfectly joined together in *the same mind*, and in *the same judgment*."

Now the question is, how was this most blessed result to be reached? Was it by each one exercising the right of private judgment? Alas! it was this very thing that gave birth to all the division and contention in the assembly at Corinth, and drew forth the sharp rebuke of the Holy Ghost. Those poor Corinthians thought they had a right to think and judge and choose for themselves, and what was the result? "It hath been declared unto me of you, my brethren, by them which are of the house of Chloe, that there are contentions among you. Now this I say, that *every one of you saith*, I am of Paul; and I of Apollos; and I of Cephas; and I of Christ. Is Christ divided?"

Here we have private judgment and its sad fruit—its necessary fruit. One man has quite as good a right to think for himself as another; and no man has any right whatsoever to force his opinion upon his fellow. Where, then, lies the remedy? In flinging to the winds our private judgments, and reverently submitting ourselves to the supreme and absolute authority of holy Scripture. If it be not thus, how could the apostle beseech the Corinthians to "speak the same thing, and to be perfectly joined together in the same mind, and in the same judgment"? Who was to prescribe the "thing" that all were to "speak"? In whose "mind" or whose "judgment" were all to be "perfectly joined together"? Had any one member of the assembly, however gifted or intelligent, the slightest shadow of a right to set forth what his brethren were to speak, to think, or to judge? Most certainly not. There was one absolute, because divine, authority to which all were bound, or rather privileged, to submit themselves. Human opinions, man's private judgment, his conscience, his reason—all these things must go for what they are worth; and most assuredly they are perfectly worthless as authority. The Word of God is the *only* authority; and if we are all governed by that, we shall "all speak the same thing," and "there will be no divisions among us;" but we shall "be perfectly joined together in the same mind, and in the same judgment."

Lovely condition! But, alas! it is not the present condition of the Church of God; and therefore it is perfectly evident that we are not all governed by the one supreme, absolute, and all-sufficient authority—the voice of holy Scripture—that most blessed voice that can never utter one discordant note—a voice ever divinely harmonious to the circumcised ear.

Here lies the root of the whole matter. The Church has departed from the authority of Christ, as set forth in His Word. Until this is seen, it is only lost time to discuss the claims of conflicting systems, ecclesiastical or theological. If a man does not see that it is his sacred duty to test every ecclesiastical system, every liturgical service, and every theological creed by the Word of God, discussion is perfectly useless. If it be allowable to settle things according to expediency—according to man's judgment, his conscience, or his reason, then verily we may as well at once give up the case as hopeless. If we have no divinely settled authority—no perfect standard— no infallible guide, we cannot see how it is possible for any one to possess the certainty that he is treading in the true path. If indeed it be true that we are left to choose for ourselves, amid the almost countless paths which lie around us, then farewell to all certainty—farewell to peace of mind and rest of heart—farewell to all holy stability of purpose and fixedness of aim. If we cannot say of the ground we occupy, of the path we pursue, and of the work in which we are engaged, "This is the thing which the Lord hath commanded," we may rest assured we are in a wrong position, and the sooner we abandon it the better.

Thank God, there is no necessity whatever for His child or His servant to continue for one hour in connection with what is wrong. "Let every one that nameth the name of Christ depart from iniquity." But how are we to know what is iniquity? By the Word of God. Whatever is contrary to Scripture, whether in morals or in doctrines, is iniquity, and I must depart from it, cost what it may. It is an individual matter.—"*Let every one.*"—"*He that hath ears.*"—"*He that overcometh.*"—"If *any* man hear My voice."

Here is the point. Let us mark it well. It is *Christ's* voice. It is not the voice of this good man or that good man; it is not the voice of the church, the voice of the fathers, the voice of general councils, but the voice of our own beloved Lord and Master. It is the individual conscience in direct, living contact with the voice of Christ—the living, eternal Word of God—the holy

Scriptures. Were it merely a question of human conscience or judgment or authority, we are at once plunged in hopeless uncertainty, inasmuch as what one man might judge to be iniquity, another might consider to be perfectly right. There must be some fixed standard to go by—some supreme authority from which there can be no appeal; and, blessed be God, there is. God has spoken; He has given us His Word; and it is at once our bounden duty, our high privilege, our moral security, our true enjoyment, to obey that Word.

Not man's interpretation of the Word, but the Word itself. This is all-important. We must have nothing—absolutely nothing between the human conscience and divine revelation. Men talk to us about the authority of the church. Where are we to find it? Suppose a really anxious, earnest, honest soul, longing to know the true way. He is told to listen to the voice of the church. He asks, Which church? Is it the Greek, Latin, Anglican, or Scotch church? Not two of them agree. Nay, more; there are conflicting parties, contending sects, opposing schools of thought, in one and the self-same body. Councils have differed, fathers have disagreed, popes have anathematized one another. In the Anglican Establishment, we have high-church, low-church, and broad-church, each differing from the rest. In the Scotch or Presbyterian church, we have the Established church, the United Presbyterian, and the Free church. And then if the anxious inquirer turns away in hopeless perplexity from those great bodies, in order to seek guidance amid the ranks of Protestant dissenters, is he likely to fare any better?

Ah! reader, it is perfectly hopeless. The whole professing church has revolted from the authority of Christ, and cannot possibly be a guide or an authority for any one. In the second and third chapters of the book of Revelation, the church is seen under judgment, and the appeal, seven times repeated, is, "He that hath an ear, let him hear"—what? The voice of the church? Impossible! The Lord could never direct us to hear the voice of that which is itself under judgment. Hear what, then? "Let him hear what the Spirit saith unto the churches."

And where is this voice to be heard? *Only* in the holy Scriptures, given of God, in His infinite goodness, to guide our souls in the way of peace and truth, notwithstanding the hopeless ruin of the church, and the thick darkness and wild confusion of baptized christendom. It lies not within the compass of human language to set forth the value and importance of having a divine and therefore an infallible and all-sufficient guide and authority for our individual path.

But be it remembered, we are solemnly responsible to bow to that authority, and follow that guide. It is utterly vain, indeed morally dangerous, to profess to have a divine guide and authority unless we are thoroughly subject thereto. This it was that characterized the Jews in the days of our Lord. They had the Scriptures, but they did not obey them. And one of the saddest features in the present condition of christendom is its boasted possession of the Bible, while the authority of that Bible is boldly set aside.

We deeply feel the solemnity of this, and would earnestly press it upon the conscience of the Christian reader. The Word of God is virtually ignored amongst us. Things are practiced and sanctioned, on all hands, which not only have no foundation in Scripture, but are diametrically opposed to it. We are not exclusively taught and absolutely governed by Scripture.

All this is most serious, and demands the attention of all the Lord's people in every place. We feel compelled to raise a warning note in the ears of all Christians in reference to this most weighty subject. Indeed, it is the sense of its gravity and vast moral importance that has led us to enter upon the service of writing these "Notes on the book of Deuteronomy." It is our earnest prayer that the Holy Ghost may use these pages to recall the hearts of the Lord's dear people to their true and proper place—even the place of reverent allegiance to His blessed Word. We feel persuaded that what will characterize all those who will walk devotedly in the closing hours of the Church's earthly history will be profound reverence for the Word of God, and genuine attachment to the Person of our Lord and Saviour Jesus Christ. The two things are inseparably bound together by a sacred and imperishable link.

"The Lord our God spake unto us in Horeb, saying, 'Ye have dwelt long enough in this mount: turn you, and take your journey, and go to the mount of the Amorites, and unto all the places nigh thereunto, in the plain, in the hills, and in the vale, and in the south, and by the sea-side, to the land of the Canaanites, and unto Lebanon, unto the great river, the river Euphrates.'" (Ver. 6, 7.)

We shall find, throughout the whole of the book of Deuteronomy, the Lord dealing much more directly and simply with the people than in any of the three preceding books; so far is it from being true that Deuteronomy is a mere repetition of what has passed before us in previous sections. For instance, in the passage just quoted there is no mention of the movement of the cloud—no reference to the sound of the trumpet. "The Lord our God spake unto us." We know, from the book of Numbers, that the movements of the camp were governed by the movements of the cloud, as communicated by the sound of the trumpet. But neither the trumpet nor the cloud is alluded to in this book. It is much more simple and familiar. "The Lord our God spake unto us in Horeb, saying, 'Ye have dwelt long enough in this mount.'"

This is very beautiful. It reminds us somewhat of the lovely simplicity of patriarchal times, when the Lord spake unto the fathers as a man speaketh to his friend. It was not by the sound of a trumpet, or by the movement of a cloud, that the Lord communicated His mind to Abraham, Isaac, and Jacob. He was so very near to them that there was no need, no room for an agency characterized by ceremony and distance. He visited them, sat with them, partook of their hospitality, in all the intimacy of personal friendship.

Such is the lovely simplicity of the order of things in patriarchal times; and this it is which imparts a peculiar charm to the narratives of the book of Genesis.

But in Exodus, Leviticus, and Numbers we have something quite different. There, we have set before us a vast system of types and shadows, rites, ordinances, and ceremonies, imposed on the people for the time being, the import of which is unfolded to us in the epistle to the Hebrews.—"The Holy Ghost this signifying, that the way into the holiest of all was not yet made manifest, while as the first tabernacle was yet standing; which was a figure for the time then present, in which were offered both gifts and sacrifices, that could not make him that did the service perfect, as pertaining to the conscience; which stood only in meats and drinks, and divers washings, and carnal ordinances, imposed on them until the time of reformation." (Heb. ix. 8-10.)

Under this system, the people were at a distance from God. It was not with them as it had been with their fathers in the book of Genesis. God was shut in from them, and they were shut out from Him. The leading features of the Levitical ceremonial, so far as the people were concerned, were bondage, darkness, distance; but on the other hand, its types and shadows pointed forward to that one great Sacrifice which is the foundation of all God's marvelous counsels and purposes, and by which He can, in perfect righteousness, and according to all the love of His heart, have a people near unto Himself, to the praise of the glory of His grace, throughout the golden ages of eternity.

Now, it has been already remarked, we shall find in Deuteronomy comparatively little of rites and ceremonies. The Lord is seen more in direct communication with the people; and even the priests, in their official capacity, come rarely before us; and if they are referred to, it is very much more in a moral than in a ceremonial way. Of this we shall have ample proof as we pass along; it is a marked feature of this beautiful book.

"The Lord our God spake unto us in Horeb, saying, 'Ye have dwelt long enough in this mount: turn you, and take your journey, and go to the mount of the Amorites.'" What a rare privilege for any people to have the Lord so near to them, and so interested in all their movements and in all their concerns, great and small! He knew how long they ought to remain in any one place, and whither they should next bend their steps. They had no need to harass themselves about their journeyings, or about any thing else. They were under the eye and in the hands of One whose wisdom was unerring, whose power was omnipotent, whose resources were inexhaustible, whose love was infinite, who had charged Himself with the care of them, who knew all their need, and was prepared to meet it, according to all the love of His heart and the strength of His holy arm.

What, then, we may ask, remained for them to do? What was their plain and simple duty? Just to obey. It was their high and holy privilege to rest in the love and obey the commandments of Jehovah, their covenant God. Here lay the blessed secret of their peace, their happiness, and their moral security. They had no need whatever to trouble themselves about their movements, no need of planning or arranging. Their journeyings were all ordered for them by One who knew every step of the way from Horeb to Kadesh-barnea, and they had just to live by the day, in happy dependence upon Him.

Happy position! Privileged path! Blessed portion! But it demanded a broken will, an obedient mind, a subject heart. If when Jehovah had said, "Ye have compassed this mountain long enough," they, on the contrary, were to form the plan of compassing it a little longer, they would have had to compass it without Him. His companionship, His counsel, and His aid could only be counted upon in the path of obedience.

Thus it was with Israel in their desert wanderings, and thus it is with us. It is our most precious privilege to leave all our matters in the hands, not merely of a covenant God, but of a loving Father. He arranges our movements for us; He fixes the bounds of our habitation; He tells us how long to stay in a place, and where to go next. He has charged Himself with all our concerns, all our movements, all our wants. His gracious word to us is, "Be careful for nothing; but in every thing by prayer and supplication with thanksgiving let your requests be made known unto God." And what then? "The peace of God, which passeth all understanding, shall keep your hearts and minds through Christ Jesus."

But it may be the reader feels disposed to ask, How does God guide His people now? We cannot expect to hear His voice telling us when to move or where to go. To this we reply, at once, It cannot surely be that the members of the Church of God—the body of Christ—are worse off in the matter of divine guidance than Israel in the wilderness. Cannot God guide His children—cannot Christ guide His servants—in all their movements and in all their service? Who would think, for a moment, of calling in question a truth so plain and so precious? True, we do not expect to hear a voice, or see the movement of a cloud; but we have what is very much better, very much higher, very much more intimate. We may rest assured our God has made ample provision for us in this, as in all beside, according to all the love of His heart.

Now, there are three ways in which we are guided: we are guided by the Word, we are guided by the Holy Ghost, and we are guided by the instincts of the divine nature; and we have to bear in mind that the instincts of the divine nature, the leadings of the Holy Ghost, and the teaching of holy Scripture will always harmonize. This is of the utmost importance to keep before us. A person might fancy himself to be led by the instincts of the divine nature, or by the Holy Spirit, to pursue a certain line of action involving consequences at issue with the Word of God. Thus his mistake would be made apparent. It is a very serious thing for any one to act on mere impulse or impression. By so doing, he may fall into a snare of the devil, and do very serious damage to the cause of Christ. We must calmly weigh our impressions in the balances of the sanctuary, and faithfully test them by the standard of the divine Word. In this way we shall be preserved from error and delusion. It is a most dangerous thing to trust impressions or act on impulse. We have seen the most disastrous consequences produced by so doing. Facts *may be* reliable. Divine authority is absolutely infallible. Our own impressions may prove as delusive as a will-o'-the-wisp, or a mirage of the desert: human feelings are most untrustworthy. We must ever submit them to the most severe scrutiny, lest they betray us into some fatally false line of action. We can trust Scripture without a shadow of misgiving; and we shall find, without exception, that the man who is led by the Holy Ghost, or guided by the instincts of the divine nature, will never act in opposition to the Word of God. This is what we may call an axiom in the divine life— an established rule in practical Christianity. Would that it had been more attended to in all ages of the Church's history! Would that it were more pondered in our own day!

But there is another point in this question of divine guidance which demands our serious attention. We not unfrequently hear people speak of "the finger of divine Providence" as something to be relied upon for guidance. This may be only another mode of expressing the idea of being guided by circumstances, which, we do not hesitate to say, is very far indeed from being the proper kind of guidance for a Christian.

No doubt, our Lord may and does, at times, intimate His mind and indicate our path by His providence; but we must be sufficiently near to Him to be able to interpret the providence aright, else we may find that what is called "an opening of Providence" may actually prove an opening by which we slip off the holy path of obedience. Surrounding circumstances, just like our inward impressions, must be weighed in the presence of God, and judged by the light of His Word, else they may lead us into the most terrible mistakes. Jonah might have considered it a remarkable providence to find a ship going to Tarshish; but had he been in communion with God, he would not have needed a ship. In short, the Word of God is the one grand test and perfect touchstone for every thing—for outward circumstances and inward impressions—for feelings, imaginations, and tendencies—all must be placed under the searching light of holy Scripture and there calmly and seriously judged. This is the true path of safety, peace, and blessedness for every child of God.

It may, however, be said, in reply to all this, that we cannot expect to find a text of Scripture to guide us in the matter of our movements, or in the thousand little details of daily life. Perhaps not; but there are certain great principles laid down in Scripture, which, if properly applied, will afford divine guidance even where we might not be able to find a particular text. And not only so, but we have the fullest assurance that our God can and does guide His children in all things. "The steps of a good man are ordered of the Lord."—"The meek will He guide in judgment; and the meek will He teach His way."—"I will guide thee with Mine eye." He can signify His mind to us as to this or that particular act or movement. If not, where are we? How are we to get on? How are we to regulate our movements? Are we to be drifted hither and thither by the tide of circumstances? Are we left to blind chance, or to the mere impulse of our own will?

Thank God, it is not so. He can, in His own perfect way, give us the certainty of His mind in any given case; and without that certainty we should never move. Our Lord Christ (all homage to His peerless name!) can intimate His mind to His servant as to where He would have him to go and what He would have him to do; and no true servant will ever think of moving or acting without such intimation. We should never act or move in uncertainty. If we are not sure, let us be quiet and wait. Very often it happens that we harass and fret ourselves about movements that God would not have us make at all. A person once said to a friend, "I am quite at a loss to know which way to turn." "Then, don't turn at all," was the friend's wise reply.

But here an all-important moral point comes in, and that is, our whole condition of soul. This, we may rest assured, has very much to do with the matter of guidance. It is "the meek He will guide in judgment, and teach His way." We must never forget this. If only we are humble and self-distrusting—if we wait on our God, in simplicity of heart, uprightness of mind, and honesty of purpose, He will most assuredly guide us. But it will never do to go and ask counsel of God in a matter about which our mind is made up, or our will is at work.

This is a fatal delusion. Look at the case of Jehoshaphat, in 1 Kings xxii.—"It came to pass in the third year, that Jehoshaphat the king of Judah came down to the king of Israel"—a sad mistake, to begin with.—"And the king of Israel said unto his servants, 'Know ye that Ramoth in Gilead is ours, and we be still, and take it not out of the hand of the king of Syria?' And he said unto Jehoshaphat, 'Wilt thou go with me to battle to Ramoth-gilead?' And Jehoshaphat said to the king of Israel, 'I am as thou art, my people as thy people, my horses as thy horses; and, (as we have it in 2 Chronicles xviii. 3,) we will be with thee in the war.'"

Here we see that his mind was made up before ever he thought of asking counsel of God in the matter. He was in a false position and a wrong atmosphere altogether. He had fallen into the snare of the enemy, through lack of singleness of eye, and hence he was not in a fit state to receive or profit by divine guidance. He was bent on his own will, and the Lord left him to reap the fruits of it; and but for infinite and sovereign mercy, he would have fallen by the sword of the Syrians, and been borne a corpse from the battle-field.

True, he did say to the king of Israel, "Inquire, I pray thee, at the word of the Lord to-day." But where was the use of this, when he had already pledged himself to a certain line of action? What folly for any one to make up his mind and then go and ask for counsel! Had he been in a right state of soul, he never would have sought counsel in such a case at all; but his state of soul was bad, his position false, and his purpose in direct opposition to the mind and will of God. Hence, although he heard, from the lips of Jehovah's messenger, His solemn judgment on the entire expedition, yet he took his own way, and well-nigh lost his life in consequence.

We see the same thing in the forty-second chapter of Jeremiah. The people applied to the prophet to ask counsel as to their going down into Egypt; but they had already made up their minds as to their course—they were bent on their own will. Miserable condition! Had they been meek and humble, they would not have needed to ask counsel in the matter; but they said unto Jeremiah the prophet, "'Let, we beseech thee, our supplication be accepted before thee, and pray for us unto the Lord *thy* God [Why not say, The Lord *our* God?] even for all this remnant; (for we are left but a few of many, as thine eyes do behold us:) that the Lord *thy* God may show us the way wherein we may walk, and the thing that we may do.' Then Jeremiah the prophet said unto them, 'I have heard you; behold, I will pray unto the Lord *your* God according to your words; and it shall come to pass, that whatsoever thing the Lord shall answer you, I will declare it unto you; I will keep nothing back from you.' Then they said to Jeremiah, 'The Lord be a true and faithful witness between us, if we do not even according to all things for the which the Lord *thy* God shall send thee to us. Whether it be good, or whether it be evil [How could the will of God be aught but good?], we will obey the voice of the Lord our God, to whom we send thee; that it may be well with us, when we obey the voice of the Lord our God.'"

Now, all this seemed very pious and very promising; but mark the sequel. When they found that the judgment and counsel of God did not tally with their will, "then spake ... *all the proud men*, saving unto Jeremiah, 'Thou speakest falsely: the Lord our God hath not sent thee to say, Go not into Egypt to sojourn there.'"

Here, the real state of the case comes clearly out. Pride and self-will were at work; their vows and promises were false. "Ye dissembled in your hearts," says Jeremiah, "when ye sent me unto the Lord your God, saying, 'Pray for us unto the Lord our God; and according unto all that the Lord our God shall say, so declare unto us, and we will do it.'" It would have been all very well had the divine response fallen in with their will in the matter; but inasmuch as it ran counter, they rejected it altogether.

How often is this the case! The Word of God does not suit man's thoughts; it judges them, it stands in direct opposition to his will, it interferes with his plans, and hence he rejects it. The human will and human reason are ever in direct antagonism to the Word of God, and the Christian must refuse both the one and the other if he really desires to be divinely guided. An unbroken will and blind reason, if we listen to them, can only lead us into darkness, misery, and desolation. Jonah *would* go to Tarshish, when he ought to have gone to Nineveh; and the consequence was that he found himself "in the belly of hell," with "the weeds wrapped about his head." Jehoshaphat *would* go to Ramoth-gilead, when he ought to have been at Jerusalem; and the consequence was that he found himself surrounded by the swords of the Syrians. The remnant, in the days of Jeremiah, *would* go into Egypt, when they ought to have remained at Jerusalem; and the consequence was that they died by the sword, by the famine, and by the pestilence in the land of Egypt, "whither they *desired* to go and to sojourn."

Thus it must ever be. The path of self-will is sure to be a path of darkness and misery; it cannot be otherwise: the path of obedience, on the contrary, is a path of peace, a path of light, a path of blessing, a path on which the beams of divine favor are ever poured in living lustre. It may, to the human eye, seem narrow, rough, and lonely; but the obedient soul finds it to be the path of life, peace, and moral security. "The path of the just is as the shining light, that shineth more and more unto the perfect day." Blessed path! May the writer and the reader ever be found treading it, with a steady step and earnest purpose.

Before turning from this great practical subject of divine guidance and human obedience, we must ask the reader to refer, for a few moments, to a very beautiful passage in the eleventh chapter of Luke. He will find it full of the most valuable instruction.

"The light of the body is the eye: therefore when thine eye is single, thy whole body also is full of light; but when thine eye is evil, thy body also is full of darkness. Take heed, therefore, that the light which is in thee be not darkness. If thy whole body therefore be full of light, having no part dark, the whole shall be full of light, as when the bright shining of a candle doth give thee light." (Ver. 34-36.)

Nothing can exceed the moral force and beauty of this passage. First of all, we have the "single eye." This is essential to the enjoyment of divine guidance. It indicates a broken will—a heart honestly fixed upon doing the will of God. There is no under-current, no mixed motive, no personal end in view. There is the one simple desire and earnest purpose to do the will of God, whatever that will may be.

Now, when the soul is in this attitude, divine light comes streaming in and fills the whole body. Hence it follows that if the body is not full of light, the eye is not single; there is some mixed motive; self-will or self-interest is at work; we are not upright before God. In this case, any light which we profess to have is darkness; and there is no darkness so gross or so terrible as that judicial darkness which settles down upon the heart governed by self-will while professing to have light from God. This will be seen in all its horrors by and by in christendom, when "that Wicked shall be revealed, whom the Lord shall consume with the spirit of His mouth, and shall destroy with the brightness of His coming; even him, whose coming is after the working of Satan with all power and signs and lying wonders, and with all deceivableness of unrighteousness in them that perish; because *they received not the love of the truth*, that they might be saved. And *for this cause* God shall send them strong delusion, that they should believe a lie; that they all might be damned who believed not the truth, but *had pleasure in unrighteousness*." (2 Thess. ii. 8-12.)

How awful is this! How solemnly it speaks to the whole professing church! How solemnly it addresses the conscience of both the writer and the reader of these lines! Light not acted upon becomes darkness.—"If the light which is in thee be darkness, how great is that darkness!" But on the other hand, a little light honestly acted upon is sure to increase; for "to him that hath shall more be given," and "the path of the just is as the shining light, that shineth more and more unto the perfect day."

This moral progress is beautifully and forcibly set forth in Luke xi. 36.—"If thy whole body therefore be full of light, having *no part dark*"—no chamber kept closed against the heavenly rays—no dishonest reserve—the whole moral being laid open, in genuine simplicity, to the action of divine light; then "the whole shall be full of light, as when the bright shining of a candle doth give thee light." In a word, the obedient soul has not only light for his own path, but the light shines out, so that others see it, like the bright shining of a candle. "Let your light so shine before men, that they may see your good works, and glorify your Father which is in heaven."

We have a very vivid contrast to all this in the thirteenth chapter of Jeremiah.—"Give glory to the Lord your God, *before He cause darkness*, and before your feet stumble upon the dark mountains, and while ye look for light, He turn it into the shadow of death, and make it gross darkness." The way to give glory to the Lord our God is to obey His Word. The path of duty is a bright and blessed path; and the one who, through grace, treads that path will never stumble on the dark mountains. The truly humble, the lowly, the self-distrusting, will keep far away from those dark mountains, and walk in that blessed path which is ever illuminated by the bright and cheering beams of God's approving countenance.

This is the path of the just, the path of heavenly wisdom, the path of perfect peace. May we ever be found treading it, beloved reader; and let us never, for one moment, forget that it is our high privilege to be divinely guided in the most minute details of our daily life. Alas! for the one who is not so guided. He will have many a stumble, many a fall, many a sorrowful experience. If we are not guided by our Father's eye, we shall be like the horse or the mule, which have no understanding, whose mouth must be held in with bit and bridle,—like the horse, impetuously rushing where he ought not, or the mule, obstinately refusing to go where he ought. How sad for a Christian to be like these! How blessed to move, from day to day, in the path marked out for us by our Father's eye!—a path which the vulture's eye hath not seen, or the lion's whelp trodden; the path of holy obedience; the path in which the meek and lowly will ever be found, to their deep joy, and the praise and glory of Him who has opened it for them and given them grace to tread it.

In the remainder of our chapter, Moses rehearses in the ears of the people, in language of touching simplicity, the facts connected with the appointment of the judges, and the mission of the spies. The appointment of the judges, Moses here attributes to his own suggestion: the mission of the spies was the suggestion of the people. That dear and most honored servant of God felt the burden of the congregation too heavy for him; and assuredly it was very heavy; though we know well that the grace of God was amply sufficient for the demand, and, moreover, that that grace could act as well by one man as by seventy.

Still, we can well understand the difficulty felt by "the meekest man in all the earth" in reference to the responsibility of so grave and important a charge; and truly the language in which he states his difficulty is affecting in the highest degree. We feel as though we must quote it for the reader.

"And I spake unto you at that time, saying, 'I am not able to bear you myself alone [Surely not; what mere mortal could? But God was there to be counted upon for exigence of every hour.]: the Lord your God hath multiplied you, and, behold, ye are this day as the stars of heaven for multitude.' (The Lord God of your fathers make you a thousand times so many more as ye are, and bless you, as He hath promised you.)" Lovely parenthesis! Exquisite breathing of a large and lowly heart! "How can I myself alone bear your cumbrance, and your burden, and *your strife*?"

Alas! here lay the secret of much of the "cumbrance" and the "burden." They could not agree among themselves,—there were controversies, contentions, and questions; and who was sufficient for these things? what human shoulder could sustain such a burden? How different it might have been with them! Had they walked lovingly together, there would have been no cases to decide, and therefore no need of judges to decide them. If each member of the congregation had sought the prosperity, the interest, and the happiness of his brethren, there would have been no "strife," no "cumbrance," no "burden." If each had done all that in him lay to promote the common good, how lovely would have been the result!

But, ah! it was not so with Israel in the desert; and, what is still more humbling, it is not so in the Church of God, although our privileges are so much higher. Hardly had the assembly been formed by the presence of the Holy Ghost ere the accents of murmuring and discontent were heard. And about what? About "neglect," whether fancied or real. Whatever way it was, *self* was at work. If the neglect was merely imaginary, the Grecians were to blame; and if it was real, the Hebrews were to blame. It generally happens, in such cases, that there are faults on both sides; but the true way to avoid all strife, contention, and murmuring is to put self in the dust and earnestly seek the good of others. Had this excellent way been understood and adopted, from the outset, what a different task the ecclesiastical historian would have had to perform! But, alas! it has not been adopted; and hence the history of the professing church, from the very beginning, has been a deplorable and humiliating record of controversy, division, and strife. In the very presence of the Lord Himself, whose whole life was one of complete self-surrender, the apostles disputed about who should be greatest. Such a dispute could never have arisen had each known the exquisite secret of putting self in the dust and seeking the good of others. No one who knows aught of the true moral elevation of self-emptiness could possibly seek a good or a great place for himself. Nearness to Christ so satisfies the lowly heart, that honors, distinctions, and rewards are little accounted of; but where self is at work, there you will have envy and jealousy, strife and contention, confusion and every evil work.

Witness the scene between the two sons of Zebedee and their ten brethren, in the tenth chapter of Mark. What was at the bottom of it? Self. The two were thinking of a good place for themselves in the kingdom, and the ten were angry with the two for thinking of any such thing. Had each set self aside, and sought the good of others, such a scene would never have been enacted,—the two would not have been thinking about themselves, and hence there would have been no ground for the "indignation" of the ten.

But it is needless to multiply examples. Every age of the church's history illustrates and proves the truth of our statement that self and its odious workings are the producing cause of strife, contention, and division, always. Turn where you will—from the days of the apostles down to the days in which our lot is cast, and you will find unmortified self to be the fruitful source of strife and schism; and on the other hand, you will find that to sink self and its interests is the true secret of peace, harmony, and brotherly love. If only we learn to set self aside, and seek earnestly the glory of Christ and the prosperity of His beloved people, we shall not have many "cases" to settle.

We must now return to our chapter.

"How can I myself alone bear your cumbrance, and your burden, and your strife? Take you wise men, and understanding, and known among your tribes, and I will make them rulers over you. And ye answered me, and said, 'The thing which thou hast spoken is good for us to do.' So I took the chief of your tribes, *wise* men, and *known*"—men fitted of God, and possessing, because entitled to, the confidence of the congregation—"and made them heads over you, captains over thousands, and captains over hundreds, and captains over fifties, and captains over tens, and officers among your tribes."

Admirable arrangement! If indeed it had to be made, nothing could be better adapted to the maintenance of order than the graduated scale of authority, varying from the captain of ten to the captain of a thousand; the lawgiver himself at the head of all, and he in immediate communication with the Lord God of Israel.

We have no allusion here to the fact recorded in Exodus xviii, namely, that the appointment of those rulers was at the suggestion of Jethro, Moses' father-in-law; neither have we any reference to the scene in Numbers xi. We call the reader's attention to this as one of the many proofs which lie scattered along the pages of Deuteronomy that it is very far indeed from being a mere repetition of the preceding sections of the Pentateuch. In short, this delightful book has a marked character of its own, and the mode in which facts are presented is in perfect keeping with that character. It is very evident that the object of the venerable lawgiver, or rather of the Holy Ghost in him, was to bring every thing to bear, in a moral way, upon the hearts of the people, in order to produce that one grand result which is the special object of the book from beginning to end, namely, a loving obedience to all the statutes and judgments of the Lord their God.

We must bear this in mind if we would study aright the book which lies open before us. Infidels, skeptics, and rationalists may impiously suggest to us the thought of discrepancies in the various records given in the different books; but the pious reader will reject, with a holy indignation, every such suggestion, knowing that it emanates directly from the father of lies, the determined and persistent enemy of the precious revelation of God. This, we feel persuaded, is the true way in which to deal with all infidel assaults upon the Bible. Argument is useless, inasmuch as infidels are not in a position to understand or appreciate its force; they are profoundly ignorant of the matter. Nor is it merely a question of profound ignorance, but of determined hostility; so that, in every way, the judgment of all infidel writers on the subject of divine inspiration is utterly worthless and perfectly contemptible. We would pity and pray for the men, while we thoroughly despise and indignantly reject their opinions. The Word of God is entirely above and beyond them. It is as perfect as its Author, and as imperishable as His throne; but its moral glories, its living depths, and its infinite perfections are only unfolded to faith and need. "I thank Thee, O Father, Lord of heaven and earth, because Thou hast hid these things from the wise and prudent, and hast revealed them unto babes."

If we are only content to be as simple as a babe, we shall enjoy the precious revelation of a Father's love, as given by His Spirit in the holy Scriptures; but on the other hand, those who fancy themselves wise and prudent—who build upon their learning, their philosophy, and their reason—who think themselves competent to sit in judgment on the Word of God, and hence on God Himself, are given over to judicial darkness, blindness, and hardness of heart. Thus it comes to pass that the most egregious folly and the most contemptible ignorance that man can display will be found in the pages of those learned writers who have dared to write against the Bible. "Where is the wise? where is the scribe? where is the disputer of this world? hath not God made foolish the wisdom of this world? For after that in the wisdom of God the world by wisdom knew not God, it pleased God by the foolishness of preaching to save them that believe." (1 Cor. i. 20, 21.)

"If any man will be wise, let him become a fool." Here lies the grand moral secret of the matter. Man must get to the end of his own wisdom, as well as of his own righteousness. He must be brought to confess himself a fool ere he can taste the sweetness of divine wisdom. It is not within the range of the most gigantic human intellect, aided by all the appliances of human learning and philosophy, to grasp the very simplest elements of divine revelation; and therefore, when unconverted men, whatever may be the force of their genius or the extent of their learning, undertake to handle spiritual subjects, and more especially the subject of the divine inspiration of holy Scripture, they are sure to exhibit their profound ignorance, and utter incompetency to deal with the question before them. Indeed, whenever we look into an infidel book, we are struck with the feebleness of their most forcible arguments; and not only so, but in every instance in which they attempt to find a discrepancy in the Bible, we see only divine wisdom, beauty, and perfectness.

We have been led into the foregoing line of thought in connection with the subject of the appointment of the elders, which is given to us in each book according to the wisdom of the Holy Ghost, and in perfect keeping with the scope and object of the book. We shall now proceed with our quotation.

"And I charged your judges at that time, saying, 'Hear the causes between your brethren, and *judge righteously* between every man and his brother, and *the stranger* that is with him. *Ye shall not respect persons* in judgment; but *ye shall hear the small as well as the great; ye shall not be afraid of the face of man*; for the judgment is God's; and the cause that is too hard for you, bring it unto me, and I will hear it.'"

What heavenly wisdom is here! what even-handed justice! what holy impartiality! In every case of difference, all the facts on both sides were to be fully heard and patiently weighed. The mind was not to be warped by prejudice, predilection, or personal feeling of any kind. The judgment was to be formed, not by impressions, but by facts—clearly established, undeniable facts. Personal influence was to have no weight whatever. The position and circumstances of either party in the cause were not to be considered. The case must be decided entirely upon its own merits. "Ye shall hear the small as well as the great." The poor man was to have the same even-handed justice meted out to him as the rich; the stranger as one born in the land. No difference was to be allowed.

How important is all this! how worthy of our attentive consideration! how full of deep and valuable instruction for us all! True, we are not all called to be judges or elders or leaders; but the great moral principles laid down in the above quotation are of the very utmost value to every one of us, inasmuch as cases are continually occurring which call for their direct application. Wherever our lot may be cast, whatever our line of life or sphere of action, we are liable, alas! to meet with cases of difficulty and misunderstanding between our brethren,—cases of wrong, whether real or imaginary; and hence it is most needful to be divinely instructed as to how we ought to carry ourselves in respect to such.

Now, in all such cases, we cannot be too strongly impressed with the necessity of having our judgment based on facts—all the facts on both sides. We must not allow ourselves to be guided by our own impressions, for we all know that mere impressions are most untrustworthy. They may be correct, and they may be utterly false. Nothing is more easily received and conveyed than a false impression, and therefore any judgment based on mere impressions is worthless. We must have solid, clearly established facts—facts established by two or three witnesses, as Scripture so distinctly enforces. (Deut. xvii. 6; Matt. xviii. 16; 2 Cor. xiii. 1; 1 Tim. v. 19.)

But further, we must never be guided in judgment by an *ex parte* statement. Every one is liable, even with the best intentions, to give a color to his statement of a case. It is not that he would intentionally make a false statement, or tell a deliberate lie; but through inaccuracy of memory, or one cause or another, he may not present the case as it really is. Some fact may be omitted, and that one fact may so affect all the other facts as to alter their bearing completely. ""*Audi alteram partem* ("Hear the other side") is a wholesome motto. And not only hear the other side, but hear all the facts on both sides, and thus you will be able to form a sound and righteous judgment. We may set it down as a standing rule, that any judgment formed without an accurate knowledge of all the facts is perfectly worthless. "Hear the causes between your brethren, and judge righteously between every man and his brother, and the stranger that is with him." Seasonable, needed words, most surely, at all times, in all places, and under all circumstances. May we apply our hearts to them.

And how important the admonition in verse 17! "Ye shall not respect persons in judgment; but ye shall hear the small as well as the great; ye shall not be afraid of the face of man." How these words discover the poor human heart! How prone we are to respect persons—to be swayed by personal influence—to attach importance to position and wealth—to be afraid of the face of man!

What is the divine antidote against all these evils? Just this: the fear of God. If we set the Lord before us, at all times, it will effectually deliver us from the pernicious influence of partiality, prejudice, and the fear of men. It will lead us to wait humbly and patiently on the Lord for guidance and counsel in all that may come before us, and thus we shall be preserved from forming hasty and one-sided judgments of men and things—that fruitful source of mischief amongst the Lord's people in all ages.

We shall now dwell for a few moments on the very affecting manner in which Moses brings before the congregation all the circumstances connected with the mission of the spies, which, like the appointment of the judges, is in perfect keeping with the scope and object of the book. This is only what we might expect. There is not, there could not be, a single sentence of useless repetition in the divine volume; still less could there be a single flaw, a single discrepancy, a single contradictory statement. The Word of God is absolutely perfect—perfect as a whole, perfect in all its parts. We must firmly hold and faithfully confess this in the face of this infidel age.

We speak not of human translations of the Word of God, in which there must be more or less of imperfection; though even here, we cannot but be "filled with wonder, love, and praise" when we mark the way in which our God so manifestly presided over our excellent English translation, so that the poor man at the back of a mountain may be assured of possessing, in his common English Bible, the revelation of God to his soul. And most surely we are warranted in saying that this is just what we might look for at the hands of our God. It is but reasonable to infer that the One who inspired the writers of the Bible would also watch over the translation of it; for inasmuch as He gave it originally, in His grace, to those who could read Hebrew and Greek, so would He not, in the same grace, give it in every language under heaven? Blessed forever be His holy name, it is His gracious desire to speak to every man in the very tongue in which he was born,—to tell us the sweet tale of His grace—the glad tidings of salvation in the very accents in which our mothers whispered into our infant ears those words of love that went right home to our very hearts. (See Acts ii. 5-8.)

Oh that men were more impressed and affected with the truth and power of all this, and then we should not be troubled with so many foolish and unlearned questions about the Bible.

Let us now hearken to the account given by Moses of the mission of the spies—its origin and its result. We shall find it full of most weighty instruction, if only the ear be open to hear and the heart duly prepared to ponder.

"And I commanded you at that time all the things which ye should do." The path of simple obedience was plainly set before them. They had but to tread it with an obedient heart and firm step. They had not to reason about consequences, or weigh the results; all these they had just to leave in the hands of God, and move on with steady purpose in the blessed path of obedience.

"And when we departed from Horeb, we went through all that *great and terrible wilderness*, which ye saw by the way of the mountain of the Amorites, as the Lord our God commanded us; and we came to Kadesh-barnea. And I said unto you, 'Ye are come unto the mountain of the Amorites, which the Lord our God doth give unto us. Behold, the Lord thy God hath set the land before thee: go up and possess it, as the Lord God of thy fathers hath said unto thee; fear not, neither be discouraged.'"

Here was their warrant for entering upon immediate possession. The Lord their God had given them the land and set it before them. It was theirs by His free gift—the gift of His sovereign grace, in pursuance of the covenant made with their fathers. It was His eternal purpose to possess the land of Canaan through the seed of Abraham His friend. This ought to have been enough to set their hearts perfectly at rest, not only as to the character of the land, but also as to their entrance upon it. There was no need of spies. Faith never wants to spy what God has given. It argues that what He has given must be worth having, and that He is able to put us in full possession of all that His grace has bestowed. Israel might have concluded that the same hand that had conducted them "through all that great and terrible wilderness" could bring them in and plant them in their destined inheritance.

So Faith would have reasoned; for it always reasons from God down to circumstances, never from circumstances up to God. "If God be for us, who can be against us?" This is Faith's argument, grand in its simplicity and simple in its moral grandeur. When God fills the whole range of the soul's vision, difficulties are little accounted of. They are either not seen, or, if seen, they are viewed as occasions for the display of divine power. Faith exults in seeing God triumphing over difficulties.

But, alas! the people were not governed by faith on the occasion now before us, and therefore they had recourse to spies. Of this Moses reminds them, and that, too, in language at once most tender and faithful.—"And ye came near unto me, *every one of you*, and said, 'We will send men before us, and they shall search us out the land, and bring us word again, by what way we must go up, and into what cities we shall come.'"

Surely, they might well have trusted God for all this. The One who had brought them up out of Egypt, made a way for them through the sea, guided them through the trackless desert, was fully able to bring them into the land. But no; they would send spies, simply because their hearts had not simple confidence in the true, the living, the almighty God.

Here lay the moral root of the matter; and it is well that the reader should thoroughly seize this point. True it is that, in the history given in Numbers, the Lord told Moses to send the spies; but why? Because of the moral condition of the people. And here we see the characteristic difference and yet the lovely harmony of the two books. Numbers gives us the public history, Deuteronomy the secret source of the mission of the spies; and as it is in perfect keeping with Numbers to give us the former, so it is in perfect keeping with Deuteronomy to give us the latter. The one is the complement of the other. We could not fully understand the subject had we only the history given in Numbers. It is the touching commentary given in Deuteronomy which completes the picture. How perfect is Scripture! All we need is the eye anointed to see and the heart prepared to appreciate its moral glories.

It may be, however, that the reader still feels some difficulty in reference to the question of the spies. He may feel disposed to ask how it could be wrong to send them when the Lord told them to do so. The answer is, The wrong was not in the act of sending them when they were told, but in the wish to send them at all. The wish was the fruit of unbelief, and the command to send them was because of that unbelief.

We may see something of the same in the matter of divorce in Matthew xix.—"The Pharisees also came unto Him, tempting Him, and saying unto Him, 'Is it lawful for a man to put away his wife for every cause?' And He answered and said unto them, 'Have ye not read, that He which made them at the beginning made them male and female, and said, For this cause shall a man leave father and mother, and shall cleave to his wife; and they twain shall be one flesh? Wherefore they are no more twain, but one flesh. What therefore God hath joined together, let not man put asunder.' They say unto Him, 'Why did Moses, then, command to give a writing of divorcement, and to put her away? He saith unto them, 'Moses *because of the hardness of your hearts* suffered you to put away your wives; but from the beginning it was not so.'"

It was not in keeping with God's original institution, or according to His heart, that a man should put away his wife; but, in consequence of the hardness of the human heart, divorce was permitted by the lawgiver. Is there any difficulty in this? Surely not; unless the heart is bent on making one. Neither is there any difficulty in the matter of the spies. Israel ought not to have needed them: simple faith would never have thought of them. But the Lord saw the real condition of things and issued a command accordingly; just as, in after ages, He saw the heart of the people bent on having a king, and He commanded Samuel to give them one.—"And the Lord said unto Samuel, 'Hearken unto the voice of the people in all that they say unto thee; for they have not rejected thee, but they have rejected Me, that I should not reign over them. According to all the works which they have done since the day that I brought them up out of Egypt even unto this day, wherewith they have forsaken Me, and served other gods, so do they also unto thee. Now therefore hearken unto their voice: *howbeit yet protest solemnly* unto them, and shew them the manner of the king that shall reign over them.'" (1 Sam. viii. 7-9.)

Thus we see that the mere granting of a desire is no proof whatever that such desire is according to the mind of God. Israel ought not to have asked for a king. Was not Jehovah sufficient? was not He their King? could not He, as He had ever done, lead them forth to battle and fight for them? Why seek an arm of flesh? why turn away from the living, the true, the almighty God to lean on a poor fellow-worm? What power was there in a king but that which God might see fit to bestow upon him? None whatever. All the power, all the wisdom, all real good, was in the Lord their God; and it was there for them—there at all times, to meet their every need. They had but to lean upon His almighty arm—to draw upon His exhaustless resources, to find all their springs in Him.

When they did get a king, according to their hearts' desire, what did he do for them? "All the people followed him trembling." The more closely we study the melancholy history of Saul's reign, the more we see that he was, almost from the very outset, a positive hindrance rather than a help. We have but to read his history, from first to last, in order to see the truth of this. His whole reign was a lamentable failure, aptly and forcibly set forth in two glowing sentences of the prophet Hosea,—"I gave thee a king in Mine anger, and took him away in My wrath." In a word, he was the answer to the unbelief and self-will of the people, and therefore all their brilliant hopes and expectations respecting him were most lamentably disappointed. He failed to answer the mind of God, and, as a necessary consequence, he failed to meet the people's need. He proved himself wholly unworthy of the crown and sceptre, and his ignominious fall on Mount Gilboa was in melancholy keeping with his whole career.

Now, when we come to consider the mission of the spies, we find it too, like the appointment of a king, ending in complete failure and disappointment. It could not be otherwise, inasmuch as it was the fruit of unbelief. True, God gave them spies, and Moses, with touching grace, says, "The saying pleased me well; and I took twelve men of you, one of a tribe," — it was Grace coming down to the condition of the people and consenting to a plan which was suited to that condition; but this by no means proves that either the plan or the condition was according to the mind of God. Blessed be His name, He can meet us in our unbelief though He is grieved and dishonored by it. He delights in a bold, artless faith; it is the only thing in all this world that gives Him His proper place. Hence, when Moses said to the people, "Behold, the Lord thy God hath set the land before thee: go up and possess it, as the Lord God of thy fathers hath said unto thee; fear not, neither be discouraged," what would have been the proper response from them? Here we are: lead on, almighty Lord — lead on to victory. Thou art enough. With Thee as our leader, we move on with joyful confidence. Difficulties are nothing to Thee, and therefore they are nothing to us. Thy word and Thy presence are all we want. In these we find at once our authority and power. It matters not in the least to us who or what may be before us: mighty giants, towering walls, frowning bulwarks — what are they all in the presence of the Lord God of Israel, but as withered leaves before the whirlwind? Lead on, O Lord.

This would have been the language of Faith; but, alas! it was not the language of Israel on the occasion before us. God was not sufficient for them. They were not prepared to go up, leaning on His arm alone: they were not satisfied with His report of the land; they would send spies. Any thing for the poor human heart but simple dependence upon the one living and true God. The natural man cannot trust God, simply because he does not know Him. "They that know Thy name will put their trust in Thee."

God must be known, in order to be trusted; and the more fully He is trusted, the better He becomes known. There is nothing in all this world so truly blessed as a life of simple faith; but it must be a reality and not a mere profession. It is utterly vain to talk of living by faith, while the heart is secretly resting on some creature-prop. The true believer has to do exclusively with God. He finds in Him all his resources. It is not that he undervalues the instruments or the channels which God is pleased to use; quite the reverse. He values them exceedingly; and cannot but value them, as the means which God uses for his help and blessing; but he does not allow them to displace God. The language of his heart is, "My soul, wait thou only upon God; for my expectation is from Him. He *only* is my rock."

There is peculiar force in the word "only." It searches the heart thoroughly. To look to the creature, directly or indirectly, for the supply of any need, is, in principle, to depart from the life of faith; and, oh! it is miserable work, this looking, in any way, to creature-streams. It is just as morally degrading as the life of faith is morally elevating. And not only is it degrading, but disappointing. Creature-props give way, and creature-streams run dry; but they that trust in the Lord shall never be confounded, and never want any good thing. Had Israel trusted the Lord instead of sending spies, they would have had a very different tale to tell; but spies they would send, and the whole affair proved a most humiliating failure.

"And they turned, and went up into the mountain, and came unto the valley of Eschol, and searched it out. And they took of the fruit of the land in their hands, and brought it down unto us, and brought us word again, and said, 'It is a good land which the Lord our God doth give us.'" How could it possibly be otherwise when God was giving it? Did they want spies to tell them that the gift of God was good? Assuredly, they ought not. An artless faith would have argued thus: Whatever God gives must be worthy of Himself; we want no spies to assure us of this. But, ah! this artless faith is an uncommonly rare gem in this world; and even those who possess it know but little of its value or how to use it. It is one thing to talk of the life of faith, and another thing altogether to live it, — the theory is one thing, the living reality quite another. But let us never forget that it is the privilege of every child of God to live by faith, and, further, that the life of faith takes in every thing that the believer can possibly need, from the starting-post to the goal of his earthly career. We have already touched upon this important point; it cannot be too earnestly or constantly insisted upon.

With regard to the mission of the spies, the reader will note with interest the way in which Moses refers to it. He confines himself to that portion of their testimony which was according to truth; he says nothing about the ten infidel spies. This is in perfect keeping with the scope and object of the book. Every thing is brought to bear, in a moral way, on the conscience of the congregation. He reminds them that they themselves had proposed to send the spies; and yet, although the spies had placed before them the fruit of the land, and borne testimony to its goodness, they would not go up. —"Notwithstanding ye would not go up, but rebelled against the commandment of the Lord your God." There was no excuse whatever. It was evident that their hearts were in a state of positive unbelief and rebellion, and the mission of the spies, from first to last, only made this fully manifest.

"And ye murmured in your tents, and said, 'Because the Lord hated us'—a terrible lie on the very face of it!—'He hath brought us forth out of the land of Egypt, to deliver us into the hand of the Amorites, to destroy us.'" What a strange proof of hatred! How utterly absurd are the arguments of unbelief! Surely, had He hated them, nothing was easier than to leave them to die amid the brick-kilns of Egypt, beneath the cruel lash of Pharaoh's taskmasters. Why take so much trouble about them? Why those ten plagues sent upon the land of their oppressors? Why, if He hated them, did He not allow the waters of the Red Sea to overwhelm them as they had overwhelmed their enemies? Why had He delivered them from the sword of Amalek? In a word, why all these marvelous triumphs of grace on their behalf if He hated them? Ah! if they had not been governed by a spirit of dark and senseless unbelief, such a brilliant array of evidence would have led them to a conclusion the direct opposite of that to which they gave utterance. There is nothing beneath the canopy of heaven so stupidly irrational as unbelief; and, on the other hand, there is nothing so sound, clear, and logical as the simple argument of a childlike faith. May the reader ever be enabled to prove the truth of this.

"And ye murmured in your tents." Unbelief is not only a blind and senseless reasoner, but a dark and gloomy murmurer. It neither gets to the right side of things nor the bright side of things. It is always in the dark—always in the wrong, simply because it shuts out God, and looks only at circumstances. They said, "Whither shall we go up? our brethren have discouraged our hearts, saying, 'The people is greater and taller than we'—but they were not greater than Jehovah—'and the cities are great and *walled up to heaven'*—the gross exaggeration of unbelief—'and moreover we have seen the sons of the Anakims there.'"

Now, Faith would say, Well, what though the cities be walled up to heaven, our God is above them, for He is *in* heaven. What are great cities or lofty walls to Him who formed the universe, and sustains it by the Word of His power? What are Anakims in the presence of the almighty God? If the land were covered with walled cities from Dan to Beersheba, and if the giants were as numerous as the leaves of the forest, they would be as the chaff of the threshing-floor before the One who has promised to give the land of Canaan to the seed of Abraham, His friend, for an everlasting possession.

But Israel had not faith, as the inspired apostle tells us in the third chapter of Hebrews, "They could not enter in because of unbelief." Here lay the great difficulty. The walled cities and the terrible Anakims would soon have been disposed of had Israel only trusted God. He would have made very short work of all these; but, ah! that deplorable unbelief! it ever stands in the way of our blessing. It hinders the outshining of the glory of God; it casts a dark shadow over our souls, and robs us of the privilege of proving the all-sufficiency of our God to meet our every need and remove our every difficulty.

Blessed be His name, He never fails a trusting heart. It is His delight to honor the very largest drafts that Faith hands in at His exhaustless treasury. His assuring word to us ever is, "Be not afraid; only believe." And again, "According to your faith be it unto you." Precious soul-stirring words! may we all realize more fully their living power and sweetness. We may rest assured of this, we can never go too far in counting on God; it would be a simple impossibility. Our grand mistake is that we do not draw more largely upon His infinite resources. "Said I not unto thee that if thou wouldest believe, thou shouldest see the glory of God?"

Thus we can see why it was that Israel failed to see the glory of God on the occasion before us,—they did not believe. The mission of the spies proved a complete failure. As it began, so it ended—in the most deplorable unbelief. God was shut out: difficulties filled their vision.

"They could not enter in." They could not see the glory of God. Hearken to the deeply affecting words of Moses. It does the heart good to read them. They touch the very deepest springs of our renewed being.—"Then I said unto you, 'Dread not, neither be afraid of them. The Lord your God which goeth before you, He shall fight for you'—only think of God fighting for people! think of Jehovah as a Man of war!—'He shall fight for you, according to all that He did for you in Egypt before your eyes; and in the wilderness, where thou hast seen how that *the Lord thy God bare thee, as a man doth bear his son*, in all the way that ye went, until ye came into this place.' Yet in this thing *ye did not believe the Lord your God*, who went in the way before you, to search you out a place to pitch your tents in, in fire by night, to show you by what way ye should go, and in a cloud by day."

What moral force, what touching sweetness in this appeal! How clearly we can see here, as indeed on every page of the book, that Deuteronomy is not a barren repetition of facts, but a most powerful commentary on those facts. It is well that the reader should be thoroughly clear as to this. If in the book of Exodus or Numbers the inspired lawgiver records the actual facts of Israel's wilderness-life, in the book of Deuteronomy he comments on those facts with a pathos that quite melts the heart. And here it is that the exquisite style of Jehovah's acts is pointed out and dwelt upon with such inimitable skill and delicacy. Who could consent to give up the lovely figure set forth in the words, "As a man doth bear his son"? Here we have the style of the action. Could we do without this? Assuredly not. It is the style of an action that touches the heart, because it is the style that so peculiarly expresses the heart. If the power of the *hand* or the wisdom of the *mind* is seen in the *substance* of an action, the love of the *heart* comes out in the *style*. Even a little child can understand this, though he might not be able to explain it.

But, alas! Israel could not trust God to bring them into the land. Notwithstanding the marvelous display of His power, His faithfulness, His goodness, and loving-kindness, from the brick-kilns of Egypt to the very borders of the land of Canaan, yet they did not believe. With an array of evidence which ought to have satisfied any heart, they still doubted. "And the Lord heard the voice of your words, and was wroth, and sware, saying, 'Surely there shall not one of these men of this evil generation see that good land, which I sware to give unto your fathers, save Caleb the son of Jephunneh; he shall see it; and to him will I give the land that he hath trodden upon, and to his children, because he hath wholly followed the Lord.'"

"Said I not unto thee that if thou wouldest believe, thou shouldest see the glory of God?" Such is the divine order. Men will tell you that seeing is believing, but in the kingdom of God, believing is seeing. Why was it that not a man of that evil generation was allowed to see the good land? Simply because they did not believe in the Lord their God. On the other hand, why was Caleb allowed to see and take possession? Simply because he believed. Unbelief is ever the great hindrance in the way of our seeing the glory of God.—"He did not many mighty works there because of their unbelief." If Israel had only believed, only trusted the Lord their God, only confided in the love of His heart and in the power of His arm, He would have brought them in and planted them in the mountain of His inheritance.

And just so is it with the Lord's people now. There is no limit to the blessings which we might enjoy, could we only count more fully upon God. "All things are possible to him that believeth." Our God will never say, You have drawn too largely; you expect too much. Impossible. It is the joy of His loving heart to answer the very largest expectations of Faith.

Let us, then, draw largely. "Open thy mouth wide, and I will fill it." The exhaustless treasury of heaven is thrown open to Faith. "*All things* whatsoever ye shall ask in prayer, believing, ye shall receive." "If any of you lack wisdom, let him ask of God, who giveth to all men liberally, and upbraideth not; and it shall be given him. But let him ask in faith, *nothing wavering*." Faith is the divine secret of the whole matter—the main-spring of Christian life from first to last. Faith wavers not, staggers not: Unbelief is ever a waverer and a staggerer, and hence it never sees the glory of God, never sees His power. It is deaf to His voice and blind to His actings; it depresses the heart and weakens the hands; it darkens the path and hinders all progress. It kept Israel out of the land of Canaan for forty years; and we have no conception of the amount of blessing, privilege, power and usefulness which we are constantly missing through its terrible influence. If faith were in more lively exercise in our hearts, what a different condition of things we should witness in our midst. What is the secret of the deplorable deadness and barrenness throughout the wide field of Christian profession? How are we to account for our impoverished condition, our low tone, our stunted growth? Why is it that we see such poor results in every department of Christian work? Why are there so few genuine conversions? Why are our evangelists so frequently cast down by reason of the paucity of their sheaves? How are we to answer all these questions? what is the cause? Will any one attempt to say it is not our unbelief?

No doubt, our divisions have much to do with it; our worldliness, our carnality, our self-indulgence, our love of ease. But what is the remedy for all these evils? How are our hearts to be drawn out in genuine love to all our brethren? By faith, that precious principle "that worketh by love." Thus the blessed apostle says to the dear young converts at Thessalonica, "Your faith groweth exceedingly." And what then? "The love of every one of you all toward each other aboundeth." Thus it must ever be. Faith puts us into direct contact with the eternal spring of love in God Himself, and the necessary consequence is that our hearts are drawn out in love to all who belong to Him—all in whom we can, in the very feeblest way, trace His blessed image. We cannot possibly be near the Lord and not love all who in every place call upon His name out of a pure heart. The nearer we are to Christ, the more intensely we must be knit, in true brotherly love, to every member of His body.

Then as to worldliness, in all its varied forms, how is it to be overcome? Hear the reply of another inspired apostle.—"For whatsoever is born of God overcometh the world; and this is the victory that overcometh the world, even our faith. Who is he that overcometh the world, but he that believeth that Jesus is the Son of God?" The new man, walking in the power of faith, lives above the world, above its motives, above its objects, its principles, its habits, its fashions; he has nothing in common with it. Though in it, he is not of it; he moves right athwart its current; he draws all his springs from heaven; his life, his hope, his all is there, and he ardently longs to be there himself when his work on earth is done.

Thus we see what a mighty principle faith is. It purifies the heart, it works by love, and it overcomes the world. In short, it links the heart in living power with God Himself, and this is the secret of true elevation, holy benevolence, and divine purity. No marvel, therefore, that Peter calls it "precious faith," for truly it is precious beyond all human thought.

See how this mighty principle acted in Caleb, and the blessed fruit it produced. He was permitted to realize the truth of those words, uttered hundreds of years afterwards, "According to your faith be it unto you." He believed that God was able to bring them into the land, and that all the difficulties and hindrances were simply bread for faith. And God, as He ever does, answered his faith. "Then the children of Judah came unto Joshua in Gilgal; and Caleb the son of Jephunneh the Kenezite said unto him, 'Thou knowest the thing that the Lord said unto Moses the man of God concerning me and thee in Kadesh-barnea. Forty years old was I when Moses the servant of the Lord sent me from Kadesh-barnea to espy out the land; and I brought him word again as it was in my heart'—the simple testimony of a bright and lovely faith.—'Nevertheless my brethren that went up with me made the heart of the people melt; but I wholly followed the Lord my God. And Moses sware on that day, saying, Surely the land whereon thy feet have trodden shall be thine inheritance, and thy children's forever, because thou hast wholly followed the Lord my God. And now, behold, the Lord hath kept me alive, *as He said*, these forty and five years, ever since the Lord spake this word unto Moses, while the children of Israel wandered in the wilderness; and now, lo, I am this day fourscore and five years old. As yet I am as strong this day as I was in the day that Moses sent me; as my strength was then, even so is my strength now, for war, both to go out, and to come in. Now therefore give me this mountain, whereof the Lord spake in that day; for thou heardest in that day how the Anakims were there, and that the cities were great and fenced: if so be the Lord will be with me, then I shall be able to drive them out, as the Lord said.'"

How refreshing are the utterances of an artless faith! How edifying! how truly encouraging! How vividly they contrast with the gloomy, depressing, withering accents of dark, God-dishonoring unbelief! "And Joshua blessed him, and gave unto Caleb the son of Jephunneh Hebron for an inheritance. Hebron therefore became the inheritance of Caleb the son of Jephunneh the Kenezite unto this day, because that he wholly followed the Lord God of Israel." (Joshua xiv.) Caleb, like his father Abraham, was strong in faith, giving glory to God; and we may say, with all possible confidence, that inasmuch as faith ever honors God, He ever delights to honor faith; and we feel persuaded that if only the Lord's people could more fully confide in God, if they would but draw more largely upon His infinite resources, we should witness a totally different condition of things from what we see around us. "Said I not unto thee that if thou wouldest believe, thou shouldest see the glory of God?" Oh for a more lively faith in God—a bolder grasp of His faithfulness, His goodness, and His power! Then we might look for more glorious results in the gospel-field; more zeal, more energy, more intense devotedness in the Church of God; and more of the fragrant fruits of righteousness in the life of believers individually.

We shall now, for a moment, look at the closing verses of our chapter, in which we shall find some very weighty instruction. And, first of all, we see the actings of divine government displayed in a most solemn and impressive manner. Moses refers, in a very touching way, to the fact of his exclusion from the promised land.—"Also the Lord was angry with me *for your sakes,* saying, 'Thou also shalt not go in thither.'"

Mark the words, "for your sakes." It was very needful to remind the congregation that it was on their account that Moses, that beloved and honored servant of the Lord, was prevented from crossing the Jordan, and setting his foot upon the land of Canaan. True, "he spake unadvisedly with his lips," but "they provoked his spirit" to do so. This ought to have touched them to the quick. They not only failed, through unbelief, to enter in themselves, but they were the cause of his exclusion, much as he longed to see "that goodly mountain and Lebanon." (See Ps. cvi. 32.)

But the government of God is a grand and awful reality. Let us never for one moment forget this. The human mind may marvel why a few ill-advised words, a few hasty sentences, should be the cause of keeping such a beloved and honored servant of God from that which he so ardently desired; but it is our place to bow the head in humble adoration and holy reverence, not to reason or judge. "Shall not the Judge of all the earth do right?" Most surely. He can make no mistake. "Great and marvelous are Thy works, Lord God Almighty; just and true are Thy ways, Thou King of nations." "God is greatly to be feared in the assembly of the saints; and to be had in reverence of all them that are about Him." "Our God is a consuming fire;" and "it is a fearful thing to fall into the hands of the living God."

Does it in any wise interfere with the action and range of the divine government that we, as Christians, are under the reign of grace? By no means. It is as true to-day as ever it was that "whatsoever *a man* soweth, that shall he also reap." Hence, therefore, it would be a serious mistake for any one to draw a plea from the freedom of divine grace to trifle with the enactments of divine government. The two things are perfectly distinct, and should never be confounded. Grace can pardon—freely, fully, eternally; but the wheels of Jehovah's governmental chariot roll on, in crushing power and appalling solemnity. Grace pardoned Adam's sin; but Government drove him out of Eden, to earn a living by the sweat of his brow, amid the thorns and thistles of a cursed earth: Grace pardoned David's sin, but the sword of Government hung over his house to the end,—Bathsheba was the mother of Solomon, but Absalom rose in rebellion.

So with Moses; Grace brought him to the top of Pisgah and showed him the land, but Government sternly and absolutely forbad his entrance thither. Nor does it in the least touch this weighty principle to be told that Moses, in his official capacity as the representative of the legal system, could not bring the people into the land. This is quite true; but it leaves wholly untouched the solemn truth now before us. Neither in the twentieth chapter of Numbers nor in the first chapter of Deuteronomy have we any thing about Moses in his official capacity. It is himself personally we have before us, and he is forbidden to enter the land because of having spoken unadvisedly with his lips.

It will be well for us all to ponder deeply, as in the immediate presence of God, this great practical truth. We may rest assured that the more truly we enter into the knowledge of grace, the more we shall feel the solemnity of government, and entirely justify its enactments. Of this we are most fully persuaded. But there is imminent danger of taking up, in a light and careless manner, the doctrines of grace while the heart and the life are not brought under the sanctifying influence of those doctrines. This has to be watched against with holy jealousy. There is nothing in all this world more awful than mere fleshly familiarity with the theory of salvation by grace. It opens the door for every form of licentiousness. Hence it is that we feel the necessity of pressing upon the conscience of the reader the practical truth of the government of God. It is most salutary at all times, but particularly so in this our day, when there is such a fearful tendency to turn the grace of our God into lasciviousness. We shall invariably find that those who most fully enter into the deep blessedness of being under the reign of grace, do also most thoroughly justify the actings of divine government.

But we learn, from the closing lines of our chapter, that the people were by no means prepared to submit themselves under the governmental hand of God; in short, they would neither have grace nor government. When invited to go up at once and take possession of the land, with the fullest assurances of the divine presence and power with them, they hesitated and refused to go. They gave themselves up completely to a spirit of dark unbelief. In vain did Joshua and Caleb sound in their ears the most encouraging words, in vain did they set before their eyes the rich fruit of the goodly land, in vain did Moses seek to move them by the most soul-stirring words; they would not go up when they were told to go. And what then? They were taken at their word. According to their unbelief, so was it unto them. "Moreover, your little ones, which ye said should be a prey, and your children, which in that day had no knowledge between good and evil, they shall go in thither, and unto them will I give it, and they shall possess it. But as for you, turn you, and take your journey into the wilderness, by the way of the Red Sea."

How sad! and yet how else could it be? If they would not, in simple faith, go up into the land, there remained nothing for them but turning back into the wilderness. But to this they would not submit. They would neither avail themselves of the provisions of grace nor bow to the sentence of judgment.—"Then ye answered and said unto me, 'We have sinned against the Lord; we will go up and fight, according to all that the Lord our God commanded us.' And when ye had girded on every man his weapon of war, ye were ready to go up into the hill."

This looked like contrition and self-judgment; but it was hollow and false. It is a very easy thing to *say*, "We have sinned." Saul said it in his day; but he said it without heart, without any genuine sense of what he was saying. We may easily gather the force and value of the words "I have sinned" from the fact that they were immediately followed by "*Honor me* now, I pray thee, before the elders of my people." What a strange contradiction!—"I have sinned," yet "Honor me." If he had really felt his sin, how different his language would have been! how different his spirit, style, and deportment! but it was all a solemn mockery. Only conceive a man full of himself, making use of a form of words, without one atom of true heart-feeling; and then, in order to get honor for himself, going through the empty formality of worshiping God. What a picture! Can any thing be more sorrowful? How terribly offensive to Him who desires truth in the inward parts, and who seeks those to worship Him who worship Him in spirit and in truth! The feeblest breathings of a broken and contrite heart are precious to God; but, oh, how offensive to Him are the hollow formalities of a mere religiousness, the object of which is to exalt man in his own eyes and in the eyes of his fellows! How perfectly worthless is the mere lip-confession of sin where the heart does not feel it! As a recent writer has well remarked, "it is an easy thing to say, 'We have sinned,' but how often we have to learn that it is not the quick, abrupt confession of sin which affords evidence that sin is felt! It is rather a proof of hardness of heart. The conscience feels that a certain act of confessing the sin is necessary, but perhaps there is hardly any thing which more hardens the heart than the habit of confessing sin without feeling it. This, I believe, is one of the great snares of christendom from of old and now, that is, the stereotyped acknowledgment of sin—the mere habit of hurrying through a formula of confession to God. I dare say we have almost all done so, without referring to any particular mode; for, alas! there is formality enough; and without having written forms, the heart may frame forms of its own, as we may have observed, if not known it, in our own experience, without finding fault with other people."[4]

Thus it was with Israel at Kadesh. Their confession of sin was utterly worthless; there was no truth in it. Had they felt what they were saying, they would have bowed to the judgment of God, and meekly accepted the consequence of their sin. There is no finer proof of true contrition than quiet submission to the governmental dealings of God. Look at the case of Moses. See how he bowed his head to the divine discipline. "The Lord," he says, "was angry with me for your sakes, saying, 'Thou also shalt not go in thither. But Joshua the son of Nun, which standeth before thee, he shall go in thither: encourage him; for he shall cause Israel to inherit it.'"

Here, Moses shows them that they were the cause of his exclusion from the land; and yet he utters not a single murmuring word, but meekly bows to the divine judgment, not only content to be superseded by another, but ready to appoint and encourage his successor. There is no trace of jealousy or envy here. It was enough for that beloved and honored servant if God was glorified and the need of the congregation met. He was not occupied with himself or his own interests, but with the glory of God and the blessing of His people.

But the people manifested a very different spirit. "We will go up and fight." How vain! How foolish! When commanded by God and encouraged by His true-hearted servants to go up and possess the land, they replied, "Whither shall we go up?" and when commanded to turn back into the wilderness, they replied, "We will go up and fight."

"And the Lord said unto me, 'Say unto them, Go not up, neither fight; for I am not among you; lest ye be smitten before your enemies.' So I spake unto you; and ye would not hear, but rebelled against the commandment of the Lord, and went presumptuously up into the hill. And the Amorites, which dwelt in that mountain, came out against you, and chased you, as bees do, and destroyed you in Seir, even unto Hormah."

It was quite impossible for Jehovah to accompany them along the path of self-will and rebellion; and, most assuredly, Israel, without the divine presence, could be no match for the Amorites. If God be for us and with us, all must be victory; but we cannot count on God if we are not treading the path of obedience. It is simply the height of folly to imagine that we can have God with us if our ways are not right. "The name of the Lord is a strong tower, the righteous runneth into it and is safe." But if we are not walking in practical righteousness, it is wicked presumption to talk of having the Lord as our strong tower.

Blessed be His name, He can meet us in the very depths of our weakness and failure, provided there be the genuine and hearty confession of our true condition; but to assume that we have the Lord with us while we are doing our own will and walking in palpable unrighteousness, is nothing but wickedness and hardness of heart. "Trust in the Lord, and do good"—this is the divine order; but to talk of trusting in the Lord while doing evil, is to turn the grace of our God into lasciviousness, and place ourselves completely in the hands of the devil, who only seeks our moral ruin. "The eyes of the Lord run to and fro throughout the whole earth, to show Himself strong in the behalf of them whose heart is perfect toward Him." When we have a good conscience, we can lift up the head and move on through all sorts of difficulties; but to attempt to tread the path of faith with a bad conscience, is the most dangerous thing in this world. We can only hold up the shield of faith when our loins are girt with truth, and the breast covered with the breastplate of righteousness.

It is of the utmost importance that Christians should seek to maintain practical righteousness, in all its branches. There is immense moral weight and value in these words of the blessed apostle Paul, "Herein do I exercise myself, to have always a conscience void of offense toward God and men." He ever sought to wear the breastplate, and to be clothed in that white linen which is the righteousness of saints. And so should we. It is our holy privilege to tread, day by day, with firm step, the path of duty, the path of obedience, the path on which the light of God's approving countenance ever shines; then, assuredly, we can count on God, lean upon Him, draw from Him, find all our springs in Him, wrap ourselves up in His faithfulness, and thus move on, in peaceful communion and holy worship, toward our heavenly home.

It is not, we repeat, that we cannot look to God in our weakness, our failure, and even when we have erred and sinned. Blessed be His name, we can; and His ear is ever open to our cry. "If we confess our sins, He is faithful and just to forgive us our sins, and to cleanse us from all unrighteousness." (1 John i.) "Out of the depths have I cried unto thee, O Lord. Lord, hear my voice: let Thine ears be attentive to the voice of my supplications. If Thou, Lord, shouldest mark iniquities, O Lord, who shall stand? But there is forgiveness with Thee, that Thou mayest be feared." (Ps. cxxx.) There is absolutely no limit to divine forgiveness, inasmuch as there is no limit to the extent of the atonement, no limit to the virtue and efficacy of the blood of Jesus Christ, God's Son, which cleanseth from all sin; no limit to the prevalency of the intercession of our adorable Advocate, our great High-Priest, who is able to save to the uttermost—right through and through to the end—them that come unto God by Him.

All this is most blessedly true; it is largely taught and variously illustrated throughout the volume of inspiration; but the confession of sin, and the pardon thereof, must not be confounded with practical righteousness. There are two distinct conditions in which we may call upon God: we may call upon Him in deep contrition and be heard, or we may call upon Him with a good conscience and an uncondemning heart and be heard. But the two things are very distinct; and not only are they distinct in themselves, but they both stand in marked contrast with that indifference and hardness of heart which would presume to count on God in the face of positive disobedience and practical unrighteousness. It is this which is so dreadful in the sight of the Lord, and which must bring down His heavy judgment. Practical righteousness He owns and approves; confessed sin He can freely and fully pardon; but to imagine that we can put our trust in God while our feet are treading the path of iniquity, is nothing short of the most shocking impiety. "Trust ye not in lying words, saying, The temple of the Lord, The temple of the Lord, The temple of the Lord, are these. For if ye throughly amend your ways and your doings; if ye throughly execute judgment between a man and his neighbor; if ye oppress not the stranger, the fatherless, and the widow, and shed not innocent blood in this place, neither walk after other gods to your hurt: then will I cause you to dwell in this place, in the land that I gave to your fathers, forever and ever. Behold, ye trust in lying words, that cannot profit. Will ye steal, murder, and commit adultery, and swear falsely, and burn incense unto Baal, and walk after other gods whom ye know not; and come and stand before Me in this house, which is called by My name, and say, 'We are delivered to do all these abominations?'" (Jeremiah vii.)

God deals in moral realities. He desires truth in the inward parts; and if men will presume to hold the truth in unrighteousness, they must look out for His righteous judgment. It is the thought of all this that makes us feel the awful condition of the professing church. The solemn passage which we have just culled from the prophet Jeremiah, though bearing primarily upon the men of Judah and the inhabitants of Jerusalem, has a very pointed application to christendom. We find, in the third chapter of 2 Timothy, that all the abominations of heathenism, as detailed in the close of Romans i, are reproduced in the last days under the garb of the Christian profession, and in immediate connection with "a form of godliness." What must be the end of such a condition of things? Unmitigated wrath. The very heaviest judgments of God are reserved for that vast mass of baptized profession which we call christendom. The moment is rapidly approaching when all the beloved and blood-bought people of God shall be called away out of this dark and sinful, though so-called "Christian world," to be forever with the Lord, in that sweet home of love prepared in the Father's house. Then the "strong delusion" shall be sent upon christendom — upon those very countries where the light of a full-orbed Christianity has shone, where a full and free gospel has been preached, where the Bible has been circulated by millions, and where all, in some way or another, profess the name of Christ and call themselves Christians.

And what then?—what is to follow this "strong delusion"? Any fresh testimony? any further overtures of mercy? any further effort of long-suffering grace? Not for christendom! not for the rejecters of the gospel of God! not for Christless, Godless professors of the hollow and worthless forms of Christianity! The heathen shall hear "the everlasting gospel"—"the gospel of the kingdom;" but as for that terrible thing, that most frightful anomaly called christendom—"the vine of the earth," nothing remains but the wine-press of the wrath of Almighty God, the blackness and darkness forever, the lake that burneth with fire and brimstone.

Reader, these are the true sayings of God. Nothing would be easier than to place before your eyes an array of Scripture proof perfectly unanswerable: this would be foreign to our present object. The New Testament, from cover to cover, sets forth the solemn truth above enunciated; and every system of theology under the sun that teaches differently will be found, on this point at least, to be totally false.

CHAPTER II

The closing lines of chapter i. show us the people weeping before the Lord.—"And ye returned and wept before the Lord; but the Lord would not hearken to your voice, nor give ear unto you. So ye abode in Kadesh many days, according unto the days that ye abode there."

There was no more reality in their tears than in their words,—their weeping was no more to be trusted than their confession. It is possible for people to confess and shed tears without any true sense of sin in the presence of God. This is very solemn. It is really mocking God. We know, blessed forever be His name, that a truly contrite heart is His delight. He makes His abode with such. "The sacrifices of God are a broken spirit: a broken and a contrite heart, O God, Thou wilt not despise." The tears that flow from a penitent heart are more precious, by far, to God than the cattle upon a thousand hills, because they prove that there is room in that heart for Him; and this is what He seeks, in His infinite grace. He wants to dwell in our hearts, and fill us with the deep, unspeakable joy of His own most blessed presence.

But Israel's confession and tears at Kadesh were not real, and hence the Lord could not accept them. The feeblest cry of a broken heart ascends directly to the throne of God, and is immediately answered by the soothing, healing balm of His pardoning love; but when tears and confession stand connected with self-will and rebellion, they are not only utterly worthless, but a positive insult to the divine Majesty.

Thus, then, the people had to turn back into the wilderness, and wander there for forty years. There was nothing else for it. They would not go up into the land, in simple faith, with God, and He would not go up with them in their self-will and self-confidence; they had, therefore, simply to accept the consequence of their disobedience. If they would not enter the land, they must fall in the wilderness.

How solemn is all this! and how solemn is the Spirit's commentary upon it in the third chapter of Hebrews! and how pointed and forcible the application to us! We must quote the passage for the benefit of the reader.— "Wherefore, as the Holy Ghost saith, 'To-day if ye will hear His voice, harden not your hearts, as in the provocation, in the day of temptation in the wilderness; when your fathers tempted Me, proved Me, and saw My works forty years. Wherefore I was grieved with that generation, and said, They do alway err *in heart*; and they have not known My ways. So I sware in My wrath, They shall not enter into My rest.' Take heed, brethren, lest there be in any of you an evil heart of unbelief, in departing from the living God. But exhort one another daily, while it is called 'To-day;' lest any of you be hardened through the deceitfulness of sin. For we are made partakers of Christ, if we hold the beginning of our confidence steadfast unto the end; while it is said, 'To-day if ye will hear His voice, harden not your hearts, as in the provocation. For some, when they had heard, did provoke; howbeit not all that came out of Egypt by Moses. But with whom was He grieved forty years? was it not with them that had sinned, whose carcases fell in the wilderness? And to whom sware He that they should not enter into His rest, but to them that believed not? So we see that they could not enter in because of unbelief. Let us therefore fear, lest, a promise being left us of entering into His rest, any of you should seem to come short of it. For unto us was the gospel preached, as well as unto them; but the word preached did not profit them, not being mixed with faith in them that heard."

Here, as in every page of the inspired volume, we learn that unbelief is *the* thing that grieves the heart and dishonors the name of God; and not only so, but it robs us of the blessings, the dignities, and the privileges which infinite grace bestows. We have very little idea of how much we lose, in every way, through the unbelief of our hearts. Just as in Israel's case the land was before them, in all its fruitfulness and beauty, and they were commanded to go and take possession, but "they could not enter in because of unbelief;" so with us — we fail to possess ourselves of the fullness of blessing which sovereign grace has put within our reach. The very treasury of heaven is thrown open to us, but we fail to appropriate. We are poor, feeble, empty, and barren when we might be rich, vigorous, full, and fruitful. We are blessed with all spiritual blessings in the heavenlies in Christ, but how shallow is our apprehension! how feeble our grasp! how poor our thoughts!

Then, again, who can calculate how much we lose, through our unbelief, in the matter of the Lord's work in our midst? We read in the gospel of a certain place in which our blessed Lord could not do many mighty works, because of their unbelief. Has this no voice for us? Do we too hinder Him by unbelief? We shall perhaps be told by some that the Lord will carry on His work irrespective of us or our faith; He will gather out His own and accomplish the number of His elect spite of our unbelief. Not all the power of earth and hell — men and devils combined can hinder the carrying out of His counsels and purposes; and as to His work, It is not by might nor by power, but by His Spirit. Human efforts are in vain; and the Lord's cause can never be furthered by Nature's excitement.

Now, all this is perfectly true; but it leaves wholly untouched the inspired statement quoted above. "He could there do not many mighty works, because of their unbelief." Did not those people lose blessing through their unbelief? did they not hinder much good being done? We must beware how we surrender our minds to the withering influence of a pernicious fatalism, which, with a certain semblance of truth, is utterly false, inasmuch as it denies all human responsibility and paralizes all godly energy in the cause of Christ. We have to bear in mind that the same One who, in His eternal counsels, has decreed the end, has also designed the means; and if we, in the sinful unbelief of our hearts and under the influence of one-sided truth, fold our arms and neglect the means, He will set us aside and carry on His work by other hands. He will work, blessed be His holy name, but we shall lose the dignity, the privilege, and the blessing of being His instruments.

Look at that striking scene in the second of Mark. It most forcibly illustrates the great principle which we desire to press upon all who may read these lines. It proves the power of faith, in connection with the carrying on of the Lord's work. If the four men whose conduct is here set forth had suffered themselves to be influenced by a mischievous fatalism, they would have argued that it was no use doing any thing—if the palsied man was to be cured he would be cured, without human effort. Why should they busy themselves in climbing up on the house, uncovering the roof, and letting down the sick man into the midst before Jesus? Ah, it was well for the palsied man and well for themselves that they did not act on such miserable reasoning as this. See how their lovely faith wrought. It refreshed the heart of the Lord Jesus; it brought the sick man into the place of healing, pardon, and blessing; and it gave occasion for the display of divine power, which arrested the attention of all present and gave testimony to the great truth that God was on earth, in the Person of Jesus of Nazareth, healing diseases and forgiving sins.

Many other examples might be adduced, but there in no need. All Scripture establishes the fact that unbelief hinders our blessing, hinders our usefulness, robs us of the rare privilege of being God's honored instruments in the carrying on of His glorious work, and of seeing the operations of His hand and His Spirit in our midst; and, on the other hand, that faith draws down power and blessing, not only for ourselves, but for others,—that it both glorifies and gratifies God, by clearing the platform of the creature and making room for the display of divine power. In short, there is no limit to the blessing which we might enjoy at the hand of our God if our hearts were more governed by that simple faith which ever counts on Him, and which He ever delights to honor. "According to your faith, be it unto you." Precious soul-stirring words! May they encourage us to draw more largely upon those exhaustless resources which we have in God. He delights to be used, blessed forever be His holy name. His word to us is, "Open thy mouth *wide*, and I will fill it." We can never expect too much from the God of all grace, who has given us His only begotten Son, and will with Him freely give us all things.

But Israel could not trust God to bring them into the land; they presumed to go in their own strength, and, as a consequence, were put to flight before their enemies. Thus it must ever be. Presumption and faith are two totally different things: the former can only issue in defeat and disaster; the latter, in sure and certain victory.

"Then we turned and took our journey into the wilderness, by the way of the Red Sea, as the Lord spake unto me; and we compassed Mount Seir many days." There is great moral beauty in the little word "*we*." Moses links himself thoroughly with the people. He and Joshua and Caleb had all to turn back into the wilderness, in company with the unbelieving congregation. This might, in the judgment of nature, seem hard; but we may rest assured it was good and profitable. There is always deep blessing in bowing to the will of God, even though we may not always be able to see the why and the wherefore of things. We do not read of a single murmuring word from these honored servants of God at having to turn back into the wilderness for forty years, although they were quite ready to go up into the land. No; they simply turned back. And well they might, when Jehovah turned back also. How could they think of complaining, when they beheld the traveling-chariot of the God of Israel facing round to the wilderness? Surely the patient grace and long-suffering mercy of God might well teach them to accept, with a willing mind, a protracted sojourn in the wilderness, and to wait for the blessed moment of entrance upon the promised land.

It is a great thing always to submit ourselves meekly under the hand of God. We are sure to reap a rich harvest of blessing from the exercise. It is really taking the yoke of Christ upon us, which, as He Himself assures us, is the true secret of rest. "Come unto Me, all ye that labor and are heavy laden, and I will give you rest. Take My yoke upon you, and learn of Me; for I am meek and lowly in heart; and ye shall find rest unto your souls. For My yoke is easy, and My burden is light."

What was this yoke? It was absolute and complete subjection to the Father's will. This we see in perfection in our adorable Lord and Saviour Jesus Christ. He could say, "Even so, Father; for so it seemed good in Thy sight." Here was the point with Him—"good in Thy sight." This settled every thing. Was His testimony rejected? did He seem to labor in vain, and spend His strength for naught and in vain? What then? "I thank Thee, O Father, Lord of heaven and earth." It was all right. Whatever pleased the Father, pleased Him. He never had a thought or wish that was not in perfect consonance with the will of God. Hence He, as a man, ever enjoyed perfect rest. He rested in the divine counsels and purposes. The current of His peace was unruffled, from first to last.

This was the yoke of Christ; and this is what He, in His infinite grace, invites us to take upon us, in order that we too may find rest unto our souls. Let us mark and seek to understand the words, "ye shall *find* rest." We must not confound the "rest" which *He gives* with the "rest" which we find. When the weary, burdened, heavy-laden soul comes to Jesus in simple faith, He gives rest—settled rest—the rest which flows from the full assurance that all is done,—sins forever put away; perfect righteousness accomplished, revealed, and possessed; every question divinely and eternally settled; God glorified; Satan silenced; conscience tranquillized.

Such is the rest which Jesus gives when we come to Him. But then we have to move through the scenes and circumstances of our daily life. There are trials, difficulties, exercises, buffetings, disappointments, and reverses of all sorts. None of these can, in the smallest degree, touch the rest which Jesus gives; but they may very seriously interfere with the rest which we are to find. They do not trouble the conscience, but they may greatly trouble the heart; they may make us very restless, very fretful, very impatient. For instance, I want to preach at Glasgow; I am announced to do so; but lo! I am shut up in a sick-room in London. This does not trouble my conscience, but it may greatly trouble my heart; I may be in a perfect fever of restlessness, ready to exclaim, How tiresome! How terribly disappointing! Whatever am I to do? It is most untoward!

And how is this state of things to be met? How is the troubled heart to be tranquillized, and the restless mind to be calmed down? What do I want? I want to find rest; how am I to find it? By stooping down and taking Christ's precious yoke upon me—the very yoke which He Himself ever wore, in the days of His flesh—the yoke of complete subjection to the will of God. I want to be able to say, without one atom of reserve—to say from the very depths of my heart, "Thy will, O Lord, be done." I want such a profound sense of His perfect love to me, and of His infinite wisdom in all His dealings with me, that I would not have it otherwise if I could—yea, that I would not move a finger to alter my position or circumstances, feeling assured that it is very much better for me to be suffering on a sick-bed in London than speaking on a platform in Glasgow.

Here lies the deep and precious secret of rest of heart, as opposed to restlessness. It is the simple ability to thank God for every thing, be it ever so contrary to our own will and utterly subversive of our own plans. It is not a mere assent to the truth that "all things work together for good to them that love God, to them who are the called according to His purpose;" it is the positive sense—the actual realization of the divine fact that the thing which God appoints is the very best thing for us; it is perfect repose in the love, wisdom, power, and faithfulness of the One who has graciously undertaken for us in every thing, and charged Himself with all that concerns us for time and eternity. We know that love will always do its very best for its object. What must it be to have God doing His very best for us? Where is the heart that would not be satisfied with God's best if only it knows aught of Him?

But He must be known ere the heart can be satisfied with His will. Eve, in the garden of Eden, beguiled by the serpent, became dissatisfied with the will of God. She *wished* for something which He had forbidden, and this something the devil undertook to supply. She thought the devil could do better for her than God. She thought to better her circumstances by taking herself out of the hands of God and placing herself in the hands of Satan. Hence it is that no unrenewed heart can ever, by any possibility, rest in the will of God. If we search the human heart to the bottom, if we submit it to a faithful analysis, we shall not find so much as a single thought in unison with the will of God—no, not one. And even in the case of the true Christian—the child of God, it is only as he is enabled, by the grace of God, to mortify his own will, to reckon himself dead, and to walk in the Spirit, that he can delight in the will of God, and give thanks in every thing. It is one of the very finest evidences of the new birth to be able, without a single shade of reserve, to say, in respect to every dealing of the hand of God, "Thy will be done." "Even so, Father; for so it seemed good in Thy sight." When the heart is in this attitude, Satan can make nothing of it. It is a grand point to be able to tell the devil and to tell the world—tell them, not in word and in tongue, but in deed and in truth; not merely with the lips, but in the heart and the life—*I am perfectly satisfied with the will of God.*

This is the way to find rest. Let us see that we understand it. It is the divine remedy for that unrest, that spirit of discontent, that dissatisfaction with our appointed lot and sphere, so sadly prevalent on all hands. It is a perfect cure for that restless ambition so utterly opposed to the mind and spirit of Christ, but so entirely characteristic of the men of this world.

May we, beloved reader, cultivate, with holy diligence, that meek and lowly spirit which is, in the sight of God, of great price, which bows to His blessed will in all things, and vindicates His dealings, come what may. Thus shall our peace flow as a river, and the name of our Lord Jesus Christ shall be magnified in our course, character, and conduct.

Ere turning from the deeply interesting and practical subject which has been engaging our attention, we would observe that there are three distinct attitudes in which the soul may be found in reference to the dealings of God, namely, subjection, acquiescence, and rejoicing. When the will is broken, there is subjection; when the understanding is enlightened as to the divine object, there is acquiescence; and when the affections are engaged with God Himself, there is positive rejoicing. Hence we read, in the tenth chapter of Luke, "In that hour Jesus *rejoiced* in spirit, and said, '*I thank Thee*, O Father, Lord of heaven and earth, that Thou hast hid these things from the wise and prudent, and hast revealed them unto babes: even so, Father; for so it seemed good in Thy sight.'" That blessed One found His perfect delight in all the will of God. It was His meat and drink to carry out that will, at all cost. In service or in suffering, in life or in death, He never had any motive but the Father's will. He could say, "I do always the things that please Him." Eternal and universal homage to His peerless name!

We shall now proceed with our chapter.

"And the Lord spake unto me, saying, 'Ye have compassed this mountain long enough; turn you northward.'"

The word of the Lord determined every thing. It fixed how long the people were to remain in any given place, and it indicated with equal distinctness whither they were next to bend their steps. There was no need whatever for them to plan or arrange their movements: it was the province and prerogative of Jehovah to settle all for them; it was theirs to obey. There is no mention here of the cloud and the trumpet; it is simply God's word and Israel's obedience.

Nothing can be more precious to a child of God, if only the heart be in a right condition, than to be guided, in all his movements, by the divine command. It saves a world of anxiety and perplexity. In Israel's case, called as they were to journey through a great and terrible wilderness, where there was no way, it was an unspeakable mercy to have their every movement, their every step, their every halting-place, ordered by on infallible Guide. There was no need whatever for them to trouble themselves about their movements, no need to inquire how long they were to stay in any given place, or where they were to go next; Jehovah settled all for them. It was for them simply to wait on Him for guidance, and to do what they were told.

Yes, reader, here was the grand point—a waiting and an obedient spirit. If this were lacking, they were liable to all sorts of questionings, reasonings, and rebellious activities. When God said, "Ye have compassed this mountain long enough," had Israel replied, No; we want to compass it a little longer: we are very comfortable here, and we do not wish to make any change; or, again, if when God said, "Turn you northward" they had replied, No; we vastly prefer going eastward; what would have been the result? Why, they would have forfeited the divine presence with them, and who could guide or help or feed them then? They could only count on the divine presence with them while they trod the path indicated by the divine command. If they chose to take their own way, there was nothing for them but famine, desolation, and darkness. The stream from the smitten rock, and the heavenly manna, were only to be found in the path of obedience.

Now, we Christians have to learn our lesson in all this—a wholesome, needed, valuable lesson. It is our sweet privilege to have our path marked out for us, day by day, by divine authority. Of this we are to be most deeply and thoroughly persuaded. We are not to allow ourselves to be robbed of this rich blessing by the plausible reasonings of unbelief. God has promised to guide us, and His promise is yea and Amen. It is for us to make our own the promise, in the artless simplicity of faith. It is as solid and as real and as true as God can make it. We cannot admit for a moment that Israel in the desert were better off in the matter of guidance than God's heavenly people in their passage through this world. How did Israel know the length of the haltings or the line of their march? By the word of God. Are we worse off? Far be the thought. Yea, we are better off by far than they. We have the Word and Spirit of God to guide us. To us pertains the high and holy privilege of walking in the footsteps of the Son of God.

Is not this perfect guidance? Yes, thank God, it is. Hear what our adorable Lord Jesus Christ saith to us,—"I am the light of the world; he that followeth Me shall not walk in darkness, but shall have the light of life." Let us mark these words, "he that *followeth Me*." He has left us "an example, that we should follow His steps." This is living guidance. How did Jesus walk? Always and only by the commandment of His Father. By that He acted; by that He moved; without it He never acted, moved, or spoke.

Now, we are called to follow Him; and in so doing, we have the assurance of His own word that we shall not walk in darkness, but shall have the light of life. Precious words!—*"the light of life."* Who can sound their living depths? who can duly estimate their worth? "The darkness is past, and the true light now shineth," and it is for us to walk in the full blaze of the light that shines along the pathway of the Son of God. Is there any uncertainty, any perplexity, any ground for hesitation here? Clearly not. How could there be if we are following Him? It is utterly impossible to combine the two ideas.

And be it remarked here that it is not by any means a question of having a literal text of Scripture for every movement or every act. For example, I cannot expect to get a text of Scripture, or a voice from heaven, to tell me to go to London or to Edinburgh; or how long I am to stay when I go. How, then, it may be asked, am I to know where I ought to go, or how long I am to stay? The answer is, Wait on God, in singleness of eye and sincerity of heart, and He will make your path as plain as a sunbeam. This was what Jesus did; and if we follow Him, we shall not walk in darkness. "I will guide thee with Mine eye" is a most precious promise; but in order to profit by it, we must be near enough to Him to catch the movement of His eye, and intimate enough with Him to understand its meaning.

Thus it is, in all the details of our daily life. It would answer a thousand questions, and solve a thousand difficulties, if we did but wait for divine guidance, and never attempt to move without it. If I have not gotten light to move, it is my plain duty to be still. We should never move in uncertainty. It often happens that we harass ourselves about moving or acting, when God would have us to be still and do nothing. We go and ask God about it, but get no answer; we betake ourselves to friends for advice and counsel, but they cannot help us, for it is entirely a question between our own souls and the Lord. Thus we are plunged in doubt and anxiety. And why? Simply because the eye is not single; we are not following Jesus, "the light of the world." We may set it down as a fixed principle, a precious axiom in the divine life, that if we are following Jesus, we shall have the light of life. He has said it, and that is enough for faith.

Hence, then, we deem ourselves perfectly warranted in concluding that the One who guided His earthly people in all their desert wanderings, can and will guide His heavenly people now in all their movements and in all their ways. But, on the other hand, let us see to it that we are not bent on doing our own will, having our own way, and carrying out our own plans. "Be ye not as the horse or as the mule, which have no understanding, whose mouth must be held in with bit and bridle, lest they come near unto thee." Be it our one grand aim to walk in the footsteps of that blessed One who pleased not Himself, but ever moved in the current of the divine will, never acted without divine authority; who, though Himself God over all, blessed forever, yet, having taken His place as a man, on the earth, surrendered completely His own will, and found His meat and His drink in doing the will of His Father. Thus shall our hearts and minds be kept in perfect peace; and we shall be enabled to move on, from day to day, with firm and decided step, along the path indicated for us by our divine and ever-present Guide, who not only knows, as God, every step of the way, but who, as man, has trodden it before us, and left us an example that we should follow His steps.

May we follow Him more faithfully in all things, through the gracious ministry of the Holy Ghost, who dwelleth in us.

We have now to invite the reader's attention to a subject of very deep interest, and one which occupies a large place in Old-Testament scripture, and is forcibly illustrated in the chapter which lies open before us, namely, God's government of the world, and His wonderful ordering of the nations of the earth. It is a grand and all-important fact to keep ever before the mind that the One whom we know as "the God and Father of our Lord Jesus Christ," and our God and Father, takes a real, lively, personal interest in the affairs of nations—that He takes cognizance of their movements and of their dealings one with another.

True, all this is in immediate connection with Israel and the land of Palestine, as we read in the thirty-second chapter of our book, and eighth verse—a passage of singular interest and of great suggestive power.—"When the Most High divided to the nations their inheritance, when He separated the sons of Adam, He set the bounds of the people according to the number of the children of Israel." Israel was and shall yet be God's earthly centre; and it is a fact of the deepest interest that, from the very outset, as we see in Genesis x, the Creator and Governor of the world formed the nations and fixed their bounds according to His own sovereign will, and with direct reference to the seed of Abraham, and that narrow strip of land which they are to possess, in virtue of the everlasting covenant made with their fathers.

But in the second chapter of Deuteronomy, we find Jehovah, in His faithfulness and righteousness, interfering to protect three distinct nations in the enjoyment of their national rights, and that, too, against the encroachments of His own chosen people. He says to Moses, "Command thou the people, saying, 'Ye are to pass through the coast of your brethren the children of Esau, which dwell in Seir; and they shall be afraid of you: take ye good heed unto yourselves therefore: meddle not with them; for I will not give you of their land, no, not so much as a foot-breadth, because I have given Mount Seir unto Esau for a possession. Ye shall buy meat of them for money, that ye may eat; and ye shall also buy water of them for money, that ye may drink.'"

Israel might imagine that they had nothing to do but seize upon the lands of the Edomite; but they had to learn something very different,—they had to be taught that the Most High is the Governor amongst the nations— that the whole earth belongs to Him, and He portions it out to one or another according to His good pleasure.

This is a very magnificent fact to keep before the mind. The great majority of men think but little of it. Emperors, kings, princes, governors, statesmen, take little account of it. They forget that God interests Himself in the affairs of nations—that He bestows kingdoms, provinces, and lands as He sees fit. They act, at times, as if it were only a question of military conquest, and as if God had nothing to do with the question of national boundaries and territorial possessions. This is their great mistake. They do not understand the meaning and force of this simple sentence, "*I have given* Mount Seir unto Esau for a possession." God will never surrender His rights in this respect. He would not allow Israel to touch a single atom of Esau's property. They were, to use a modern phrase, to pay ready cash for whatever they needed, and go quietly on their way. Indiscriminate slaughter and plunder were not to be thought of by the people of God.

And mark the lovely reason for all this. "For the Lord thy God hath blessed thee in all the works of thy hand; He knoweth thy walking through this great wilderness; these forty years the Lord thy God hath been with thee, thou hast lacked nothing." They could well afford, therefore, to let Esau alone, and leave his possessions untouched. They were the favored objects of Jehovah's tender care. He took knowledge of every step of their weary journey through the desert. He had, in His infinite goodness, charged Himself with all their necessities. He was going to give them the land of Canaan, according to His promise to Abraham; but the self-same hand which was giving them Canaan had given Mount Seir to Esau.

We see the same thing exactly in reference to Moab and Ammon.—"The Lord said unto me, 'Distress not the Moabites, neither contend with them in battle; for I will not give thee of their land for a possession, because I have given Ar unto the children of Lot for a possession.'" And again, "And when thou comest nigh over against the children of Ammon, distress them not, nor meddle with them; for I will not give thee of the land of the children of Ammon any possession, because I have given it onto the children of Lot for a possession."

The possessions here alluded to had been, of old time, in the hands of giants; but it was God's purpose to give up their territories to the children of Esau and Lot, and therefore He destroyed these giants; for who or what can stand in the way of the divine counsels? "That also was accounted a land of giants: giants dwelt therein in old time; ... a people great, and many, and tall, as the Anakims; but the Lord destroyed them before them; and they succeeded them, and dwelt in their stead: as He did to the children of Esau which dwelt in Seir, when He destroyed the Horims from before them; and they succeeded them, and dwelt in their stead even unto this day." (Ver. 20-23.)

Hence, then, Israel were not permitted to meddle with the possessions of any of these three nations—the Edomites, Ammonites, and Moabites; but in the very next sentence, we see another thing altogether in the case of the Amorites.—"Rise ye up, take your journey, and pass over the river Arnon: behold, I have given into thine hand Sihon the Amorite, king of Heshbon, and his land: begin to possess it, and contend with him in battle."

The great principle, in all these varied instructions to Israel, is that God's word must settle every thing for His people. It was not for Israel to inquire why they were to leave the possessions of Esau and Lot untouched, and to seize upon those of Sihon. They were simply to do what they were told. God can do as He pleases. He has His eye upon the whole scene: He scans it all. Men may think He has forsaken the earth, but He has not, blessed be His name. He is, as the apostle tells us in his discourse at Athens, "Lord of heaven and earth;" and "He hath made of one blood all nations of men, for to dwell on all the face of the earth; and hath determined the times before appointed, and the bounds of their habitations." And, further, "He hath appointed a day, in the which He will judge the habitable earth [οἰκουμένην] in righteousness, by that Man whom He hath ordained; whereof He hath given assurance [given proof] unto all, in that He hath raised Him from the dead."

Here we have a most solemn and weighty truth, to which men of all ranks and conditions would do well to take heed. God is the Sovereign Ruler of the world. He giveth no account of any of His matters. He puts down one and sets up another. Kingdoms, thrones, governments, are all at His disposal. He acts according to His own will in the ordering and arrangement of human affairs. But, at the same time, He holds men responsible for their actings in the various positions in which His providence has placed them. The ruler and the ruled, the king, the governor, the magistrate, the judge— all classes and grades of men will have, sooner or later, to give account to God. Each one, as if he were the only one, will have to stand before the judgment-seat of Christ, and there review his whole course, from first to last. Every act, every word, every secret thought, will there come out with awful distinctness. There will be no escaping in a crowd. The Word declares that they shall be judged "*every man* according to his works." It will be intensely individual, and unmistakably discriminating. In a word, it will be a divine judgment, and therefore absolutely perfect. Nothing will be passed over. "Every idle word that men shall speak, they shall give account thereof at the day of judgment." Kings, governors, and magistrates will have to account for the way in which they have used the power with which they were intrusted, and the wealth which passed through their hands. The noble and the wealthy who have spent their fortune and their time in folly, vanity, luxury, and self-indulgence will have to answer for it all before the throne of the Son of Man, whose eyes are as a flame of fire, to read men through and through; and His feet as fine brass, to crush, in unsparing judgment, all that is contrary to God.

Infidelity may sneeringly inquire, *How* can these things be? *How* could the untold millions of the human race find room before the judgment-seat of Christ? and *how* could there be time to enter so minutely into the details of each personal history? Faith replies, God says it shall be so, and this is conclusive; and as to the "How?" the answer is, God! Infinity! Eternity! Bring God in, and all questions are hushed and all difficulties disposed of in a moment. In fact, the one grand, triumphant answer to all the objections of the infidel, the skeptic, the rationalist, and the materialist, is just that one majestic word, "God!"

We press this upon the reader; not, indeed, to enable him to reply to infidels, but for the rest and comfort of his own heart. As to infidels, we are increasingly persuaded that our highest wisdom is to act on our Lord's words in Matthew xv.—"Let them alone." It is perfectly useless to argue with men who despise the Word of God, and have no other foundation to build upon than their own carnal reasonings. But, on the other hand, we deem it to be of the very last possible importance that the heart should ever repose, in all the artless simplicity of a child, in the truth of God's Word. "Hath He said, and shall He not do it? or hath He spoken, and shall He not make it good?"

Here is the sweet and hallowed resting-place of faith, the calm haven where the soul can find refuge from all the conflicting currents of human thought and feeling. "The Word of the Lord endureth forever; and this is the Word which by the gospel is preached unto you." Nothing can touch the Word of our God. It is settled forever in heaven; and all we want is to have it hidden in our hearts, as our own very possession—the treasure which we have received from God—the living fountain where we may ever drink for the refreshment and comfort of our souls. Then shall our peace flow as a river, and our path shall be as the shining light, which shineth more and more unto the perfect day.

Thus may it be, O Lord, with all Thy beloved people, in these days of growing infidelity. May Thy holy Word be increasingly precious to our hearts. May our consciences feel its power. May its heavenly doctrines form our character and govern our conduct in all the relationships of life, that Thy name may be glorified in all things.

CHAPTER III

"Then we turned, and went up the way to Bashan; and Og the king of Bashan came out against us, he and all his people, to battle at Edrei. And the Lord said unto me, 'Fear him not: for I will deliver him, and all his people, and his land, into thy hand; and thou shalt do unto him as thou didst unto Sihon king of the Amorites, which dwelt at Heshbon.' So the Lord our God delivered into our hands Og also, the king of Bashan, and all his people; and we smote him until none was left to him remaining. And we took all his cities at that time, there was not a city which we took not from them, threescore cities, all the region of Argob, the kingdom of Og in Bashan. All these cities were fenced with high walls, gates, and bars; beside unwalled towns a great many. And we utterly destroyed them, as we did unto Sihon king of Heshbon, utterly destroying the men, women, and children of every city. But all the cattle, and the spoil of the cities, we took for a prey to ourselves." (Ver. 1-7.)

The divine instructions as to Og, king of Bashan, were precisely similar to those given, in the preceding chapter, with respect to Sihon the Amorite; and in order to understand both, we must look at them purely in the light of the government of God—a subject but little understood, though one of very deep interest and practical importance. We must accurately distinguish between grace and government. When we contemplate God in government, we see Him displaying His power in the way of righteousness—punishing evil-doers, pouring out vengeance upon His enemies, overthrowing empires, upturning thrones, destroying cities, sweeping away nations, tribes, and peoples. We find Him commanding His people to slay men, women, and little children with the edge of the sword; to set fire to their houses, and turn their cities into desolate heaps.

Again, we hear Him addressing the prophet Ezekiel in the following remarkable words: "Son of man, Nebuchadrezzar king of Babylon caused his army to serve a great service against Tyrus: every head was made bald, and every shoulder was peeled; yet had he no wages, nor his army, for Tyrus, for the service that he had served against it. Therefore, thus saith the Lord God, Behold, I will give the land of Egypt unto Nebuchadrezzar king of Babylon; and he shall take her multitude, and take her spoil, and take her prey; and it shall be the wages for his army. I have given him the land of Egypt for his labor wherewith he served against it, because they wrought for Me, saith the Lord God." (Ezek. xxix. 18-20.)

This is a very wonderful passage of Scripture; setting before us a subject which runs through the entire volume of Old-Testament scripture—a subject demanding our profound and reverent attention. Whether we turn to the five books of Moses, to the historical books, to the Psalms, or to the prophets, we find the inspiring Spirit giving us the most minute details of God's actings in government. We have the deluge in the days of Noah, when the whole earth, with all its inhabitants, with the exception of eight persons, was destroyed by an act of divine government. Men, women, children, cattle, fowl, and creeping things were all swept away and buried beneath the billows and waves of God's righteous judgment.

Then we have, in the days of Lot, the cities of the plain, with all their inhabitants—men, women, and children—in a few short hours, consigned to utter destruction, overthrown by the hand of Almighty God, and buried beneath the deep, dark waters of the Dead Sea. Those guilty cities, "Sodom and Gomorrha, and the cities about them in like manner, giving themselves over to fornication, and going after strange flesh, are set forth for an example, suffering the vengeance of eternal fire."

Then, again, as we pass down along the page of inspired history, we see the seven nations of Canaan—men, women, and children—given over into the hands of Israel for unsparing judgment; nothing that breathed was to be left alive.

But, we may truly say, time would fail us even to refer to all the passages of holy Scripture which set before our eyes the solemn actings of the divine government. Suffice it to say that the line of evidence runs from Genesis to Revelation—beginning with the deluge and ending with the burning up of the present system of things.

Now, the question is, Are we competent to understand these ways of God in government? Is it any part of our business to sit in judgment upon them? Are we capable of unraveling the profound and awful mysteries of divine providence? Can we—are we called upon to—account for the tremendous fact of helpless babes involved in the judgment of their guilty parents? Impious infidelity may sneer at these things; morbid sentimentality may stumble over them; but the true believer, the pious Christian, the reverent student of holy Scripture, will meet them all with this one simple but safe and solid question, "Shall not the Judge of all the earth do right?"

This, we may rest assured, reader, is the only true way in which to meet such questions. If man is to sit in judgment upon the actings of God in government—if he can take upon himself to decide as to what is and what is not worthy of God to do, then, verily, we have lost the true sense of God altogether. And this is just what the devil is aiming at. He wants to lead the heart away from God; and to this end, he leads men to reason and question and speculate in a region which lies as far beyond their ken as heaven is above the earth. Can we comprehend God? If we could, we should ourselves be God.

> "We comprehend Him not,
> Yet earth and heaven tell,
> God sits as Sovereign on the throne,
> And ruleth all things well."

It is at once absurd and impious, in the very highest degree, for puny mortals to dare to question the counsels, enactments, and ways of the almighty Creator and all-wise Governor of the universe. Assuredly, all who do so must sooner or later find out their terrible mistake. Well would it be for all questioners and cavilers to give heed to the pungent question of the inspired apostle in Romans ix.—"Nay but, O man, who art thou that repliest against God? Shall the thing formed say to him that formed it, Why hast thou made me thus? Hath not the potter power over the clay, of the same lump to make one vessel unto honor, and another unto dishonor?"

How simple! How forcible! How unanswerable! This is the divine method of meeting all the hows and whys of infidel reason. If the potter has power over the lump of clay which he holds in his hand—a fact which none would think of disputing—how much more has the Creator of all things power over the creatures which His hand has formed! Men may reason and argue interminably as to why God permitted sin to enter; why He did not at once annihilate Satan and his angels; why He allowed the serpent to tempt Eve; why He did not keep her back from eating the forbidden fruit. In short, the hows and whys are endless; but the answer is one—"Who art thou, O man, that repliest against God?" How monstrous for a poor worm of the earth to attempt to sit in judgment upon the unsearchable judgments and ways of the Eternal God! What blind and presumptuous folly for a creature, whose understanding is darkened by sin, and who is thus wholly incapable of forming a right judgment about any thing divine, heavenly, or eternal, to attempt to decide how God should act in any given case! Alas! alas! it is to be feared that thousands who now argue with great apparent cleverness against the truth of God, will find out their fatal mistake when it will be too late to correct it.

And as to all those who, though very far from taking common ground with the infidel, are nevertheless troubled with doubts and misgivings as to some of God's ways in government, and as to the awful question of eternal punishment,[5] we would earnestly recommend them to study and drink in the spirit of that lovely little psalm, cxxxi.—"Lord, my heart is not haughty, nor mine eyes lofty: neither do I exercise myself in great matters, or in things too high for me. Surely I have behaved and quieted myself as a child that is weaned of his mother: my soul is even as a weaned child."

Then, when the heart has in some measure taken in this exquisite breathing, it may turn with real profit to the words of the inspired apostle (2 Cor. x.)—"For the weapons of our warfare are not carnal, but mighty through God to the pulling down of strong holds; casting down imaginations, and every high thing that exalteth itself against the knowledge of God, and bringing into captivity every thought to the obedience of Christ."

Doubtless, the philosopher, the scholar, the profound thinker, would smile contemptuously at such a childish mode of dealing with such great questions; but this is a very small matter in the judgment of the devout disciple of Christ. The same inspired apostle makes very short work of all this world's wisdom and learning. He says, "Let no man deceive himself. If any man among you seemeth to be wise in this world, let him become a fool, that he may be wise. For the wisdom of this world is foolishness with God. For it is written, 'He taketh the wise in their own craftiness.' And again, 'The Lord knoweth the thoughts of the wise, that they are vain.'" (1 Cor. iii.) And again, "It is written, 'I will destroy the wisdom of the wise, and will bring to nothing the understanding of the prudent.' Where is the wise? where is the scribe? where is the disputer of this world? hath not God made foolish the wisdom of this world? For after that in the wisdom of God the world by wisdom knew not God, it pleased God by the foolishness of the preaching *to save them that believe.*" (1 Cor. i. 19-21.)

Here lies the grand moral secret of the whole matter. Man has to find out that he is simply a fool, and that all the wisdom of the world is foolishness. Humbling but wholesome truth! Humbling, because it puts man in his right place; wholesome, yea, most precious, because it brings in the wisdom of God. We hear a great deal nowadays about science, philosophy, and learning. "Hath not God made foolish the wisdom of this world?"

Do we fully take in the meaning of these words? Alas! it is to be feared they are but little understood. There are not wanting men who would fain persuade us that science has gone far beyond the Bible.[6] Alas! for the science, and for all those who give heed to it. If it has gone beyond the Bible, whither has it gone? In the direction of God, of Christ, of heaven, of holiness, of peace? Nay; but quite in the opposite direction. And where must it all end? We tremble to think, and feel reluctant to pen the reply.

Still, we must be faithful, and declare solemnly that the sure and certain end of that path along which human science is conducting its votaries is the blackness of darkness forever.

"The world by wisdom knew not God." What did the philosophy of Greece do for its disciples? It made them the ignorant worshipers of "an unknown God." The very inscription on their altar published to the universe their ignorance and their shame.

And may we not lawfully inquire if philosophy has done better for christendom than it did for Greece? Has it communicated the knowledge of the true God? Who could dare to say, Yes? There are millions of baptized professors throughout the length and breadth of christendom who know no more of the true God than those philosophers who encountered Paul in the city of Athens.

The fact is this: every one who really knows God, is the privileged possessor of eternal life. So our Lord Jesus Christ declares, in the most distinct manner, in the seventeenth chapter of John.—"This is life eternal, that they might know Thee the only true God, and Jesus Christ, whom Thou hast sent." This is most precious to every soul that, through grace, has gotten this knowledge. To know God, is to have life—life eternal.

But how can I know God? where can I find Him? Can science and philosophy tell me? Have they ever told any one? have they ever guided any poor wanderer into this way of life and peace? No; never. "The world by wisdom knew not God." The conflicting schools of ancient philosophy could only plunge the human mind into profound darkness and hopeless bewilderment; and the conflicting schools of modern philosophy are not a whit better. They can give no certainty, no safe anchorage, no solid ground of confidence, to the poor benighted soul. Barren speculation, torturing doubt, wild and baseless theory, is all that human philosophy, in any age or of any nation, has to offer to the earnest inquirer after truth.

How, then, are we to know God? If such a stupendous result hangs on this knowledge, if to know God is life eternal—and Jesus says it is—then how is He to be known? "No man hath seen God at any time; the only begotten Son, which is in the bosom of the Father, He hath declared Him." (John i. 18.)

Here we have an answer divinely simple, divinely sure. Jesus reveals God to the soul—reveals the Father to the heart. Precious fact! We are not sent to creation to learn who God is, though we see His power, wisdom, and goodness there; we are not sent to the law, though we see His justice there; we are not sent to providence, though we see the profound mysteries of His government there. No; if we want to know who and what God is, we are to look in the face of Jesus Christ, the only begotten Son of God, who dwelt in His bosom before all worlds, who was His eternal delight, the object of His affections, the centre of His counsels. He it is who reveals God to the soul. We cannot have the slightest idea of what God is apart from the Lord Jesus Christ. "In Him dwelleth all the fullness of the Godhead [θεοτης] bodily." "God who commanded the light to shine out of darkness, hath shined in our hearts, to give the light of the knowledge of the glory of God, in the face of Jesus Christ."

Nothing can exceed the power and blessedness of all this. There is no darkness here, no uncertainty. "The darkness is past and the true light now shineth." Yes; it shineth in the face of Jesus Christ. We can gaze, by faith, on that blessed One; we can trace His marvelous path on the earth; see Him going about doing good, and healing all that were oppressed of the devil; mark His very looks, His words, His works, His ways; see Him healing the sick, cleansing the leper, opening the eyes of the blind, unstopping the ears of the deaf, causing the lame to walk, the maimed to be whole, raising the dead, drying the widow's tears, feeding the hungry, binding up broken hearts, meeting every form of human need, soothing human sorrow, hushing human fears; and doing all these things in such a style, with such touching grace and sweetness, as to make each one feel, in his very inmost soul, that it was the deep delight of that loving heart thus to minister to his need.

Now, in all this He was revealing God to man; so that if we want to know what God is, we have simply to look at Jesus. When Philip said, "Lord, shew us the Father, and it sufficeth us," the prompt reply was, "Have I been so long time with you, and yet hast thou not known Me, Philip? he that hath seen Me hath seen the Father; and how sayest thou then, 'Shew us the Father?' Believest thou not that I am in the Father, and the Father in Me? the words that I speak unto you I speak not of Myself; but the Father that dwelleth in Me, He doeth the works. Believe Me that I am in the Father, and the Father in Me: or else believe Me for the very works' sake."

Here is true rest for the heart. We know the true God, and Jesus Christ, whom He hath sent; and this is life eternal. We know Him as our own very God and Father, and Christ as our own personal, loving Lord and Saviour; we can delight in Him, walk with Him, lean on Him, trust in Him, cling to Him, draw from Him, find all our living springs in Him, rejoice in Him all the day long, find our meat and our drink in doing His blessed will, furthering His cause, and promoting His glory.

Reader, do you know all this for yourself? Say, is it a living, divinely real thing in your own soul this moment? This is true Christianity, and you should not be satisfied with any thing less. You will perhaps tell us we have wandered far from the third chapter of Deuteronomy. But whither have we wandered? To the Son of God and to the soul of the reader. If this be wandering, be it so; it most assuredly is not wandering from the object for which we are penning these "Notes," which is, to bring Christ and the soul together, or to bind them together, as the case may be. We would never, for one moment, lose sight of the fact that, both in writing and speaking, we have not merely to expound Scripture, but to seek the salvation and blessing of souls. Hence it is that we feel constrained, from time to time, to appeal to the heart and conscience of the reader, as to his practical state, and as to how far he has made his very own of these imperishable realities which pass in review before us. And we earnestly beseech the reader, whoever he may be, to seek a deeper acquaintance with God in Christ; and, as a sure consequence of this, a closer walk with Him and more thorough consecration of heart to Him.

This, we are thoroughly persuaded, is what is needed in this day of unrest and unreality in the world, and of lukewarmness and indifference in the professing church. We want a very much higher standard of personal devotedness, more real purpose of heart to cleave to the Lord and follow Him. There is much—very much to discourage and hinder in the condition of things around us. The language of the men of Judah in the days of Nehemiah may, with some measure of appropriateness and force, be applied to our times,—"The strength of the bearers of burdens is decayed, and there is much rubbish." But, thank God, the remedy now, as then, is to be found in this soul-stirring sentence, "Remember the Lord."

We now return to our chapter, in the remainder of which the lawgiver rehearses in the ears of the congregation the story of their dealings with the two kings of the Amorites, together with the facts connected with the inheritance of the two tribes and a half on the wilderness side of Jordan. And with regard to the latter subject, it is interesting to notice that he raises no question as to the right or the wrong of their choosing their possession short of the land of promise. Indeed, from the narrative given here, it could not be known that the two tribes and a half had expressed any wish in the matter. So far is our book from being a mere repetition of its predecessors.

Here are the words: "And this land, which we possessed at that time, from Aroer, which is by the river Arnon, and half Mount Gilead, and the cities thereof, *gave I unto the Reubenites and to the Gadites*. And the rest of Gilead, and all Bashan, being the kingdom of Og, *gave I unto the half tribe of Manasseh*; all the region of Argob, with all Bashan, which was called the land of giants.... And *I gave* Gilead unto Machir. And unto the Reubenites and unto the Gadites *I gave* from Gilead even unto the river Arnon half the valley, and the border even unto the river Jabbok, which is the border of the children of Ammon.... And I commanded you at that time, saying, *The Lord your God hath given you this land to possess it:"* —not a word about their having asked it—"ye shall pass over armed before your brethren the children of Israel, all that are meet for the war. But your wives, and your little ones, and your cattle (for I know that ye have much cattle), shall abide in your cities *which I have given you;* until the Lord have given rest unto your brethren, as well as unto you, and until they also possess the land which the Lord your God hath given them beyond Jordan; and then shall ye return every man unto his possession, which I have given you."

In our studies on the book of Numbers, we have dwelt upon certain facts connected with the settlement of the two tribes and a half, proving that they were below the mark of the Israel of God in choosing their inheritance any where short of the other side of Jordan; but in the passage we have just quoted, there is no allusion at all to this side of the question, because the object of Moses is to set before the whole congregation the exceeding goodness, loving-kindness, and faithfulness of God, not only in bringing them through all the difficulties and dangers of the wilderness, but also in giving them, even already, such signal victories over the Amorites, and putting them in possession of regions so attractive and so suited to them. In all this, he is laying down the solid basis of Jehovah's claim upon their hearty obedience to His commandments; and we can at once see and appreciate the moral beauty of overlooking entirely, in such a rehearsal, the question as to whether Reuben, Gad, and the half tribe of Manasseh were wrong in stopping short of the land of promise. It is, to every devout Christian, a striking proof, not only of the touching and exquisite grace of God, but also of the divine perfectness of Scripture.

No doubt, every true believer enters upon the study of Scripture with the full and deeply wrought conviction of its absolute perfectness in every part. He reverently believes that there is not, from the opening of Genesis to the close of Revelation, a single flaw, a single hitch, a single discrepancy— not one; all is as perfect as its divine Author.

But then the cordial belief of the divine perfectness of Scripture as a whole can never lessen our appreciation of the evidences which come out in detail; nay, it enhances it exceedingly. Thus, for example, in the passage now before us, is it not perfectly beautiful to mark the absence of all reference to the failure of the two tribes and a half in the matter of choosing their inheritance, seeing that any such reference would be entirely foreign to the object of the lawgiver and to the scope of the book? Is it not the joy of our hearts to trace such infinite perfections, such exquisite and inimitable touches? Assuredly it is; and not only so, but we are persuaded that the more the moral glories of the volume dawn upon our souls, and its living and exhaustless depths are unfolded to our hearts, the more we shall be convinced of the utter folly of infidel assaults upon it, and of the feebleness and gratuitousness of many well-meant efforts to prove that it does not contradict itself. Thank God, His Word stands in no need of human apologists. It speaks for itself, and carries with it its own powerful evidences; so that we can say of it what the apostle says of his gospel, that "if it be hid, it is hid to them that are lost; in whom the god of this world hath blinded the minds of them which believe not, lest the light of the glorious gospel of Christ, who is the image of God, should shine unto them." We are more and more convinced each day, that the most effective method of answering all infidel attacks upon the Bible is, to cherish a more profound faith in its divine power and authority, and to use it as those who are most thoroughly persuaded of its truth and preciousness. The Spirit of God alone can enable any one to believe in the plenary inspiration of the holy Scriptures. Human arguments may go for what they are worth; they may doubtless silence gainsayers, but they cannot reach the heart—they cannot bring the genial rays of divine revelation to bear down in living, saving power upon the soul. This is a work divine; and until it is done, all the evidences and arguments in the world must leave the soul in the moral darkness of unbelief; but when it is done, there is no need of human testimony in defense of the Bible. External evidences, however interesting and valuable (and they are both), cannot add a single jot or tittle to the glory of that peerless revelation, which bears on every page, every paragraph, every sentence, the clear impress of its divine Author. As with the sun in the heavens, its every ray tells of the Hand that made it, so of the Bible, its every sentence tells of the Heart that inspired it. But inasmuch as a blind man cannot see the sunlight, so neither can the unconverted soul see the force and beauty of holy Scripture. The eye must be anointed with heavenly eye-salve ere the infinite perfections of the divine volume can be discerned or appreciated.

Now, we must own to the reader that it is the deep and ever-deepening sense of all this that has led us to the determination not to occupy his time or our own by reference to the attacks which have been made by rationalistic writers on that portion of the Word of God with which we are now engaged. We leave this to other and abler hands. What we desire for ourselves and our readers is, that we may feed in peace upon the green pastures which the Shepherd and Bishop of our souls has graciously thrown open to us; that we may help each other, as we pass along, to see more and more of the moral glory of that which lies before us, and thus to build each other up on our most holy faith. This will be far more grateful work to us, and we trust also to our readers, than replying to men who, in all their puny efforts to find out flaws in the holy volume, only prove, to those capable of judging, that they understand neither what they say nor whereof they affirm. If men *will* abide in the dark vaults and tunnels of a dreary infidelity, and there find fault with the sun, or deny that it shines at all, let it be ours to bask in the light, and help others to do the same.

We shall now dwell for a little on the remaining verses of our chapter, in which we shall find much to interest, instruct, and profit us.

And first, Moses rehearses in the ears of the people his charge to Joshua.—"And I commanded Joshua at that time, saying, 'Thine eyes have seen all that the Lord our God hath done unto these two kings; so shall the Lord do unto all the kingdoms whither thou passest. Ye shall not fear them; for the Lord your God He shall fight for you.'" (Ver. 21, 22.)

The remembrance of the Lord's dealings with us in the past should strengthen our confidence in going on. The One who had given His people such a victory over the Amorites, who had destroyed such a formidable foe as Og, king of Bashan, and given into their hands all the land of the giants, what could He not do for them? They could hardly expect to encounter in all the land of Canaan any enemy more powerful than Og, whose bedstead was of such enormous dimensions as to call for the special notice of Moses; but what was he in the presence of his almighty Creator? Dwarfs and giants are all alike to Him. The grand point is to keep God Himself ever before our eyes; then difficulties vanish. If He covers the eyes, we can see nothing else; and this is the true secret of peace, and the real power of progress. "Thine eyes have seen all that the Lord your God hath done." And as He has done, *so* He will do. He *hath* delivered, and He *doth* deliver, and He *will* deliver. Past, present, and future are all marked by divine deliverance.

Reader, art thou in any difficulty? Is there any pressure upon thee? Art thou anticipating, with nervous apprehension, some formidable evil? Is thine heart trembling at the very thought of it? It may be thou art like one who has come to the far end, like the apostle Paul in Asia—"Pressed out of measure, above strength, insomuch that we despaired even of life." If so, beloved friend, accept a word of encouragement. It is our deep and earnest desire to strengthen your hands in God, and to encourage your heart to trust Him for all that is before you. "Fear not:" only believe. He never fails a trusting heart—no, never. Make use of the resources which are treasured up for you in Him. Just put yourself, your surroundings, your fears, your anxieties, all into His hands, *and leave them there.*

Yes, leave them there. It is of little use your putting your difficulties, your necessities, into His hands and then, almost immediately, taking them into your own. We often do this. When in pressure, in need, in deep trial of some kind or other, we go to God in prayer, we cast our burden upon Him and seem to get relief; but, alas! no sooner have we risen from our knees than we begin again to look at the difficulty, ponder the trial, dwell upon all the sorrowful circumstances, until we are again at our very wits' end.

Now, this will never do. It sadly dishonors God, and, of course, leaves us unrelieved and unhappy. He would have our minds as free from care as the conscience is free from guilt. His word to us is, "Be careful for nothing; but in every thing by prayer and supplication with thanksgiving let your requests be made known unto God." And what then? "The peace of God, which passeth all understanding, shall keep [or garrison—φρουρήσει] your hearts and minds through Christ Jesus."

Thus it was that Moses, that beloved man of God and honored servant of Christ, sought to encourage his fellow-laborer and successor, Joshua, in reference to all that was before him.—"Ye shall not fear them; for the Lord your God He shall fight for you." Thus, too, did the blessed apostle Paul encourage his beloved son and fellow-servant Timothy to trust in the living God; to be strong in the grace which is in Christ Jesus; to lean, with unshaken confidence, on God's sure foundation; to commit himself, with unquestioning assurance, to the authority, teaching, and guidance of the holy Scriptures; and thus armed and furnished, to give himself, with holy diligence and true spiritual courage, to that work to which he was called. And thus, too, the writer and the reader can encourage one another, in these days of increasing difficulty, to cling, in simple faith, to that Word which is settled forever in heaven; to have it hidden in the heart as a living power and authority in the soul—something that will sustain us, though heart and flesh should fail, and though we had not the countenance or support of a human being. "All flesh is as grass, and all the glory of man as the flower of grass. The grass withereth, and the flower thereof falleth away; but the Word of the Lord endureth forever. And this is the Word which by the gospel is preached unto you." (1 Pet. i. 24, 25.)

How precious is this! What comfort and consolation! What stability and rest! What real strength, victory, and moral elevation! It is not within the compass of human language to set forth the preciousness of the Word of God, or to define, in adequate terms, the comfort of knowing that the self-same Word which is settled forever in heaven, and which shall endure throughout the countless ages of eternity, is that which has reached our hearts in the glad tidings of the gospel, imparting to us eternal life, and giving us peace and rest in the finished work of Christ, and a perfectly satisfying object in His adorable Person. Truly, as we think of all this, we cannot but own that every breath should be a halleluiah. Thus it shall be by and by, and that forever, all homage to His peerless name!

The closing verses of our chapter present a peculiarly touching passage between Moses and his Lord, the record of which, as given here, is in lovely keeping, as we might expect, with the character of the entire book of Deuteronomy.—"And I besought the Lord at that time, saying, 'O Lord God, Thou hast begun to show Thy servant Thy greatness, and Thy mighty hand; for what god is there in heaven or in earth that can do according to Thy works and according to Thy might? I pray Thee, let me go over, and see the good land that is beyond Jordan, that goodly mountain, and Lebanon.' But the Lord was wroth with me for your sakes, and would not hear me: and the Lord said unto me, 'Let it suffice thee; speak no more unto Me of this matter. Get thee up into the top of Pisgah, and lift up thine eyes westward, and northward, and southward, and eastward, and behold it with thine eyes: for thou shalt not go over this Jordan. But charge Joshua, and encourage him, and strengthen him; for he shall go over before this people, and he shall cause them to inherit the land which thou shalt see.'" (Ver. 23-28.)

It is very affecting to find this eminent servant of God urging a request which could not be granted. He longed to see that good land beyond Jordan. The portion chosen by the two tribes and a half could not satisfy his heart; he desired to plant his foot upon the proper inheritance of the Israel of God. But it was not to be. He had spoken unadvisedly with his lips at the waters of Meribah; and, by the solemn and irreversible enactment of the divine government, he was prohibited from crossing the Jordan.

All this, the beloved servant of Christ most meekly rehearses in the ears of the people. He does not hide from them the fact that the Lord had refused to grant his request. True, he had to remind them that it was on their account—that was morally needful for them to hear; still he tells them, in the most unreserved manner, that Jehovah was wroth with him, and that He refused to hear him—refused to allow him to cross the Jordan, and called upon him to resign his office and appoint his successor.

Now, it is most edifying to hear all this from the lips of Moses himself. It teaches us a fine lesson, if only we are willing to learn it. Some of us find it very hard indeed to confess that we have done or said any thing wrong—very hard to own before our brethren that we have entirely missed the Lord's mind in any particular case. We are careful of our reputation; we are touchy and tenacious. And yet, with strange inconsistency, we admit, or seem to admit, in general terms, that we are poor, feeble, erring creatures; and that, if left to ourselves, there is nothing too bad for us to say or to do. But it is one thing to make a most humiliating general confession, and another thing altogether to own that, in some given case, we have made a gross mistake. This latter is a confession which very few have grace to make. Some can hardly ever admit that they have done wrong.

Not so that honored servant whose words we have just quoted. He, notwithstanding his elevated position as the called, trusted, and beloved servant of Jehovah—the leader of the congregation, whose rod had made the land of Egypt to tremble, was not ashamed to stand before the whole assembly of his brethren and confess his mistake—own that he had said what he ought not, and that he had earnestly urged a request which Jehovah could not grant.

Does this lower Moses in our estimation? The very reverse: it raises him immensely. It is morally lovely to hear his confession, to see how meekly he bows his head to the governmental dealings of God, to mark the unselfishness of his acting toward the man who was to succeed him in his high office. There was not a trace of jealousy or envy; no exhibition of mortified pride. With beautiful self-emptiness he steps down from his elevated position, throws his mantle over the shoulders of his successor, and encourages him to discharge, with holy fidelity, the duties of that high office which he himself had to resign.

"He that humbleth himself shall be exalted." How true was this in Moses' case! He humbled himself under the mighty hand of God. He accepted the holy discipline imposed upon him by the divine government. He uttered not a murmuring word at the refusal of his request; he bows to it all, and hence he was exalted in due time. If government kept him out of Canaan, grace conducted him to Pisgah's top, from whence, in company with his Lord, he was permitted to see that good land, in all its fair proportions—see it, not as inherited by Israel, but as given of God.

The reader will do well to ponder deeply the subject of grace and government. It is indeed a very weighty and practical theme, and one largely illustrated in Scripture, though but little understood amongst us. It may seem wonderful to us, hard to be understood, that one so beloved as Moses should be refused an entrance into the promised land; but in this we see the solemn action of the divine government, and we have to bow our heads and worship. It was not merely that Moses, in his official capacity, or as representing the legal system, could not bring Israel into the land. This is true; but it is not all. Moses spake unadvisedly with his lips. He and Aaron his brother failed to glorify God, in the presence of the congregation, and for this cause "the Lord spake unto Moses and Aaron, 'Because ye believed Me not, to sanctify Me in the eyes of the children of Israel, therefore ye shall not bring this congregation into the land which I have given them.'" And again, we read, "The Lord spake unto Moses and Aaron in Mount Hor, by the coast of the land of Edom, saying, 'Aaron shall be gathered unto his people; for he shall not enter into the land which I have given unto the children of Israel, because ye rebelled against My word at the water of Meribah. Take Aaron and Eleazar his son, and bring them up unto Mount Hor; and strip Aaron of his garments, and put them upon Eleazar his son; and Aaron shall be gathered unto his people, and shall die there.'"

All this is most solemn. Here we have the two leading men in the congregation, the very men whom God had used to bring His people out of the land of Egypt, with mighty signs and wonders—"that Moses and Aaron"—men highly honored of God, and yet refused entrance into Canaan. And for what? Let us mark the reason.—*"Because ye rebelled against My word."*

Let these words sink down into our hearts. It is a terrible thing to rebel against the Word of God; and the more elevated the position of those who so rebel, the more serious it is in every way, and the more solemn and speedy must be the divine judgment. "For rebellion is as the sin of witchcraft, and stubbornness is as iniquity and idolatry."

These are weighty words, and we ought to ponder them deeply. They were uttered in the ears of Saul, when he had failed to obey the word of the Lord; and thus we have before us examples of a prophet, a priest, and a king, all judged, under the government of God, for an act of disobedience. The prophet and the priest were refused entrance into the land of Canaan, and the king was deprived of his throne, simply because they disobeyed the word of the Lord.

Let us remember this. We, in our fancied wisdom, might deem all this very severe. Are we competent judges? This is a grand question in all such matters. Let us beware how we presume to sit in judgment on the enactments of divine government. Adam was driven out of paradise, Aaron was stripped of his priestly robes, Moses was sternly refused entrance into Canaan, and Saul was deprived of his kingdom—and for what? Was it for what men would call a grave moral offense—some scandalous sin. No; it was, in each case, for neglecting the word of the Lord. This is the serious thing for us to keep before us, in this day of human willfulness, in which men undertake to set up their own opinions, to think for themselves, and judge for themselves, and act for themselves. Men proudly put the question, "Has not every man a right to think for himself?" We reply, Most certainly not. We have a right to obey. To obey what? Not the commandments of men, not the authority of the so-called church, not the decrees of general councils—in a word, not any merely human authority, call it what you please, but simply the Word of the living God—the testimony of the Holy

Ghost—the voice of holy Scripture. This it is that justly claims our implicit, unhesitating, unquestioning obedience. To this we are to bow down our whole moral being. We are not to reason, we are not to speculate, we are not to weigh consequences, we have nothing to do with results, we are not to say "Why?" or "Wherefore?" It is ours to obey, and leave all the rest in the hands of our Master. What has a servant to do with consequences? what business has he to reason as to results? It is of the very essence of a servant to do what he is told, regardless of all other considerations. Had Adam remembered this, he would not have been turned out of Eden; had Moses and Aaron remembered it, they might have crossed the Jordan; had Saul remembered it, he would not have been deprived of his throne. And so, as we pass down along the stream of human history, we see this weighty principle illustrated over and over again; and we may rest assured, it is a principle of abiding and universal importance.

And be it remembered, we are not to attempt to weaken this great principle by any reasonings grounded upon God's foreknowledge of all that was to happen, and all that man would do, in the course of time. Men do reason in this way, but it is a fatal mistake. What has God's foreknowledge to do with man's responsibility? Is man responsible, or not? This is the question. If, as we most surely believe, he is, then nothing must be allowed to interfere with this responsibility. Man is called to obey the plain word of God; he is in no wise responsible to know aught about God's secret purposes and counsels. Man's responsibility rests upon what is revealed, not upon what is secret. What, for example, did Adam know about God's eternal plans and purposes when he was set in the garden of Eden and forbidden to eat of the tree of the knowledge of good and evil? Was his transgression in any wise modified by the stupendous fact that God took occasion from that very transgression to display, in the view of all created intelligences, His glorious scheme of redemption through the blood of the Lamb? Clearly not. He received a plain commandment, and by that commandment his conduct should have been absolutely governed. He disobeyed, and was driven out of paradise into a world which has, for well-nigh six thousand years, exhibited the terrible consequences of one single act of disobedience—the act of taking the forbidden fruit.

True it is, blessed be God, that grace has come into this poor sin-stricken world and there reaped a harvest which could never have been reaped in the fields of an unfallen creation. But man was judged for his transgression; he was driven out by the hand of God in government, and by an enactment of that government, he has been compelled to eat bread in the sweat of his brow. "Whatsoever *a man* [no matter who] soweth, that shall he also reap."

Here we have the condensed statement of the principle which runs all through the Word, and is illustrated on every page of the history of God's government. It demands our very gravest consideration. It is, alas! but little understood. We allow our minds to get under the influence of one-sided and therefore false ideas of grace, the effect of which is most pernicious. Grace is one thing, and government is another: they must never be confounded. We would earnestly impress upon the heart of the reader the weighty fact that the most magnificent display of God's sovereign grace can never interfere with the solemn enactments of His government.

CHAPTER IV

"Now therefore *hearken*, O Israel, unto the statutes and unto the judgments which I teach you, for to *do* them, that ye may *live*, and go in and *possess* the land which the Lord God of your fathers giveth you."

Here we have very prominently before us the special characteristic of the entire book of Deuteronomy.—"Hearken" and "do," that ye may "live" and "possess." This is a universal and abiding principle. It was true for Israel, and it is true for us. The pathway of life and the true secret of possession is simple obedience to the holy commandments of God. We see this all through the inspired volume, from cover to cover. God has given us His Word, not to speculate upon it or discuss it, but, that we may obey it. And it is as we, through grace, yield a hearty and happy obedience to our Father's statutes and judgments, that we tread the bright pathway of life, and enter into the reality of all that God has treasured up for us in Christ. "He that hath My commandments, and keepeth them, he it is that loveth Me; and he that loveth Me shall be loved of My Father, and I will love him, and will manifest Myself to him."

How precious is this! Indeed, it is unspeakable. It is something quite peculiar. It would be a very serious mistake to suppose that the privilege here spoken of is enjoyed by all believers. It is not. It is only enjoyed by such as yield a loving obedience to the commandments of our Lord Jesus Christ. It lies within the reach of all, but all do not enjoy it, because all are not obedient. It is one thing to be a child, and quite another to be an obedient child; it is one thing to be saved, and quite another thing to love the Saviour, and delight in all His most precious precepts.

We may see this continually illustrated in our family circles. There, for example, are two sons, and one of them only thinks of pleasing himself, doing his will, gratifying his own desires. He takes no pleasure in his father's society, does not take any pains to carry out his father's wishes, knows hardly any thing of his mind, and what he does know he utterly neglects or despises. He is ready enough to avail himself of all the benefits which accrue to him from the relationship in which he stands to his father— ready enough to accept clothes, books, money—all, in short, that the father gives; but he never seeks to gratify the father's heart by a loving attention to his will, even in the smallest matters. The other son is the direct opposite to all this. He delights in being with his father; he loves his society, loves his ways, loves his words; he is constantly taking occasion to carry out his father's wishes, to get him something that he knows will be agreeable to him. He loves his father, not for his gifts, but for himself; and he finds his richest enjoyment in being in his father's company and in doing his will.

Now, can we have any difficulty in seeing how very differently the father will feel towards those two sons? True, they are both his sons, and he loves them both, with a love grounded upon the relationship in which they stand to him; but beside the love of relationship common to both, there is the love of complacency peculiar to the obedient child. It is impossible that a father can find pleasure in the society of a willful, self-indulgent, careless son. Such a son may occupy much of his thoughts, he may spend many a sleepless night thinking about him and praying for him, he would gladly spend and be spent for him; but he is not agreeable to him, does not possess his confidence, cannot be the depositary of his thoughts.

All this demands the serious consideration of those who really desire to be acceptable or agreeable to the heart of our heavenly Father and our Lord Jesus Christ. We may rest assured of this, that obedience is grateful to God; and "His commandments are not grievous"—nay, they are the sweet and precious expression of His love, and the fruit and evidence of the relationship in which He stands to us. And not only so, but He graciously rewards our obedience by a fuller manifestation of Himself to our souls, and His dwelling with us. This comes out in great fullness and beauty in our Lord's reply to Judas, not Iscariot, for whose question we may be thankful— "'Lord, how is it that Thou wilt manifest Thyself unto us, and not unto the world?' Jesus answered and said unto him, 'If a man love Me, he will keep My words; and My Father will love him, and We will come unto him, and make Our abode with him.'" (John xiv.)

Here we are taught that it is not a question of the difference between "the world" and "us," inasmuch as the world knows nothing either of relationship or obedience, and is therefore in no wise contemplated in our Lord's words. The world hates Christ, because it does not know Him. Its language is, "Depart from us; for we desire not the knowledge of Thy ways." "We will not have this Man to reign over us."

Such is the world, even when polished by civilization, and gilded with the profession of Christianity. There is, underneath all the gilding, all the polish, a deep-seated hatred of the Person and authority of Christ. His sacred, peerless name is tacked on to the world's religion, at least throughout baptized christendom; but behind the drapery of religious profession, there lurks a heart at enmity with God and His Christ.

But our Lord is not speaking of the world in John xiv. He is shut in with "His own," and it is of them He is speaking. Were He to manifest Himself to the world, it could only be for judgment and eternal destruction. But, blessed be His name, He does manifest Himself to His own obedient children, to those who have His commandments and keep them, to those who love Him and keep His words.

And, let the reader thoroughly understand that when our Lord speaks of His commandments, His words, and His sayings, He does not mean the ten commandments, or law of Moses. No doubt, those ten commandments form a part of the whole canon of Scripture—the inspired Word of God; but to confound the law of Moses with the commandments of Christ would be simply turning things upside down, it would be to confound Judaism with Christianity—law and grace. The two things are as distinct as any two things can be, and must be so maintained by all who would be found in the current of the mind of God.

We are sometimes led astray by the mere sound of words; and hence, when we meet with the word "commandments," we instantly conclude that it must needs refer to the law of Moses. But this is a very great and mischievous mistake. If the reader is not clear and established as to this, let him close this volume and turn to the first eight chapters of the epistle to the Romans, and the whole of the epistle to the Galatians, and read them calmly and prayerfully, as in the very presence of God, with a mind freed from all theological bias and the influence of all previous religious training. There he will learn, in the fullest and clearest manner, that the Christian is not under law in any way, or for any object whatsoever, either for life, for righteousness, for holiness, for walk, or for any thing else. In short, the teaching of the entire New Testament goes to establish, beyond all question, that the Christian is not under law, not of the world, not in the flesh, not in his sins. The solid ground of all this is the accomplished redemption which we have in Christ Jesus, in virtue of which we are sealed by the Holy Ghost, and thus indissolubly united to, and inseparably identified with a risen and glorified Christ; so that the apostle John can say of all believers, all God's dear children, "*As* He [Christ] *is, so are we* in this world." This settles the whole question, for all who are content to be governed by holy Scripture. And as to all beside, discussion is worse than useless.

We have digressed from our immediate subject, in order to meet any difficulty arising from a misunderstanding of the word "commandments." The reader cannot too carefully guard against the tendency to confound the commandments spoken of in John xiv. with the commandments of Moses, given in Exodus xx. And yet we reverently believe that Exodus xx. is as truly inspired as John xiv.

And now, ere we finally turn from the subject which has been engaging us, we would ask the reader to refer, for a few moments, to a piece of inspired history which illustrates, in a very striking way, the difference between an obedient and disobedient child of God. He will find it in Genesis xviii, xix. It is a profoundly interesting study, presenting a contrast instructive, suggestive, and practical beyond expression. We are not going to dwell upon it, having in some measure done so in our "Notes on the Book of Genesis;" but we would merely remind the reader that he has before him, in these two chapters, the history of two saints of God. Lot was just as much a child of God as Abraham. We have no more doubt that Lot is amongst "the spirits of just men made perfect" than that Abraham is there. This, we think, cannot be called in question, inasmuch as the inspired apostle Peter tells us that Lot's "righteous soul was vexed with the filthy conversation of the wicked."

But mark the grave difference between the two men. The Lord Himself visited Abraham, sat with him, and partook readily of his hospitality. This was a high honor indeed, a rare privilege—a privilege which Lot never knew, an honor to which he never attained. The Lord never visited him in Sodom; He merely sent His angels, His ministers of power, the agents of His government. And even they, at first, sternly refused to enter Lot's house or to partake of his proffered hospitality. Their withering reply was, "Nay, but we will abide in the street all night." And when they did enter his house, it was only to protect him from the lawless violence with which he was surrounded, and to drag him out of the wretched circumstances into which, for worldly gain and position, he had plunged himself. Could contrast be more vivid?

But further, the Lord delighted in Abraham, manifested Himself to him, opened His mind to him, told him of His plans and purposes—what He was about to do with Sodom. "Shall I," said He, "hide from Abraham that thing which I do; seeing that Abraham shall surely become a great and mighty nation, and all the nations of the earth shall be blessed in him? For *I know him, that he will command his children and his household after him, and they shall keep the way of the Lord, to do justice and judgment,* that the Lord may bring upon Abraham that which he hath spoken of him."

We could hardly have a more telling illustration of John xiv. 21, 23, although the scene occurred two thousand years before the words were uttered. Have we aught like this in the history of Lot? Alas! no. It could not be. He had no nearness to God, no knowledge of His mind, no insight into His plans and purposes. How could he? Sunk, as he was, in the low moral depths of Sodom, how could he know the mind of God? Blinded by the murky atmosphere which inwrapped the guilty cities of the plain, how could he see into the future? Utterly impossible. If a man is mixed up with the world, he can only see things from the world's stand-point; he can only measure things by the world's standard, and think of them with the world's thoughts. Hence it is that the Church, in its Sardis condition, is *threatened* with the coming of the Lord as a thief, instead of being *cheered* with the hope of His coming as the bright and morning star. If the professing church has sunk to the world's level—as, alas! she has—she can only contemplate the future from the world's point of view. This accounts for the feeling of dread with which the great majority of professing Christians look at the subject of the Lord's coming. They are looking for Him as a thief, instead of the blessed Bridegroom of their hearts. How few there are, comparatively, who *love His appearing*! The great majority of professors (we grieve to have to pen the words) find their type in Lot rather than in Abraham. The Church has departed from her proper ground; she has gone down from her true moral elevation, and mingled herself with that world which hates and despises her absent Lord.

Still, thank God, there are "a few names, even in Sardis, which have not defiled their garments"—a few living stones, amid the smouldering ashes of lifeless profession—a few lights twinkling amid the moral gloom of cold, nominal, heartless, worldly Christianity. And not only so, but in the Laodicean phase of the Church's history, which presents a still lower and more hopeless condition of things, when the whole professing body is about to be spued out of the mouth of "the faithful and true witness"—even at this advanced stage of failure and departure, those gracious words fall, with soul-stirring power, on the attentive ear, "Behold, I stand at the door, and knock: if *any man* hear My voice, and open the door, I will come in *to him*, and will sup with him, and he with Me."[7]

Thus, in the days of professing Christianity, as in the days of the patriarchs—in the times of the New Testament, as in those of the Old, we see the same value and importance attached to a hearing ear and an obedient heart. Abraham, in the plains of Mamre, the pilgrim and the stranger, the faithful and obedient child of God, tasted the rare privilege of entertaining the Lord of glory—a privilege which could not be known by one who had chosen his place and his portion in a sphere doomed to destruction. So, also, in the days of Laodicean indifference and boastful pretension, the truly obedient heart is cheered with the sweet promise of sitting down to sup with Him who is "the Amen, the faithful and true witness, the beginning of the creation of God." In a word, let the condition of things be what it may, there is no limit to the blessing of the individual soul who will only hearken to the voice of Christ, and keep His commandments.

Let us remember this. Let it sink down into the very deepest depths of our moral being. Nothing can rob us of the blessings and privileges flowing from obedience. The truth of this shines out before our eyes in every section and on every page of the volume of God. At all times, in all places, and under all circumstances, the obedient soul was happy in God, and God was happy in him. It always holds good, whatever be the character of the dispensation, that, "To this man will I look, even to him who is of a contrite spirit, and trembles at My word." Nothing can ever alter or touch this. It meets us in the fourth chapter of our blessed book of Deuteronomy, in the words with which this section opens—"Now therefore *hearken*, O Israel, unto *the statutes* and unto *the judgments which I teach you*, for *to do*, that ye may live, and go in and possess the land which the Lord God of your fathers giveth you." It meets us in those precious words of our Lord, in John xiv, on which we have been dwelling—"He that hath *My commandments* and keepeth them, he it is that loveth Me," etc. And again, "If a man love Me, *he will keep My sayings*."[8] It shines with peculiar brightness in the words of the inspired apostle John—"Beloved, if our heart condemn us not, then have we confidence toward God. And whatsoever we ask, we receive of Him, *because we keep His commandments*, and *do those things that are pleasing in His sight*. And this is His commandment, that we should believe on the name of His Son Jesus Christ, and love one another, as he gave us commandment. And he that keepeth His commandments dwelleth in Him, and He in him." (1 John iii. 21-24.)

Passages might easily be multiplied, but there is no need. Those which we have quoted set before us, in the clearest and fullest way possible, the very highest motive for obedience, namely, its being agreeable to the heart of our Lord Jesus Christ—well-pleasing to God. True, we owe a hearty obedience on every ground. "We are not our own; we are bought with a price." We owe our life, our peace, our righteousness, our salvation, our everlasting felicity and glory, all to Him; so that nothing can exceed the moral weight of His claims upon us for a life of whole-hearted obedience. But above and beyond His moral claims stands the marvelous fact that His heart is gratified, His spirit refreshed, by our keeping His commandments and doing those things that are pleasing in His sight.

Beloved Christian reader, can any thing exceed the moral power of such a motive as this? Only think of our being privileged to give pleasure to the heart of our beloved Lord! What sweetness, what interest, what preciousness, what holy dignity, it imparts to every little act of obedience to know that it is grateful to the heart of our Father! How far beyond the legal system is this! It is a most perfect contrast, in its every phase and every feature. The difference between the legal system and Christianity is the difference between death and life, bondage and liberty, condemnation and righteousness, distance and nearness, doubt and certainty. How monstrous the attempt to amalgamate these two things—to work them up into one system, as though they were but two branches from the one stem! What hopeless confusion must be the result of any such effort! How terrible the effect of seeking to place souls under the influence of the two things! As well might we attempt to combine the sun's meridian beams with the profound darkness of midnight. Looked at from a divine and heavenly stand-point, judged in the light of the New Testament, measured by the standard of the heart of God, the mind of Christ, there could not be a more hideous anomaly than that which presents itself to our view in christendom's effort to combine law and grace. And as to the dishonor done to God, the wound inflicted on the heart of Christ, the grief and despite offered to the Holy Ghost, the damage done to the truth of God, the grievous wrong perpetrated upon the beloved lambs and sheep of the flock of Christ, the terrible stumbling-block thrown in the way of both Jew and Gentile, and, in short, the serious injury done to the entire testimony of God during the last eighteen centuries, the judgment-seat of Christ can alone declare it; and oh, what an awful declaration that will be! It is too tremendous to contemplate.

But there are many pious souls throughout the length and breath of the professing church who conscientiously believe that the only possible way to produce obedience, to attain to practical holiness, to secure a godly walk, to keep our evil nature in order, is to put people under the law. They seem to fear that if souls are taken from under the school-master, with his rod and rudiments, there is an end to all moral order. In the absence of the authority of law, they look for nothing but hopeless confusion. To take away the ten commandments as a rule of life, is, in their judgment, to remove those grand moral embankments which the hand of God has erected to stem the tide of human lawlessness.

We can fully understand their difficulty. Most of us have had to encounter it, in one shape or another. But we must seek to meet it in God's way. It is of no possible use to cling, with fond tenacity, to our own notions, in the face of the plainest and most direct teaching of holy Scripture. We must, sooner or later, give up all such notions. Nothing will, nothing can, stand but the Word of our God—the voice of the Holy Ghost—the authority of Scripture—the imperishable teachings of that peerless revelation which our Father has, in His infinite grace, put into our hands. To that we must listen, with profound and reverent attention; to it we must bow down, with unquestioning and unqualified obedience. We must not presume to hold a single opinion of our own: God's opinion must be ours. We must clear out all the rubbish, which, by the influence of mere human teaching, has accumulated in our minds, and have every chamber thoroughly cleansed by the action of the Word and Spirit of God, and thoroughly ventilated by the pure and bracing air of the new creation.

Furthermore, we must learn to confide implicitly in every word that proceedeth out of the mouth of God. We must not reason, we must not judge, we must not discuss: we must simply believe. If man speaks, if it be a mere question of human authority, then indeed we must judge, because man has no right to command. We must judge what he says, not by our own opinions, or by any human standard, creed, or confession of faith, but by the Word of God. But when Scripture speaks, all discussion is closed.

This is an unspeakable consolation. It is not within the compass of human language to set forth adequately the value or the moral importance of this great fact. It delivers the soul completely from the blinding power of self-will on the one hand, and of mere subjection to human authority on the other. It brings us into direct, personal, living contact with the authority of God; and this is life, peace, liberty, moral power, true elevation, divine certainty, and holy stability. It puts an end to doubts and fears, to all the fluctuations of mere human opinion, so perplexing to the mind, so torturing to the heart. We are no longer tossed about with every wind of doctrine, every wave of human thought. *God has spoken.* This is quite enough. Here the heart finds its deep and settled repose. It has made its escape from the stormy ocean of theological controversy, and cast anchor in the blessed haven of divine revelation.

Hence, therefore, we would say to the pious reader of these lines, if you would know the mind of God on the subject before us—if you would know the ground, character, and object of Christian obedience, you must simply listen to the voice of holy Scripture. And what does it say? Does it send us back to Moses, to teach us how to live? Does it send us back "to the palpable mount," in order to secure holy living? Does it put us under the law, to keep the flesh in order? Hear what it says. Yes; hearken and ponder. Take the following words from Romans vi.—words of emancipating, holy power: "For sin shall not have dominion over you; for *ye are not under law,* but under grace."

Now, we most earnestly entreat the reader to let these words enter into the very depths of his soul. The Holy Ghost declares, in the simplest and most emphatic manner, that Christians are not under law. If we were under law, sin would have dominion over us. Indeed, we invariably find, in Scripture, that "sin," "law," and "flesh" are linked together. A soul under law cannot possibly enjoy full deliverance from the dominion of sin; and in this we can see at a glance the fallacy of the whole legal system, and the utter delusion of seeking to produce holy living by putting souls under the law. It is simply putting them into the very place where sin can lord it over them, and rule them with absolute sway. How is it possible, then, to produce holiness by law? It is absolutely hopeless.

But let us turn, for a moment, to Romans vii. "Wherefore, my brethren, ye also"—and all true believers, all God's people—"are become *dead to the law* by the body of Christ; that ye should be married to another, even to Him who is raised from the dead, that we should bring forth fruit unto God." Now, it is perfectly plain that we cannot be "dead to the law" and "under the law" at the same time. It may perhaps be argued that the expression, "dead to the law" is merely a figure. Well, supposing it be so, we ask, A figure of what? Surely it cannot be a figure of persons under law. Nay, it is a figure of the very opposite.

And let us mark particularly, the apostle does not say the law is dead. Nothing of the kind. The law is not dead, but we are dead to it. We have passed, by the death of Christ, out of the sphere to which the law belongs. Christ took our place; He was made under the law; and, on the cross, He was made sin for us. But He died for us, and we died in Him; and He has thus taken us clean out of the position in which we were under the dominion of sin, and under law, and introduced us into an entirely new position, in living association and union with Himself, so that it can be said. "As He is, so are we in this world." Is He under law? Assuredly not. Well, neither are we. Has sin any claim upon Him? None whatever. Neither has it any upon us. We are, as to our standing, as He is in the presence of God; and therefore to put us back under law would be a complete overturning of the entire Christian position, and a most positive and flagrant contradiction of the very plainest statements of holy Scripture.

Now, we would, in all simplicity and godly sincerity, ask, How could holy living be promoted by removing the very foundation of Christianity? How could indwelling sin be subdued by putting us under the very system that gave sin power over us? How could true Christian obedience ever be produced by flying in the face of holy Scripture? We confess we cannot conceive any thing more thoroughly preposterous. Surely a divine end can only be gained by pursuing a divine way. Now, God's way of giving us deliverance from the dominion of sin is by delivering us from under law; and hence all those who teach that Christians are under law are plainly at issue with God. Tremendous consideration for all who desire to be teachers of the law!

But let us hear further words from the seventh chapter of Romans. The apostle goes on to say, "For *when we were in the flesh*, the motions of sins, which were by the law, did work in our members to bring forth fruit unto *death*. But now *we are delivered from the law*, being dead [or, having died] to that wherein we were held: *that we should serve* in newness of spirit, and not in the oldness of the letter."[9]

Here, again, all is as clear as a sunbeam. What means the expression, "When we *were* in the flesh"? Does it—can it mean that we *are* still in that condition? Clearly not. If I were to say, When I *was* in London, would any one understand that I am in London still? The thought is absurd.

But what does the apostle mean by the expression, "When we were in the flesh"? He simply refers to a thing of the past—to a condition that no longer obtains. Are believers, then, not in the flesh? So Scripture emphatically declares. But does this mean that they are not in the body? Assuredly not. They are in the body as to the fact of their existence, but not in the flesh as to the ground of their standing before God.

In chapter viii. we have the most distinct statement of this point.—"So then they that are in the flesh cannot please God. *But ye are not in the flesh,* but in the Spirit, if so be that the Spirit of God dwell in you." Here we have the statement of a most solemn fact, and the setting forth of a most precious, glorious privilege. "They that are in the flesh *cannot please God.*" They may be very moral, very amiable, very religious, very benevolent; but they cannot please God. Their entire position is false. The source whence all the streams flow is corrupt; the root and stem whence all the branches emanate are rotten—hopelessly bad. They cannot produce a single atom of good fruit—fruit that God can accept. "They cannot please God." They must get into an entirely new position; they must have a new life, new motives, new objects—in a word, they must be a new creation. How solemn is all this! Let us weigh it thoroughly, and see if we understand the apostle's words.

But on the other hand, mark the glorious privilege of all true believers. *"Ye are not in the flesh."* Believers are no longer in a position in which they cannot please God. They have a new nature—a new life, every movement, every outflow, of which is agreeable to God. The very feeblest breathing of the divine life is precious to God. Of this life, the Holy Ghost is the power, Christ the object, glory the goal, heaven the home. All is divine, and therefore perfect. True, the believer is liable to err, prone in himself to wander, capable of sinning. In him (that is, in his flesh,) dwelleth no good thing. But his *standing* is based on the eternal stability of the grace of God, and his *state* is met by the divine provision which that grace has made for him in the precious atonement and all-prevailing advocacy of our Lord Jesus Christ. Thus he is forever delivered from that terrible system in which the prominent figures are, "Flesh," "Law," "Sin," "Death"—melancholy group, most surely!—and he is brought into that glorious scene in which the prominent figures are, "Life," "Liberty," "Grace," "Peace," "Righteousness," "Holiness," "Glory," "Christ." "For *ye are not come* to the mount that might be touched"—that is, the palpable mount—"and that burned with fire, nor unto blackness, and darkness, and tempest, and the sound of a trumpet, and the voice of words; which voice they that heard, entreated that the word should not be spoken to them any more: (For they could not endure that which was commanded, 'And if so much as a beast touch the mountain, it shall be stoned, or thrust through with a dart:' and so terrible was the sight, that Moses said, 'I exceedingly fear and quake:') but *ye are come* unto Mount Sion, and unto the city of the living God, the heavenly Jerusalem, and to an innumerable company of angels, the general assembly, the church of the first-born [ones] which are written in heaven, and to God the Judge of all, and to the spirits of just men made perfect, and to Jesus the Mediator of the new covenant, and to the blood of sprinkling, that speaketh better things than Abel." (Heb. xii.)

Thus we have endeavored to meet the difficulty of any conscientious reader who up to the moment in which he opened this volume had cherished the conviction that it is only by putting believers under the law that practical holiness and true obedience can be attained. We trust he has followed us through the line of Scripture evidence which we have laid before him. If so, he will see that to place believers in such a position is to do away with the very foundations of Christianity—to abandon grace—to give up Christ—to go back to the flesh, in which we cannot please God, and to place ourselves under the curse. In short, the legal system of men is diametrically opposed to the teaching of the entire New Testament. It was against this system and its upholders that the blessed apostle Paul, during his whole life, ever testified. He absolutely abhorred it, and continually denounced it. The law-teachers were ever seeking to sap and undermine his blessed labors, and subvert the souls of his beloved children in the faith. It is impossible to read his burning sentences in the epistle to the Galatians, his withering references in his epistle to the Philippians, or his solemn warnings in the epistle to the Hebrews, and not see how intense was his abhorrence of the whole legal system of the law-teachers, and how bitterly he wept over the ruins of the testimony so dear to his large, loving, devoted heart.

But it is possible that after all we have written, and notwithstanding the full tide of Scripture evidence to which we have called the reader's attention, he may still feel disposed to ask, Is there not a danger of unholy laxity and levity if the restraining power of the law be removed? To this we reply, God is wiser than we are. He knows best how to cure laxity and levity, and how to produce the right sort of obedience. He tried the law, and what did it do?

It worked wrath; it caused the offense to abound; it developed "the motions of sins;" it brought in death; it was the strength of sin; it deprived the sinner of all power; it slew him; it was condemnation; it cursed all who had to do with it—"As many as are of the works of the law are under the curse;" and all this, not because of any defect in the law, but because of man's total inability to keep it.

Is it not plain to the reader that neither life nor righteousness nor holiness nor true Christian obedience could ever be attained under law? Is it possible, after all that has passed in review before us, that he can have a single question, a single doubt, a single difficulty? We trust not. No one who is willing to bow down to the teaching and authority of the New Testament can adhere to the legal system for one hour.

However, ere we turn from this weighty and all-important subject, we shall place before the reader a passage or two of Scripture in which the moral glories of Christianity shine forth with peculiar lustre, in vivid contrast to the entire Mosaic economy.

First of all, let us take that familiar passage at the opening of the eighth of Romans, "There is therefore now *no condemnation* to them which are *in Christ Jesus*. For the law of the spirit of life in Christ Jesus *hath made me free* from the law of sin and death. For what the law could not do, in that it was weak through the flesh, God sending His own Son *in the likeness* of sinful flesh, and for sin, condemned sin in the flesh; that the righteousness [δικαίωμα] of the law might be fulfilled in us, who walk not after the flesh, but after the Spirit." (Ver. 1-4.)

Now, we must bear in mind that verse 1 sets forth the *standing* of every Christian—his *position* before God. He is "in Christ Jesus." This settles every thing. He is not in the flesh; he is not under law; he is absolutely and eternally "in Christ Jesus." Hence there is, there can be, no condemnation. The apostle is not speaking of or referring to our *walk* or our *state*. If he were, he could not possibly speak of "no condemnation." The most perfect Christian walk that ever was exhibited, the most perfect Christian state that ever was attained, would afford some ground for judgment and condemnation. There is not a Christian on the face of the earth who has not daily to judge his state and his walk—his moral condition and his practical ways. How, then, could "no condemnation" ever stand connected with, or be based upon, Christian walk? Utterly impossible. In order to be free from all condemnation, we must have what is divinely perfect, and no Christian walk is or ever was that. Even a Paul had to withdraw his words (Acts xxiii. 5.). He repented of having written a letter (2 Cor. vii. 8.). A perfect walk and a perfect state were only found in One. In all beside—even the holiest and best, failure is found.

Hence, therefore, the second clause of Romans viii. 1 must be rejected: it is not Scripture. This, we think, would be seen by any one really taught of God, apart from all question of mere criticism. Any spiritual mind would detect the incongruity between the words "no condemnation" and "walk." The two things cannot be made to harmonize. And here, we doubt not, is just where thousands of pious souls have been plunged into difficulty as to this really magnificent and emancipating passage. The joyful sound, "No condemnation," has been robbed of its deep, full, and blessed significance by a clause introduced by some scribe or copyist whose feeble vision was doubtless dazzled by the brightness of that free, absolute, sovereign grace which shines in the opening statement of the chapter. How often have we heard such words as these!—"Oh, yes; I know there is no condemnation to them that are in Christ Jesus; but that is if they walk not after the flesh, but after the Spirit. Now, I cannot say that I walk thus. I long to do so, and I mourn over my failure. I would give worlds to be able to walk more perfectly; but, alas! alas! I have to judge myself—my state, my walk, my ways—each day, each hour. This being so, I dare not apply to myself the precious words, 'no condemnation.' I hope to be able to do so some day, when I have made more progress in personal holiness; but in my present state, I should deem it the very height of presumption to appropriate to myself the precious truth contained in the first clause of Romans viii."

Such thoughts as these have passed through the minds of most of us, if they have not been clothed in words. But the simple and conclusive answer to all such legal reasonings is found in the fact that the second clause of Romans viii. 1 is not Scripture at all, but a very misleading interpolation, foreign to the spirit and genius of Christianity, opposed to the whole line of argument in the context where it occurs, and utterly subversive of the solid peace of the Christian. It is a fact well known to all who are conversant with biblical criticism, that all the leading authorities are agreed in rejecting the second clause of Romans viii. 1.[10] And in this, it is simply a matter of criticism confirming, as all sound criticism must do, the conclusion at which a really spiritual mind would arrive without any knowledge of criticism at all.

But in addition to all that has been advanced in reference to this question, we cannot but think that the occurrence of the clause, "who walk not after the flesh, but after the Spirit," in verse 4, affords abundant evidence of its misplacement in verse 1. We cannot, for a moment, admit the thought of redundancy in holy Scripture. Now, in verse 4 it *is* a question of walk—a question of our fulfilling "the righteousness [mark the word—δικαίωμα] of the law," and hence the clause is in its right, because divinely fitted, place. A person who walks in the Spirit—as every Christian ought—fulfills the righteousness of the law. Love is the fulfilling of the law; and love will lead us to do what the ten commandments could never effect, namely, to love our enemies. No lover of holiness, no advocate of practical righteousness, need ever be the least afraid of losing aught by abandoning the legal ground, and taking his place on the elevated platform of true Christianity—by turning from Mount Sinai to Mount Zion—by passing from Moses to Christ. No; he only reaches a higher source, a deeper spring, a wider sphere of holiness, righteousness, and practical obedience.

And then, if any one should feel disposed to ask, Does not the line of argument which we have been pursuing tend to rob the law of its characteristic glory? We reply, Most assuredly not. So far from this, the law was never so magnified, never so vindicated, never so established, never so glorified, as by that precious work which forms the imperishable foundation of all the privileges, the blessings, the dignities, and the glories of Christianity. The blessed apostle anticipates and answers this very question in the earlier part of his epistle to the Romans. "Do we then," he says, "make void the law through faith? Far be the thought; yea, we establish the law." How could the law be more gloriously vindicated, honored, and magnified than in the life and death of the Lord Jesus Christ? Will any one seek, for a moment, to maintain the extravagant notion that it is magnifying the law to put Christians under it? We fondly trust the reader will not. Ah! no; all this line of things must be completely abandoned by those whose privilege it is to walk in the light of the new creation; who know Christ as their life and Christ as their righteousness, Christ their sanctification, Christ their great exemplar, Christ their model, Christ their all and in all; who find their motive for obedience, not in the fear of the curses of a broken law, but in the love of Christ, according to those exquisitely beautiful words, "The love of Christ"—not the law of Moses—"constraineth us; because we thus judge, that if one died for all, then were all dead. And He died for all, that they which live should not henceforth live unto themselves, but unto Him which died for them and rose again." (2 Cor. v.)

Could the law ever produce aught like this? Impossible. But, blessed forever be the God of all grace, "what the law could not do," not because it was not holy, just, and good, but "in that it was weak through the flesh"— the workman was all right, but the material was rotten, and nothing could be made of it; but "God sending His own Son in the likeness of sinful flesh, and for sin, condemned sin in the flesh, that the righteousness of the law might be fulfilled in us, who," as risen with Christ, linked with Him by the

Holy Ghost, in the power of a new and everlasting life, "walk not after the flesh, but after the Spirit."

This, and only this, is true, practical Christianity; and if the reader will turn to the second of Galatians, he will find another of those fine, glowing utterances of the blessed apostle, setting forth, with divine force and fullness, the special glory of Christian life and walk. It is in connection with his faithful rebuke of the apostle Peter at Antioch, when that beloved and honored servant of Christ, through his characteristic weakness, had been led to step down, for a moment, from the elevated moral ground on which the gospel of the grace of God places the soul. We cannot do better than quote the entire paragraph for the reader: every sentence of it is pregnant with spiritual power.

"But when Peter was come to Antioch, I withstood him *to the face.*" He did not go behind his back, to disparage and depreciate him in the view of others, even though "he was to be blamed. For before that certain came from James, he did eat with the Gentiles; but when they were come, he withdrew and separated himself, fearing them which were of the circumcision. And the other Jews dissembled likewise with him, insomuch that Barnabas also was carried away with their dissimulation. But when I saw that they walked not uprightly according to the truth of the gospel, I said unto Peter before them all, If thou, being a Jew, livest after the manner of Gentiles, and not as do the Jews, why compellest thou the Gentiles to live as do the Jews? We who are Jews by nature, and not sinners of the Gentiles, knowing that a man is not justified by works of law, but by the faith of Jesus Christ, even we have believed in Jesus Christ, that we might be justified by the faith of Christ, and not by works of law; for by works of law shall no flesh be justified. But if, while we seek to be justified by Christ, we ourselves also are found sinners, is therefore Christ the minister of sin? God forbid [or, Far be the thought—μη γενοιτο.]. For if I build again the things which I destroyed, I make myself a transgressor." For if the things were right, why destroy them? and if they were wrong, why build them again? "For I, through law, am *dead to law,* that I might live unto God. I am crucified with Christ: nevertheless I live; yet not I, but Christ liveth in me; and the life which I now live in the flesh, I live [not by the law, as a rule of life, but] by the faith of the Son of God, *who loved me,* and gave *Himself for me.* I do not frustrate the grace of God; for if righteousness come by law, then Christ is dead in vain [or, has died for nothing—δωρεὰν.]." (Gal. ii. 11-21.)

Here, then, we have one of the very finest statements of the truth as to practical Christianity any where to be found. But what specially claims our attention just now is, the very marked and beautiful way in which the gospel of God opens up the path of the true believer between the two fatal errors of legality on the one side and carnal laxity on the other. Verse 19, in the passage just quoted, contains the divine remedy for both these deadly evils. To all—whoever or wherever they are—who would seek to put the Christian under the law, in any shape or for any object whatsoever, our apostle exclaims, in the ears of dissembling Jews, with Peter at their head, and as an answer to all the law-teachers of every age, "*I am dead to law.*"

What can the law have to say to a dead man? Nothing. The law applies to a living man, to curse him and kill him because he has not kept it. It is a very grave mistake indeed to teach that the law is dead or abolished. It is nothing of the sort. It is alive in all its force, in all its stringency, in all its majesty, in all its unbending dignity. It would be a very serious mistake to say that the law of England against murder is dead; but if a man is dead, the law no longer applies to him, inasmuch as he has passed entirely out of its range.

But how is the believer dead to law? The apostle replies, "I through law am dead to law." The law had brought the sentence of death into his conscience, as we read in Romans vii, "I was alive without the law once; but when the commandment came, sin revived and I died. And the commandment, which was ordained to life, I found to be into death. For sin, taking occasion by the commandment, deceived me, and by it slew me."

But there is more than this. The apostle goes on to say, "I am crucified with Christ: nevertheless I live; yet not I, but Christ liveth in me." And here is the triumphant answer of the Christian to those who say that inasmuch as the Mosaic law is abrogated, there is no longer any demand for the legal restraint under which the Jews were called to live. To all who would seek liberty for self-indulgence, the answer is, "I am dead to law, [not that I might give a loose rein to the flesh, but] that I might live unto God."

Thus nothing can be more complete, nothing more morally beautiful, than the answer of true Christianity to legality on the one hand and licentiousness on the other. Self crucified; sin condemned; new life in Christ; a life to be lived to God; a life of faith in the Son of God; the motive-spring of that life, the constraining love of Christ—what can exceed this? Will any one, in view of the moral glories of Christianity, contend for putting believers under the law, putting them back into the flesh—back into the old creation—back to the sentence of death in the conscience—back to bondage, darkness, distance, fear of death, condemnation?

Is it possible that any one who has ever tasted, even in the very feeblest measure, the heavenly sweetness of God's most blessed gospel, can accept the wretched mongrel system, composed of half law and half grace, which christendom offers to the soul? How terrible to find the children of God—

members of the body of Christ—temples of the Holy Ghost—robbed of their glorious privileges, and burdened with a heavy yoke, which, as Peter says, "neither our fathers nor we were able to bear." We earnestly entreat the Christian reader to consider what has been placed before him. Search the Scriptures; and if you find these things to be so, then fling aside forever the grave-clothes in which christendom inwraps its deluded votaries, and walk in the liberty wherewith Christ makes His people free; tear off the bandage with which it covers the eyes of men, and gaze on the moral glories which shine with such heavenly brilliancy in the gospel of the grace of God.

And then let us prove, by a holy, happy, gracious walk and conversation, that grace can do what law never could. Let our practical ways from day to day, in the midst of the scenes, circumstances, relationships, and associations in which we are called to live, be the most convincing reply to all who contend for the law as a rule of life.

Finally, let it be our earnest, loving desire and aim to seek, in so far as in us lies, to lead all the dear children of God into a clearer knowledge of their standing and privileges in a risen and glorified Christ. May the Lord send out His light and His truth, in the power of the Holy Ghost, and gather His beloved people around Himself, to walk in the joy of His salvation, in the purity and light of His presence, and to wait for His coming.

We do not attempt to offer any apology for what may perhaps appear to some of our readers to be a very lengthened digression from the fourth chapter of Deuteronomy. The fact is, we have been led into what we judge to be a very needed line of practical truth by the very first verse of the chapter, as quoted at the opening of this section. We felt it absolutely necessary, in speaking of the weighty question of obedience, to seek to place it on its true basis. If Israel was called to "hearken and do," how much more are we, who are so richly blessed—yea, "blessed with *all* spiritual blessings in the heavenlies in Christ Jesus." We are called to obedience, even to the obedience of Jesus Christ, as we have it in 1 Peter i, "Elect according to the foreknowledge of God the Father, through sanctification of the Spirit, unto obedience and sprinkling of the blood of Jesus Christ." We are called to the very same character of obedience as that which marked the life of our blessed Lord Jesus Christ Himself. Of course, in Him there was no hindering influence as, alas! there is in us; but as to the character of the obedience, it is the same.

This is an immense privilege. We are called to walk in the footsteps of Jesus. "He that saith he abideth in Him ought himself also so to walk even as He walked." Now, in pondering the path of our Lord, in considering His marvelous life, there is one point which demands our profound and reverent attention—a point which connects itself, in a very special manner, with the book of Deuteronomy—and that is, the way in which He ever used the Word of God—the place which He ever gave to the holy Scriptures. This we consider to be a subject of the last possible importance at the present moment. It holds a prominent place throughout the lovely book with which we are at present engaged. Indeed, as we have already remarked, it characterizes the book, and marks it off from the three books which precede it in the divine canon. We shall find proofs and illustrations of this in abundance as we pass along. Every where, the Word of God gets its own paramount place, as the only rule, the only standard, the only authority, for man. It meets him in every position, in every relationship, in every sphere of action, and in every stage of his moral and spiritual history. It tells him what he ought to do, and what he ought not. It furnishes him with ample guidance in every difficulty. It descends, as we shall see, to the most minute details—such details, indeed, as fill us with amazement to think that the High and Mighty One that inhabiteth eternity could occupy Himself with them—to think that the Omnipotent Creator and Sustainer of the vast universe could stoop to legislate about a bird's nest. (Chap. xxii. 6.)

Such is the Word of God—that peerless revelation—that perfect and inimitable volume which stands alone in the history of literature. And we may say that one special charm of the book of Deuteronomy—one peculiar feature of interest is, the way in which it exalts the Word of God, and enforces upon us the holy and happy duty of unqualified and unhesitating obedience.

Yes; we repeat and would fervently emphasize the words—unqualified and unhesitating obedience. We would have these wholesome words sounded in the ears of Christian professors throughout the length and breadth of the earth. We live in a day specially marked by the setting up of man's reason, man's judgment, man's will; in short, we live in what the inspired apostle calls "man's day." On all hands we are encountered by lofty and boastful words about human reason, and the right of every man to judge and reason and think for himself. The thought of being absolutely and completely governed by the authority of holy Scripture is treated with sovereign contempt by thousands of men who are the religious guides and teachers of the professing church. For any one to assert his reverent belief in the plenary inspiration, the all-sufficiency, and the absolute authority of Scripture, is quite sufficient to stamp him as an ignorant, narrow-minded man, if not a semi-lunatic, in the judgment of some who occupy the very highest position in the professing church. In our universities, our colleges, and our schools, the moral glory of the Divine Volume is fast fading away, and instead thereof our young people are led and taught to walk in the light of science—the light of human reason. The Word of God itself is impiously placed at the bar of man's judgment, and reduced to the level of the human understanding. Every thing is rejected which soars beyond man's feeble vision.

Thus the Word of God is virtually set aside. For, clearly, if Scripture is to be submitted to human judgment, it ceases to be the Word of God. It is the very height of folly to think of submitting a divine and therefore perfect revelation to any tribunal whatsoever. Either God has given us a revelation or He has not. If He has, that revelation must be paramount, supreme, above and beyond all question, absolutely unquestionable, unerring, divine. To its authority all must bow down, without a single question. To suppose for a moment that man is competent to judge the Word of God, able to pronounce upon what is or what is not worthy of God to say or to write, is simply to put man in God's place. And this is precisely what the devil is aiming at, although many of his instruments are not aware that they are helping on his designs.

But the question is continually cropping up before us, "How can we be sure that we have, in our English Bible, the *bona-fide* revelation of God?" We reply, God can make us sure of it. If He does not, no one can: if He does, no one need. This is our ground, and we deem it unassailable. We should like to ask all those who start this infidel question (for such we must honestly call it), Supposing that God cannot give us the absolute certainty that, in our common English Bible, we do actually possess His own most precious, priceless revelation, then whither are we to turn? Of course, in such a weighty matter, on which momentous and eternal consequences hang, a single doubt is torture and misery. If I am not sure of possessing a revelation from God, I am left without a single ray of light for my path; I am plunged in darkness, gloom, and mental misery. What am I to do? Can man help me by his learning, his wisdom, or his reason? Can he satisfy my soul by his decision? Can he solve my difficulty, answer my question, remove my doubt, dissipate my fear? Is man better able than God to give me the assurance that God has spoken?

The idea is absolutely monstrous—monstrous in the very highest degree. The plain fact is this, reader: If God cannot give us the certainty that He has spoken, we are left without His word altogether. If we must turn to human authority, call it what you please, in order to guarantee the Word of God to our souls, then that authority is higher and greater, safer and more trustworthy, than the Word which it guarantees. Blessed be God, it is not so. He has spoken to our hearts. He has given us His Word, and that Word carries its own credentials with it. It stands in no need of letters of commendation from a human hand. What! turn to man to accredit the

Word of the living God!—apply to a worm to give us the assurance that our God has spoken to us in His Word! Away forever with the blasphemous notion, and let our whole moral being—all our ransomed powers adore the matchless grace, the sovereign mercy, that has not left us to grope in the darkness of our own minds, or to be bewildered by the conflicting opinions of men; but has given us His own perfect and most precious revelation, the divine light of His Word, to guide our feet into the path of certainty and peace, to enlighten our understandings and comfort our hearts, to preserve us from every form of doctrinal error and moral pravity, and finally, to conduct us into the rest, blessedness, and glory of His own heavenly kingdom. All praise to His name throughout the everlasting ages!

But we must bear in mind that the marvelous privilege of which we have spoken—and truly it is most marvelous—is the basis of a most solemn responsibility. If it be true that God has, in His infinite goodness, given us a perfect revelation of His mind, then what should be our attitude in reference to it? Are we to sit in judgment upon it? Are we to discuss, argue, or reason? Alas! for all who do so. They will find themselves on terribly dangerous ground. The only true, the only proper, the only safe attitude for man in the presence of God's revelation is, obedience—simple, unqualified, hearty obedience. This is the only right thing for us, and this is the thing which is pleasing to God. The path of obedience is the path of sweetest privilege, rest, and blessing. This path can be trodden by the merest babe in Christ, as well as by the "young men" and the "fathers." There is the one straight and blessed path for all. Narrow it is, no doubt; but, oh! it is safe, bright, and elevated. The light of our Father's approving countenance ever shines upon it; and in this blessed light the obedient soul finds the most triumphant answer to all the reproaches of those who talk, in high-sounding words, about breadth of mind, liberality of thought, freedom of opinion, progress, development, and such like. The obedient child of God can afford to put up with all this, because he feels and knows, he believes and is sure, that he is treading a path indicated for him by the precious Word of God. He is not careful to explain or apologize, feeling assured that those who object, oppose, and reproach are utterly incapable of understanding or appreciating his explanation. And, moreover, he feels that it is no part of his duty to explain or defend. He has but to obey; and as for objectors and opposers, he has but to refer them to his Master.

This makes it all so simple, so plain, so certain. It delivers the heart from a thousand difficulties and perplexities. If we were to set about replying to all who undertake to raise questions or start difficulties, our whole life would be spent in the profitless task. We may rest assured the best possible answer to all infidel objectors is, the steady, earnest, onward path of unqualified obedience. Let us leave infidels, skeptics, and rationalists to their own worthless theories, while we, with unswerving purpose and firm step, pursue that blessed path of childlike obedience which, like the shining light, shineth more and more unto the perfect day. Thus shall our minds be kept tranquil, for the peace of God, which passeth all understanding, shall garrison our hearts and minds through Christ Jesus. When the Word of God, which is settled forever in heaven, is hidden deep down in our hearts, there will be a calm certainty, a holy stability, and a marked progress in our Christian career, which will afford the best possible answer to the gainsayer, the most effectual testimony to the truth of God, and the most convincing evidence and solid confirmation to every wavering heart.

The chapter before us abounds in the most solemn exhortation to Israel, grounded upon the fact of their having heard the word of God. Thus in the second verse we have a sentence or two which should be deeply engraved on the tablets of every Christian's heart.—"Ye shall not add unto the word which I command you, neither shall ye diminish aught from it."

These words involve two grand facts with regard to the Word of God. It is not to be added to, for the simplest of all reasons, because there is nothing lacking; it is not to be diminished, because there is nothing superfluous. Every thing we want is there, and nothing that is there can be done without. "Add thou not unto His words, lest He reprove thee, and thou be found a liar." To suppose that aught can be added to God's Word is, upon the very face of it, to deny that it is God's Word; and, on the other hand, if we admit that it is the Word of God, then it follows of necessity (blessed necessity!) that we could not afford to do without a single sentence of it. There would be a blank in the volume which no human hand could fill up, if a single clause were dropped from its place in the canon. We have all we want, and hence we must not add: we want it all, and hence we must not diminish.

How deeply important is all this, in this day of human tampering with the Word of God! How blessed to know that we have in our possession a book so divinely perfect that not a sentence, not a clause, not a word, can be added to it. We speak not, of course, of translations or versions, but of the Scriptures as originally given of God—His own perfect revelation. To this, not a touch can be given. As well might a human finger have dared to touch the creation of God, on the morning when all the sons of God sang together, as to add a jot or a tittle to the inspired Word of God. And on the other hand, to take away a jot or a tittle from it, is to say that the Holy Ghost has penned what was unnecessary. Thus the holy volume is divinely guarded at both ends. It is securely fenced round about, so that no rude hand should touch its sacred contents.

What! it may be said in reply, do you mean to say that every sentence, from the opening lines of Genesis to the close of Revelation, is divinely inspired? Yes; that is precisely the ground we take. We claim for every line between the covers of the volume a divine origin. To question this is to attack the very pillars of the Christian faith. A single flaw in the canon would be sufficient to prove it not of God. To touch a single stone in the arch is to bring down the whole fabric in ruins around us. "All Scripture is divinely inspired, and" being so, must be "profitable for doctrine, for reproof, for correction, for instruction in righteousness; that the man of God may be perfect [αρτιος], throughly furnished unto all good works." (2 Tim. iii.)

This stronghold must on no account be surrendered; nay, it must be tenaciously held, in the face of every infidel assault. If it be given up, all is hopelessly lost—we have nothing to lean upon. Either the Word of God is perfect, or we are left without any divine foundation for our faith. If there be a word too much or a word too little in the revelation which God has given us, then verily we are left, like a ship without compass, rudder, or chart, to be drifted about on the wild, tumultuous ocean of infidel thought; in short, if we have not an absolutely perfect revelation, we are of all men most miserable.

But we may still be challenged with such a question as this: Do you believe that the long string of names in the opening chapters of 1 Chronicles— those genealogical tables are divinely inspired? were they written for our learning? and if so, what are we to learn from them? We unhesitatingly declare our reverent belief in the divine inspiration of all these; and we have no doubt whatever but that their value, interest, and importance will be fully proved by and by in the history of that people to whom they specially apply.

And then, as to what we are to learn from those genealogical records, we believe they teach us a most precious lesson as to Jehovah's faithful care of His people Israel, and His loving interest in them and in all that concerns them. He watches over them from generation to generation, even though they are scattered and lost to human view. He knows all about "the twelve tribes," and He will manifest them in due time, and plant them in their destined inheritance, in the land of Canaan, according to His promise to Abraham, Isaac, and Jacob.

Now, is not all this full of blessed instruction for us? Is it not full of comfort for our souls? Is it not most confirmatory of our faith to mark the gracious pains-taking of our God, His minute care and vigilance in reference to His earthly people? Most assuredly it is. And ought not our hearts to be interested in all that interests the heart of our Father? Are we not to take an interest in any thing save what directly concerns ourselves? Where is there a loving child who would not take an interest in all his father's concerns, and delight to read every line that drops from his father's pen?

Let us not be misunderstood. We do not, by any means, attempt to imply that all portions of the Word of God are of like interest and importance to us. We do not presume to assert that we are to hang with equal interest over the first chapter of 1 Chronicles and the seventeenth chapter of John or the eighth chapter of Romans. It seems hardly necessary to make such a statement, inasmuch as no such question is raised. But what we assert is that each of the above scriptures is divinely inspired, one just as much as another; and not only so, but we further assert that 1 Chronicles i. and such like passages fill a niche which John xvii. cannot fill, and do a work which Romans viii. cannot do.

And finally, above and beyond all, we must remember that we are not competent to judge what is and what is not worthy of a place in the inspired canon. We are ignorant and short-sighted; and the very portion which we might deem beneath the dignity of inspiration may have some very important bearing upon the history of God's ways with the world at large or with His people in particular.

In short, it simply resolves itself into this with every truly pious soul — every really spiritual mind: We reverently believe in the divine inspiration of every line of our precious Bible, from beginning to end; and we believe this not on the ground of any human authority whatsoever. To believe in holy Scripture because it comes to us accredited by any authority upon earth, would be to set that authority above holy Scripture, inasmuch as that which guarantees has more weight — more value than the thing guaranteed. Hence, we should no more think of looking to human authority to confirm the Word of God than we should of bringing out a rush-light to prove that the sun was shining.

No, reader; we must be clear and decided as to this. It must be, in the judgment of our souls, a great cardinal truth which we hold dearer than life itself — the plenary inspiration of holy Scripture. Thus shall we have wherewithal to answer the cool audacity of modern skepticism, rationalism, and infidelity. We do not mean to say that we shall be able to convince infidels. God will deal with them in His own way, and convince them with His own unanswerable arguments in His own time. It is labor and time lost to argue with such men. But we feel persuaded that the most dignified and effective answer to infidelity, in its every phase, will be found in the calm repose of the heart that rests in the blessed assurance that "all Scripture is given by inspiration of God;" and again, "Whatsoever things were written aforetime were written for our learning; that we through patience and comfort of the Scriptures might have hope." The former of these precious quotations proves that Scripture has come from God; the latter, that it has come to us. Both together go to prove that we must neither add to nor take from the Word of God. There is nothing lacking, and nothing superfluous. The Lord be praised for this solid foundation-truth, and for all the comfort and consolation that flows from it to every true believer!

We shall now proceed to quote for the reader a few of the passages in this fourth chapter of Deuteronomy which so emphatically set forth the value, importance, and authority of the Word of God. In them, as in the whole of this book, we shall see that it is not so much a question of any particular ordinance, rite, or ceremony, but of the weight, solemnity, and dignity of the Word of God itself, whatever that Word may set before us.

"Behold, I have taught you statutes and judgments, even as the Lord my God commanded me, that ye should do so in the land whither ye go to possess it." Their conduct was to be ruled and formed, in all things, by the divine commandments. Immense principle for them, for us, for all! "Keep, therefore, and do them; for *this is your wisdom* and *your understanding* in the sight of the nations, which shall hear all these statutes, and say, Surely this great nation is a wise and understanding people."

Let us specially weigh these words. Their wisdom and their understanding were to consist in their simply keeping and doing the divine statutes and judgments. It was not by learned discussion or arguments that their wisdom was to be displayed, but by childlike, unquestioning obedience. All the wisdom was in the statutes and judgments, not in their thoughts and reasonings respecting them. The profound and marvelous wisdom of God was seen in His Word, and this was what the nations were to see and admire. The light of the divine judgments shining in the conduct and character of the people of God was to draw forth the admiring testimony of the nations around.

Alas! alas! how differently it turned out! How little did the nations of the earth learn, from the actings of Israel, about God and His Word! Yea, His name was blasphemed continually through their ways. Instead of occupying the high and holy and happy ground of loving obedience to the divine commandments, they descended to the level of the nations around them—adopted their habits, worshiped their gods, and walked in their ways; so that those nations, instead of seeing the lofty wisdom, purity, and moral glory of the divine statutes, saw only the weakness, folly, and moral degradation of a people who made their boast in being the depositary of those oracles which condemned themselves. (Rom. ii, iii.)

Still, blessed be God, His Word must stand forever, however His people may fail to carry it out. His standard is perfect, and therefore must never be lowered; and if the power of His Word be not seen in the ways of His people, it will shine in the condemnation of those ways, and ever abide for the guidance, comfort, strength, and blessing of any who desire, however feebly or falteringly, to tread the path of obedience.

However, in the chapter with which we are at present occupied, the lawgiver seeks to set the divine standard faithfully before the people, in all its dignity and moral glory. He fails not to unfold to them the true effect of obedience, while he solemnly warns them against the danger of turning away from the holy commandments of God. Hear his powerful pleadings with their hearts. "What nation is there so great," he says, "who hath God so nigh unto them, as the Lord our God is in all things that we call upon Him for? And what nation is there so great, that hath statutes and judgments so righteous as all this law, which I set before you this day?"

Here is true moral greatness, at all times and in all places, for a nation, for a people, for a household, or for an individual. To have the living God nigh unto us; to have the sweet privilege of calling upon Him, in all things; to have His power and His mercy ever exercised toward us; to have the light of His blessed countenance shining approvingly upon us, in all our ways; to have the moral effect of His righteous statutes and holy commandments seen in our practical career, from day to day; to have Him manifesting Himself to us, and making His abode with us.

What human language can adequately set forth the deep blessedness of such privileges as these? and yet they are placed, by infinite grace, within the reach of every child of God on the face of the earth. We do not mean to assert that every child of God enjoys them. Far from it. They are reserved, as we have already seen, for those who, through grace, are enabled to render a loving, hearty, reverent obedience to the divine word. Here lies the precious secret of the whole matter. It was true for Israel of old, and it is true for the Church now—it was true for the individual soul then, and it is true for the individual soul now, that divine complacency is the priceless reward of human obedience. And we may further add that obedience is the bounden duty and high privilege of all God's people, and of each in particular. Come what may, implicit obedience is our privilege and our duty, divine complacency our present sweet reward.

But the poor human heart is prone to wander, and manifold influences are at work around us to draw us off from the narrow path of obedience. We need not marvel, therefore, at the solemn and oft-repeated admonitions addressed by Moses to the hearts and consciences of his hearers. He pours his large, loving heart out to the congregation so dear to him, in glowing, earnest, soul-stirring accents. "Only take heed to thyself," he says, "and keep thy soul diligently, lest thou forget the things which thine eyes have seen, and lest they depart from thy heart all the days of thy life; but teach them thy sons, and thy sons' sons."

These are weighty words for all of us. They set before us two things of unspeakable importance, namely, individual and domestic responsibility — personal and household testimony. God's people of old were responsible to keep the heart with all diligence, lest it should let slip the precious Word of God. And not only so, but they were solemnly responsible to instruct their children and their grandchildren in the same. Are we, with all our light and privilege, less responsible than Israel of old? Surely not. We are imperatively called upon to give ourselves to the careful study of the Word of God — to apply our hearts to it. It is not enough that we hurry over a few verses or a chapter, as a piece of daily religious routine. This will not meet the case at all. We want to make the Bible our supreme and absorbing study, — that in which we delight — in which we find our refreshment and recreation.

It is to be feared that some of us read the Bible as a matter of duty, while we find our delight and refreshment in the newspaper and light literature. Need we wonder at our shallow knowledge of Scripture? How could we know aught of the living depths or the moral glories of a volume which we merely take up as a cold matter of duty, and read a few verses with a yawning indifference, while, at the same time, the newspaper or the sensational novel is literally devoured?

It will perhaps be said, in reply, We cannot be always reading the Bible. Would those who thus speak say, We cannot be always reading the newspaper or the novel? And, we would further inquire, what must be the actual state of a person who can say, "We cannot be always reading the Bible"? Can he be in a healthy condition of soul? Can he really love the Word of God? Can he have any just sense of its preciousness, its excellence, its moral glories? Impossible.

What mean the following words to Israel: "Therefore shall ye lay up these My words *in your heart*, and *in your soul*, and bind them for a sign upon *your hand*, that they may be as frontlets between *your eyes*"? The "heart," the "soul," the "hand" the "eyes" — all engaged about the precious Word of God. This was real work. It was to be no empty formality, no barren routine. The whole man was to be given up, in holy devotion, to the statutes and judgments of God.

"And ye shall teach them your children, speaking of them when thou sittest in thine house, and when thou walkest by the way, when thou liest down, and when thou risest up. And thou shalt write them upon the door-posts of thine house, and upon thy gates." Do we, Christians, enter into such words as these? Has the Word of God such a place in our hearts, in our homes, and in our habits? Do those who enter our houses, or come in contact with us in daily life, see that the Word of God is paramount with us? Do those with whom we do business see that we are governed by the precepts of holy Scripture? Do our servants and our children see that we live in the very atmosphere of Scripture, and that our whole character is formed and our conduct governed by it?

These are searching questions for our hearts, beloved Christian reader. Let us not put them away from us. We may rest assured there is no more correct indicator of our moral and spiritual condition than that afforded by our treatment of the Word of God. If we do not love it—love to study it—thirst after it—delight in it—long for the quiet hour in the which we can hang over its sacred page and drink in its most precious teaching—meditate upon it, in the closet, in the family, in the street; in short, if we do not breathe its holy atmosphere—if we could ever give utterance to such a sentiment as that given above, that "we cannot be always reading the Bible," then, verily, we have urgent need to look well to our spiritual state, for we are sadly out of health. The new nature loves the Word of God—earnestly desires it, as we read in 1 Peter ii.—"As new-born babes, desire the sincere milk of the Word, that ye may grow thereby."

This is the true idea. If the sincere milk of the Word be not sought after, diligently used and eagerly fed upon, we must be in a low, unhealthy, dangerous condition of soul. There may not be any thing outwardly wrong in our conduct, we may not be publicly dishonoring the Lord in our ways, but we are grieving His loving heart by our gross neglect of His Word, which is but another term for the neglect of Himself. It is the very height of folly to talk of loving Christ if we do not love and live upon His Word. It is a delusion to imagine that the new life can be in a healthy, prosperous condition where the Word of God is habitually neglected in the closet and the family.

We do not, of course, mean that no other book but the Bible should be read, or we should not pen these "Notes;" but nothing demands greater watchfulness than the matter of reading. All things are to be done in the name of Jesus, and to the glory of God, and this is amongst the "all things." We should read no book that we cannot read to the glory of God, and on which we cannot ask God's blessing.

We feel that this entire subject demands the most serious consideration of all God's people, and we trust that the Spirit of God may use our meditation on the chapter before us to stir up our hearts and consciences in reference to what is due to the Word of God, both in our hearts and in our houses.

No doubt, if it has its right place in the heart, it will have its right place also in the house; but if there be no acknowledgment of the Word of God in the bosom of the family, it is hard to believe that it has its right place in the heart. Heads of houses should ponder this matter seriously. We are most fully persuaded that there ought to be, in every Christian household, a daily acknowledgment of God and His Word. Some may perhaps look upon it as bondage, as legality, as religious routine, to have regular family worship. We would ask such objectors, Is it bondage for the family to assemble at meals? Are the family reunions around the social board ever regarded as a wearisome duty—a piece of dull routine? Certainly not, if the family be a well-ordered and happy one. Why, then, should it be regarded as a burdensome thing for the head of a Christian household to gather his children and his servants around him and read a few verses of the precious Word of God, and breathe a few words of prayer before the throne of grace? We believe it to be a habit in perfect accordance with the teaching of both the Old and the New Testaments—a habit grateful to the heart of God—a holy, blessed, edifying habit.

What should we think of a professing Christian who never prayed, never read the Word of God, in private? Could we possibly regard him as a happy, healthy, true Christian? Assuredly not. Indeed we should seriously question the existence of divine life in such a soul. Prayer and the Word of God are absolutely essential to healthy, vigorous Christian life; so that a man who habitually neglects these must be in an utterly dead state.

Now, if it be thus in reference to an individual, how can a family be regarded as in a right state where there is no family reading, no family prayer, no family acknowledgment of God or His Word? Can we conceive a God-fearing household going on from Lord's day morning to Saturday night without any collective recognition of the One to whom they owe every thing? Day after day rolls on, domestic duties are attended to, the family assemble regularly at meals, but there is no thought of summoning the household around the Word of God, or around the mercy-seat. We ask, Where is the difference between such a family and any poor heathen household? Is it not most sad—most deplorable to find those who make the very highest profession, and who take their places at the Lord's table, yet living in the gross neglect of family reading—family worship?

Reader, are you the head of a household? If so, what are your thoughts on the subject? and what is your line of action? Have you family reading and family prayer, daily in your house? If not, (bear with us when we ask you,) why not? Search and see what is the real root of the matter. Has your heart declined from God, from His Word and His ways? Do you read and pray in private? Do you love the Word and prayer? do you find delight in them? If so, how is it you neglect them in your household? Perhaps you seek to excuse yourself on the ground of nervousness and timidity; if so, look to the Lord to enable you to overcome the weakness. Just cast yourself on His unfailing grace, and gather your household around you at a certain hour each day, read a few verses of Scripture and breathe half a dozen words of prayer; or, if you cannot do this at first, just let the family kneel for a few moments in silence before the throne.

Any thing, in short, like a family acknowledgment, a family testimony: any thing but a godless, careless, prayerless life in your household. Do, dear friend, suffer the word of exhortation in this matter. Let us entreat you to begin at once, looking to God to help you, as He most assuredly will, for He never fails a really trusting, dependent heart. Do not any longer go on neglecting God and His Word in your family circle. It is really terrible. Let no arguments about bondage, legality, or formalism weigh with you for a moment. We almost feel disposed to exclaim, Blessed bondage! If indeed it be bondage to read the Word, we cordially welcome it, and fearlessly glory in it.

But, no; we cannot for a moment regard it in any such light. We believe it to be a most delightful privilege for every one whom God has set at the head of a household to gather all the members of that household around him and read a portion of the blessed book, and pour out his heart in prayer to God. We believe it is *specially* the duty of the head so to do. It is by no means necessary to make it a long, wearisome service. As a rule, both in our houses and in our public assemblies, short, fresh, fervent exercises are by far the most edifying.

But this, of course, is an open question, as to which we merely give our judgment, which must go for what it is worth. The length and character of the service must, in every case, be left to the person who conducts it. But we do most earnestly trust that if these lines should be scanned by any one who is the head of a household, and if he has hitherto neglected the holy privilege of family worship—family reading, he will, henceforth, do so no more. May he be enabled to say, with Joshua, "Let others do as they will, as for me and my house, we will serve the Lord."

It is not, surely, that we would lead any to imagine that the mere act of family reading takes in all that is comprehended in that weighty sentence, "We will serve the Lord." Far from it. That blessed service takes in every thing belonging to our private and domestic history: it takes in the most minute details of practical daily life. All this is most true and invaluable. But we are most thoroughly persuaded that nothing can go right in any household in which family reading and family prayer are habitually neglected.

It may be said that there are many families who seem very particular about their morning and evening reading and prayer, and yet their whole domestic history, from morning till night, is a flagrant contradiction of their so-called religious service. It may be that the head of the house, instead of shedding sunlight upon the family circle, is morose in his temper, rude and coarse in his manners, rough and contradictory to his wife, arbitrary and severe to his children, unreasonable and exacting to his servants, finding fault with what is laid on the table, after having asked God's blessing upon it; and, in short, in every way giving the lie to his reading and his prayer in the family. So also as to the wife and the mother, and the children and the servants. The whole domestic economy is out of order. There is disorder and confusion; meals are unpunctual; there is a want of kindly consideration one of another; the children are rude, selfish, and willful; the servants are thoughtless, wasteful, and disobedient, if not much worse; the tone, atmosphere, and style of the entire establishment are unchristian, ungodly, utterly unbecoming.

And then, when you travel outside the domestic circle, and mark the conduct of the heads and members of the family toward those outside— mark their business, if they be in business, hear the testimony of those who deal with them, as to the quality of their goods, the style and character of their work; the spirit and temper in which they carry on their business; such grasping and griping, such covetousness, such commercial trickery; nothing of God, nothing of Christ, nothing to distinguish them from the most thorough worldlings around; yea, the conduct of those very worldlings, of those who would never think of such a thing as family worship, would put them to shame.

Under such painful and humiliating circumstances, what of the family worship—the family reading—the family altar? Alas! it is an empty formality—a powerless, worthless, unseemly proceeding; in place of being a morning and evening sacrifice, it is a morning and evening lie—a solemn mockery—an insult to God.

All this is sadly true. There is a terrible lack of household testimony—of common, practical righteousness in our families and in the entire economy of our houses. There is but little of the white raiment—the fine linen, which is the righteousness of saints. We seem to forget those weighty words of the inspired apostle in Romans xiv.—"The kingdom of God is not meat and drink; but *righteousness*, and peace, and joy in the Holy Ghost." Some of us seem to think that whenever we meet with the word "righteousness," it must needs mean the righteousness of God in which we stand, or righteousness imputed to us. This is a very great mistake indeed. We must remember there is a practical and human side of this question; there is the subjective as well as the objective—the walk as well as the standing—the condition as well as the position.

These things must never be separated. It is of little use to set up or seek to maintain a family altar amid the ruins of family testimony. It is nothing short of a hideous caricature to begin and end with so-called family worship a day characterized throughout by ungodliness and unrighteousness, levity, folly, and vanity. Can aught be more unsightly or more miserably inconsistent than an evening spent in song-singing, charades, and other light games, closed up with a contemptible bit of religion in the shape of reading and prayer?

All this line of things is most deplorable. It ought not to be found in connection with the holy name of Christ, with His assembly, or the holy exercises of His table. We must measure every thing in our private life, in our domestic economy, in our daily history, in all our intercourse, and in all our business transactions, with that one standard, namely, the glory of Christ. Our one grand question, in reference to every thing that comes before us or solicits our attention, must be, Is this worthy of the holy name which is called upon me? If not, let us not touch it; yea, let us turn our back upon it with stern decision, and flee from it with holy energy. Let us not listen for a moment to the contemptible question, "What harm is there in it?" Nothing but harm if Christ be not in it. No truly devoted heart would ever entertain, much less put, such a question. Whenever you hear any one speaking thus, you may at once conclude that Christ is not the governing object of the heart.

We trust the reader is not weary of all this homely, practical truth. We believe it is loudly called for in this day of high profession. We have all of us much need to consider our ways, to look well to the real state of our hearts as to Christ; for here lies the true secret of the whole matter. If the heart be not true to Him, nothing can be right—nothing in the private life, nothing in the family, nothing in the business, nothing in the assembly, nothing any where; but if the heart be true to Him, *all* will be—must be right.

No marvel, therefore, if the blessed apostle, when he reaches the close of that wonderful epistle to the Corinthians, sums all up with this solemn declaration: "If any man love not the Lord Jesus Christ, let him be Anathema

Maran-atha." In the course of his letter, he deals with various forms of doctrinal error and moral pravity; but when he comes to the close, instead of pronouncing his solemn sentence upon any particular error or evil, he hurls it with holy indignation against any one, no matter who or what, who does not love the Lord Jesus Christ. Love to Christ is the grand safeguard against every form of error and evil. A heart filled with Christ has no room for aught beside; but if there be no love to Him, there is no security against the wildest error or the worst form of moral evil.

We must now return to our chapter.

The attention of the people is specially called to the solemn scenes at Mount Horeb—scenes which should surely have deeply and abidingly impressed their hearts. "Specially the day that thou stoodest before the Lord thy God in Horeb, when the Lord said unto me, Gather Me the people together, and *I will make them hear My words.*" The grand and all-important point for Israel of old, for the Church now, for each, for all, at all times and in all places, is, to be brought into direct, living contact with the eternal Word of the living God, to the end "that they may learn to fear Me all the days that they shall live upon the earth, and *that they may teach their children.*"

It is very beautiful to note the intimate connection between hearing God's Word and fearing His name. It is one of those great root-principles which never change, never lose their power or their intrinsic value. The Word and the name go together; and the heart that loves the one will reverence the other, and bow down to its holy authority in all things. "He that loveth Me not keepeth not My sayings." "He that saith, I know Him, and keepeth not His commandments, is a liar, and the truth is not in him. But whoso keepeth His word, in him verily is the love of God perfected." (John xiv; 1 John ii.) Every true lover of God will treasure up His Word in the heart, and where the Word is thus lovingly treasured in the heart, its hallowed influence will be seen in the whole life, character, and conduct. God's object in giving His Word is that it may govern our conduct, form our character, and shape our ways; and if His Word has not this practical effect upon us, it is utterly vain for us to speak of loving Him—yea, it is nothing short of positive mockery, which He must sooner or later resent.

And let us note particularly the solemn responsibility of Israel as to their children. They were not only to "hear" and "learn" for themselves, but they were also to teach their children. This is a universal and abiding duty, which cannot be neglected with impunity. God attaches very great importance to this matter. We hear Him saying as to Abraham, "I know him, that he will *command his children and his household* after him, and they shall keep the way of the Lord, to do justice and judgment; that the Lord may bring upon Abraham that which He hath spoken of him." (Gen. xviii.)

These words are most important, as setting before us the divine estimate of domestic training and family piety. In all ages, and under all dispensations, God has been pleased to give expression to His approbation of the proper education of the children of His people—their faithful training according to His holy Word. We find no such thing sanctioned in Scripture as children being allowed to grow up in ignorance and carelessness and willfulness. Some professing Christians, under the baneful influence of a certain school of theology, seem to think that it is, in some way, an interference with the sovereignty of God, with His purposes and counsels, to instruct their children in the truth of the gospel and the letter of holy Scripture. They consider that the children ought to be left to the action of the Holy Ghost, which they are sure to experience in God's own time if indeed they are of God's elect, and if not, all human effort is perfectly useless.

Now, we must, in all faithfulness to the truth of God and to the souls of our readers, bear the clearest and strongest testimony against this one-sided view of the great practical subject before us. There is nothing more mischievous, nothing more pernicious in its effect upon the conscience, the heart, the life, the whole practical career and moral character, than one-sided theology. It does not matter what side you take, so long as you only take one. It is sure to produce what we must term a spiritual malformation. We feel we cannot too strongly and earnestly warn the reader against this sore evil. It can only lead to the most disastrous results; and as to its effect in reference to the training of our children and the management of our households—the subject now before us—it is mischievous in the extreme. Indeed we have seen the most deplorable consequences follow the carrying out of this line of thought. We have known the children of Christian parents to grow up in utter ignorance of divine things, in carelessness, recklessness, and open infidelity; and if a word of admonition were offered, it has been met by arguments based upon the dogmas of a one-sided divinity—and the one side turned the wrong way. It has been said, "We cannot make Christians of our children, and we must not make them formalists or hypocrites. It must be a divine work or nothing. When God's time comes, He will effectually call them, if indeed they are among the number of His elect; if not, all our efforts are perfectly useless."

To all this we reply, that this line of argument, if carried to its fullest extent, would prevent the farmer from plowing his ground or sowing his seed. It is very plain that he cannot make the seed to germinate or fructify. He could no more cause a solitary grain of wheat to grow than he could create the universe. Does this prevent his plowing and sowing? does it cause him to fold his arms and say, I can do nothing. I cannot, by any effort of mine, make corn grow. It is a divine operation, and therefore I must wait God's time. Does any farmer reason and act like this? Surely not, unless he be a lunatic. Every sound-minded person knows that plowing and sowing must go before the reaping; and if the former be neglected, it is the height of extravagant folly to look for the latter.

Nor is it otherwise in the matter of training our children. We know God is sovereign; we believe in His eternal counsels and purposes; we fully recognize the grand doctrines of election and predestination—yea, we are as thoroughly persuaded of them as of the truth that God is, or that Christ died and rose again. Moreover, we believe that the new birth must take place in every instance—in the case of our children as of all beside; we are convinced that this new birth is entirely a divine operation, effected by the Holy Ghost, through the Word, as we are distinctly taught in our Lord's discourse with Nicodemus in John iii, and also in James i. 18 and 1 Peter i. 23.

But does all this touch, in the most remote way, the solemn responsibility of Christian parents to teach and train their children, diligently and faithfully, from their earliest moments? Most certainly not. Woe be to the parents who, on any plea or on any ground whatsoever, be it one-sided theology, misapplied Scripture, or aught else, deny their responsibility, or neglect their plain, bounden duty, in this holy business. True, we cannot make our children Christians, and we ought not to make them formalists or hypocrites; but we are not called to *make* them any thing. We are simply called to do our duty by them, and leave results to God. We are instructed and commanded to bring up our children "in the nurture and admonition of the Lord." When is this "bringing up" to commence? when are we to begin the sacred work of training our little ones? Surely, at the beginning. The very moment we enter upon a relationship, we enter also upon the responsibility which that relationship entails. We cannot deny this; we cannot shake it off. We may neglect it, and have to reap the sad consequences of our neglect, in various ways. It is a very serious thing to stand in the sacred relationship of a parent—very interesting and very delightful, no doubt; but most serious, because of the responsibility involved. True it is, blessed be God, His grace is sufficient for us in this as in all beside, and "if any man lack wisdom, let him ask of God, who giveth to all liberally, and upbraideth not; and it shall be given him." "We are not sufficient of ourselves," in this weighty matter, to think or to do any thing as ourselves, but our sufficiency is of God, and He will meet our every need. We have simply to draw upon Him, for exigence of every hour.

But we must do our duty. Some do not like the homely word "duty." They think it has a legal ring about it. We trust the reader does not think so, for it is a very great mistake indeed. We look upon the word as a very sound and morally wholesome one, and we believe that every true Christian loves it. One thing is certain, it is only in the path of duty we can count on God. To talk of trusting God, when out of the path of duty, is a miserable conceit, and a delusion; and in the matter of our relationship as parents, to neglect our duty is to bring down upon us the most disastrous consequences.

We believe the whole business of Christian education is summed up in two brief sentences, namely, Count on God for your children, and, Train your children for God. To take the first without the second is antinomianism; to take the second without the first is legality; to take both together is sound, practical Christianity—true religion in the sight of God and man.

It is the sweet privilege of every Christian parent to count, with all possible confidence, upon God for his children. But then we must remember that there is, in the government of God, an inseparable link connecting this privilege with the most solemn responsibility as to training. For a Christian parent to speak of counting on God for the salvation of his children, and for the moral integrity of their future career in this world, while the duty of training is neglected, is simply a miserable delusion.

We press this most solemnly upon all Christian parents, but especially upon those who have just entered upon the relationship. There is great danger of shirking our duty to our children, of shifting it over upon others, or neglecting it altogether. We do not like the trouble of it; we shrink from the constant worry as it seems to us. But we shall find that the trouble and the worry and the sorrow and the heart-scalding arising from the neglect of our duty will be a thousand times worse than all that can be involved in the discharge of it. To every true lover of God there is deep delight in treading the path of duty. Every step taken in that path strengthens our confidence to go on. And then we can always count upon the infinite resources that we have in God when we are keeping His commandments. We have simply to betake ourselves, morning by morning, yea, hour by hour, to our Father's exhaustless treasury, and there get all we want, in the way of grace and wisdom and moral power, to enable us to discharge aright the holy functions of our relationship. "He giveth more grace." This always holds good. But if we, instead of seeking grace to discharge our duty, seek ease in neglecting it, we are simply laying up a store of sorrow which will accumulate rapidly and fall upon us heavily at a future day. "Be not deceived; God is not mocked; for whatsoever a man soweth, that shall he also reap. For he that soweth to his flesh, shall of the flesh reap corruption; but he that soweth to the Spirit, shall of the Spirit reap life everlasting." (Gal. vi.)

This is the condensed statement of a great principle of God's moral government—a principle of universal application, and one which applies, with singular force, to the subject before us. *As* we sow, in the matter of the education of our children, *so* we shall, most assuredly, reap. There is no getting out of this.

But let not any dear Christian parent, whose eye may scan these lines, be at all discouraged or faint-hearted. There is no reason whatever for this, but, on the contrary, every reason for the most joyful confidence in God. "The name of the Lord is a strong tower; the righteous runneth into it, and is safe." Let us tread, with firm step, the path of duty; and then we can count, with unwavering confidence, upon our ever-faithful and gracious God for the need of each day as it rolls along. And in due time we shall reap the precious fruit of our labor, according to the appointment of God, and in pursuance of the enactments of His moral government.

We do not attempt to lay down any rules or regulations for the training. We do not believe in such. Children cannot be trained by dry rules. Who could attempt to embody in rules all that is wrapped up in that one sentence, "Bring them up in the nurture and admonition of the Lord"?

Here we have, indeed, a golden rule which takes in every thing from the cradle to matured manhood. Yes, we repeat, "from the cradle;" for we are most fully persuaded that all true Christian training begins at the very beginning. Some of us have little idea of how soon and how sharply children begin to observe, and how much they take in as they gaze at us through their dear expressive eyes.

And then how marvelously susceptible they are of the moral atmosphere which surrounds them! Yes; and it is this very moral atmosphere that constitutes the grand secret of training our families. Our children should be permitted to breathe, from day to day, the atmosphere of love and peace, purity, holiness, and true practical righteousness. This has an amazing effect in forming the character. It is a great thing for our children to see their parents walking in love, in harmony, in tender care one for the other, in kind consideration for the servants, in love and sympathy for the poor. Who can measure the moral effect upon a child of the very first angry look, or unkind word, between father and mother? And in cases where the daily history is one of unsightly strife and contention—the father contradicting the mother, and the mother disparaging the father—how are children to grow in such an atmosphere as this?

The fact is, it is not within the compass of human language to set forth all that is involved in the moral tone of the entire family circle—the spirit, style, and atmosphere of the whole household, the drawing-room, the dining-room, the nursery, the kitchen; where circumstances admit of such distinctions, or where the family have to confine themselves to two rooms. It is not a question of rank, position, or wealth, but of the beauteous grace of God shining out in all. There may be the stalled ox or the dinner of herbs—these are not, at present, in question. But what we press on all fathers and mothers—all heads of households, high and low, rich and poor, learned and ignorant, is the necessity of training their children in an atmosphere of love and peace, truth and holiness, purity and kindness. Thus will our households be the practical exhibition of the character of God; and all who come in contact with them will, at least, have before their eyes a practical witness to the truth of Christianity.

But, ere we turn from the subject of domestic government, there is one special point to which we desire to call the attention of Christian parents—a point of the utmost possible moment, yet too much neglected amongst us, and that is, the need of inculcating upon our children the duty of implicit obedience. This cannot be too strongly insisted upon, inasmuch as it not only affects the order and comfort of our households, but, what is infinitely more important, it concerns the glory of God and the practical carrying out of His truth. "Children, obey your parents in the Lord; for this is right." And again, "Children, obey your parents *in all things*; for this is well pleasing unto the Lord." (Eph. vi.; Col. iii.)

This is absolutely essential, and must be firmly insisted upon from the very outset. The child must be taught to obey from his earliest moments. He must be trained to submit himself to divinely appointed authority, and that, as the apostle puts it, "in all things." If this be not attended to from the very first, it will be found almost impossible to attend to it afterwards. If the will be allowed to act, it grows, with terrible rapidity, and each day's growth increases the difficulty of bringing it under control. Hence, the parent should begin at once to establish his authority on a basis of moral strength and firmness; and when this is done, he may be as gentle and tender as the most loving heart could desire. We do not believe in sternness, harshness, or severity. They are by no means necessary, and are generally the accompaniments of bad training and the proofs of bad temper. God has put into the parent's hand the reins of government and the rod of authority, but it is not needful—if we may so express it—to be continually chucking the reins and brandishing the rod, which are the sure proofs of moral weakness. Whenever you hear a man continually talking about his authority, you may be sure his authority is not properly established. There is a quiet dignity about true moral power which is perfectly unmistakable.

Furthermore, we judge it to be a mistake for a parent to be perpetually crossing a child's will in matters of no moment. Such a line of action tends to break the child's spirit, whereas the object of all sound training is to break the will. The child should ever be impressed with the idea that the parent seeks *only* his real good, and that if he has to refuse or prohibit any thing, it is not for the purpose of curtailing the child's enjoyment, but simply for the promotion of his true interests.

One grand object of domestic government is to protect each member of the household in the enjoyment of his privileges, and in the proper discharge of his relative duties. Now, inasmuch as it is the divinely appointed duty of a child to obey, the parent is responsible to see this duty discharged, for if it be neglected, some other members of the domestic circle must suffer.

There can be no greater nuisance in a house than a naughty, willful child; and, as a general rule, wherever you find such, it is to be traced to bad training. We are aware, of course, that children differ in temper and disposition—that some children have peculiarly strong wills and sturdy tempers, and are therefore specially hard to manage.

All this we quite understand; but it leaves wholly untouched the question of the parent's responsibility to insist upon implicit obedience. He can always count on God for the needed grace and power to carry out this point. Even in the case of a widowed mother, we believe, most assuredly, she can look to God to enable her to command her children and her household. In no case, therefore, should parental authority be surrendered for a moment.

It sometimes happens that, through injudicious fondness, the parent is tempted to pamper the will of the child; but it is sowing to the flesh, and must yield corruption. It is not true love at all to indulge a child's will, neither can it possibly minister to his true happiness or legitimate enjoyment. An over-indulged, self-willed child is miserable himself and a grievous infliction on all who have to do with him. Children should be taught to think of others, and to seek to promote their comfort and happiness in every way. How very unseemly it is, for example, for a child to enter the house and ascend the stairs whistling, singing, and shouting, in total disregard of other members of the household who may be seriously disturbed and annoyed by such conduct! No properly trained child would think of acting in such a way; and where such unsubdued, unruly, inconsiderate conduct is allowed, there is a serious defect in the domestic government.

It is essential to family peace, harmony, and comfort, that all the members should "consider one another." We are responsible to seek the good and the happiness of those around us, and not our own. If all would but remember this, what different households we should have! and what a different tale would families have to tell! Every Christian household should be the reflection of the divine character. The atmosphere should just be the very atmosphere of heaven. How is this to be? Simply by each one—parent, child, master, and servant—seeking to walk in the footsteps of Jesus, and manifest His spirit. He never pleased Himself, never sought His own interest in any thing; He did always the thing that pleased the Father; He came to serve and to give; He went about doing good, and healing all that were oppressed of the devil. Thus it was ever with that most blessed One—the gracious, loving, sympathizing Friend of all the sons and daughters of want, weakness, and sorrow; and if only the various members of each Christian family were formed on this perfect model, we should, at least, realize something of the power and efficacy of personal and domestic Christianity, which, blessed be God, can ever be maintained and exhibited notwithstanding the hopeless ruin of the professing church. "Thou and thy house" suggests a great golden principle which runs through the volume of God, from beginning to end. In every age, under every dispensation, in the days of the patriarchs, in the days of the law, and in the days of Christianity, we find, to our exceeding comfort and encouragement, that personal and domestic godliness has its place as something grateful to the heart of God and to the glory of His holy name.

This we consider to be most consolatory at all times, but more particularly at a time like the present, when the professing church seems so rapidly sinking into gross worldliness and open infidelity; and not this only, but when those who most earnestly desire to walk in obedience to the Word of God, and to act on the grand foundation-truth of the unity of the body, find it so difficult to maintain a a corporate testimony. In view of all this, we may well bless God, with overflowing hearts, that personal and family piety can always be maintained, and that from the heart and the home of every Christian a constant stream of praise may ascend to the throne of God, and a stream of active benevolence flow out to a needy, sorrowful, sin-stricken world. May it be so more and more, through the mighty ministry of God the Holy Ghost, that God, in all things, may be glorified in the hearts and homes of His beloved people.

We have now to consider the very solemn warning addressed to the congregation of Israel against the terrible sin of idolatry—a sin to which, alas! the poor human heart is ever prone, in one way or another. It is quite possible to be guilty of the sin of idolatry without bowing down before a graven image; wherefore it behooves us to weigh well the words of warning which fell from the lips of Israel's venerable lawgiver. They are most assuredly written for our learning.

"And ye came near and stood under the mountain; and the mountain burned with fire unto the midst of heaven, with darkness, clouds, and thick darkness." Solemn and suited accompaniments of the occasion! "And the Lord spake unto you out of the midst of the fire." Oh, how differently He speaks in the gospel of His grace! "Ye heard the voice of the words, but saw no similitude." Important fact for them to ponder! *"Only a voice."* And "faith cometh by hearing, and hearing by the Word of God." "And He declared unto you His covenant, which He commanded you to perform — ten commandments; and He wrote them upon two tables of stone. And the Lord commanded me at that time to teach you statutes and judgments," not that they might discuss them, sit in judgment upon them, or argue about them, but "that *ye might do them*" — the grand old story, the Deuteronomic theme of *obedience*, most precious! whether out of or "in the land whither ye go over to possess it."

Here lies the solid ground of the appeal against idolatry. They *saw* nothing. God did not show Himself to them. He did not assume any bodily shape, of which they might form an image. He gave them His word — His holy commandments, so plain that a child could understand them, and the wayfaring men though fools need not err therein. There was no need for them, therefore, to set about imagining what God was like; nay, this was *the* very sin against which they were so faithfully warned. They were called to hear God's voice, not to see His shape — to obey His commandment, not to make an image of Him. Superstition vainly seeks to do honor to God by forming and worshiping an image; Faith, on the contrary, lovingly receives and reverently obeys His holy commandments. "If a man love Me," says our blessed Lord, "he will" — what? make an image of Me, and worship it? Nay, but "he will keep My words." This makes it so simple, so safe, so certain. We are not called to work up our minds to form any conception of God; we have simply to hear His word and keep His commandments. We can have no idea whatever of God but as He has been pleased to reveal Himself. — "No man hath seen God at any time; the only begotten Son, which is in the bosom of the Father, He hath declared Him." — "God, who commanded the light to shine out of darkness, hath shined in our hearts, to give the light of the knowledge of the glory of God in the face of Jesus Christ."

Jesus is declared to be the brightness of God's glory and the exact impression of His substance. He could say, "He that hath seen Me hath seen the Father." Thus the Son reveals the Father; and it is by the Word, through the power of the Holy Ghost, that we know any thing of the Son; and therefore for any one to attempt, by any efforts of his mind or workings of his imagination, to conceive an image of God, or of Christ, is simply idolatry. To endeavor to arrive at any knowledge of God or of Christ save by Scripture, is simply mysticism and confusion; nay, more, it is to put ourselves directly into the hands of the devil, to be led by him into the wildest, darkest, and deadliest delusion.

Hence, therefore, as Israel, at Mount Horeb, was shut up to the "*voice*" of God and warned against any similitude, so we are shut up to holy Scripture and warned against every thing which would draw us away, the breadth of a hair, from that holy and all-sufficient standard. We must not listen to the suggestions of our own minds, nor to those of any other human mind: we must absolutely and sternly refuse to listen to any thing but the voice of God—the voice of holy Scripture. Here is true security, true rest; here we have absolute certainty, so that we can say, "I know *whom*"—not merely *what*—"I have believed; and am persuaded that *He*," etc.

"Take ye therefore good heed unto yourselves, (for ye saw no manner of similitude on the day that the Lord spake unto you in Horeb out of the midst of the fire,) lest ye corrupt yourselves, and make you a graven image, the similitude of any figure, the likeness of male or female, the likeness of any beast that is on the earth, the likeness of any winged fowl that flieth in the air, the likeness of any thing that creepeth on the ground, the likeness of any fish that is in the waters beneath the earth; and lest thou lift up thine eyes unto heaven, and when thou seest the sun, and the moon, and the stars, even all the host of heaven, shouldest be driven to worship them, and serve them, which the Lord thy God hath divided unto all nations under the whole heaven. But the Lord hath taken you, and brought you forth out of the iron furnace, even out of Egypt, to be unto Him a people of inheritance, as ye are this day."

There is a very weighty truth set before us here. The people are expressly taught that in making any image and bowing down thereto, they, in reality, lowered and corrupted themselves. Hence, when they made the golden calf, the Lord said unto Moses, "Go, get thee down; for thy people, which thou broughtest out of the land of Egypt, have corrupted themselves." It could not be otherwise. The worshiper must be inferior to the object of his worship; and therefore, in worshiping a calf, they actually put themselves below the level of the beasts that perish. Well, therefore, might He say, They "have corrupted themselves; they have turned aside quickly out of the way which I commanded them; they have made them a molten calf, and have worshiped it, and have sacrificed thereunto, and said, 'These be thy gods, O Israel, which have brought thee up out of the land of Egypt.'"

What a spectacle! A whole congregation, led by Aaron the high-priest, bowing in worship before a thing formed by a graving tool out of the earrings which had just been taken from the ears of their wives and daughters! Only conceive a number of intelligent beings—people endowed with reason, understanding, and conscience—saying of a molten calf, "These be thy gods, O Israel, which have brought thee up out of the land of Egypt"! They actually displaced Jehovah by an image graven by art and man's device! And these were the people who had seen the mighty works of Jehovah in the land of Egypt. They had seen plague after plague falling upon Egypt and its obdurate king; they had seen the land, as it were, shaken to its very centre by the successive strokes of Jehovah's governmental rod; they had seen Egypt's first-born laid in death by the sword of the destroying angel; they had seen the Red Sea divided by one stroke of Jehovah's rod, and they had passed through upon dry ground between those crystal walls which afterwards fell, in crushing power, upon their enemies—all these things had passed before their eyes, and yet they could so soon forget all and say of a molten calf, "These be thy gods, O Israel, which have brought thee up out of the land of Egypt." Did they really believe that a molten image had made the land of Egypt to tremble, humbled its proud monarch, and brought them forth victoriously? Had a calf divided the sea for them, and led them majestically through its depths? So, at least, they said; for what will people not say when the eye and the heart are turned away from God and His Word?

But we may perhaps be asked, Has all this a voice for us? Are Christians to learn any thing from Israel's molten calf? and do the warnings addressed to Israel against idolatry convey any voice to the ear of the Church? Are we in danger of bowing down to a graven image? Is it possible that we, whose high privilege it is to walk in the full-orbed light of New-Testament Christianity, could ever worship a molten calf?

To all this we reply, first of all, in the language of Romans xv. 4, "*Whatsoever things* were written aforetime"—Exodus xxxii. and Deuteronomy iv. included—"were written for our learning, that we through patience and comfort of the Scriptures might have hope." This brief passage contains our chartered right to range through the wide field of Old-Testament scripture and gather up and appropriate its golden lessons, to feed upon its "exceeding great and precious promises," to drink in its deep and varied consolation, and to profit by its solemn warnings and wholesome admonitions.

And then, as to our being capable of or liable to the gross sin of idolatry, we have a striking answer in 1 Corinthians x, where the inspired apostle uses the very scene at Mount Horeb as a warning to the Church of God. We cannot do better than quote the entire passage for the reader. There is nothing like the Word of God; may we love, prize, and reverence it more and more each day.

"Moreover, brethren, I would not that ye should be ignorant, how that *all* our fathers were under the cloud"—those whose carcasses fell in the wilderness, as well as those who reached the land of promise,—"and all passed through the sea; and were all baptized unto Moses in the cloud and in the sea; and did all eat the same spiritual meat; and did all drink the same spiritual drink: for they drank of that spiritual Rock that followed them; and that Rock was Christ." How strong, how solemn, and how searching is this for all professors! "But with many of them God was not well pleased; for they were overthrown in the wilderness. Now these things were *our examples*" (let us carefully mark this), "to the intent we should not lust after *evil things*"—things in any way contrary to the mind of Christ, "as they also lusted. Neither *be ye idolaters*" (so that professing Christians may be idolaters) "as were some of them; as it is written, 'The people sat down to eat and drink, and rose up to play.' Neither let us commit fornication, as some of them committed, and fell in one day three and twenty thousand. Neither let us tempt Christ, as some of them also tempted, and were destroyed of serpents. Neither murmur ye, as some of them also murmured, and were destroyed of the destroyer. Now *all these things* happened unto them for ensamples; and *they are written for our admonition*, upon whom the ends of the ages are come. Wherefore let him that thinketh he standeth take heed lest he fall."

Here we learn, in the plainest manner, that there is no depth of sin and folly, no form of moral pravity, into which we are not capable of plunging, at any moment, if not kept by the mighty power of God. There is no security for us save in the moral shelter of the divine presence. We know that the Spirit of God does not warn us against things to which we are not liable. He would not say to us, "Neither be ye idolaters," if we were not capable of being such. Idolatry takes various shapes. It is not, therefore, a question of the shape of the thing, but the thing itself—not the outward form, but the root or principle of the thing. We read that "covetousness is idolatry," and that a covetous man is an idolater; that is, a man desiring to possess himself of more than God has given him is an idolater—is actually guilty of the sin of Israel when they made the golden calf and worshiped it. Well might the blessed apostle say to the Corinthians—say to us, "Wherefore, my dearly beloved, flee from idolatry." Why be warned to *flee* from a thing to which we are not liable? Are there any idle words in the volume of God? What mean those closing words of the first epistle of John—"Little children, keep yourselves from idols"? Do they not tell us that we are in danger of worshiping idols? Assuredly they do. Our treacherous hearts are capable of departing from the living God, and setting up some other object beside Him; and what is this but idolatry? Whatever commands the heart is the heart's idol, be it what it may—money, pleasure, power, or aught else,—so that we may well see the urgent need for the many warnings given us by the Holy Ghost against the sin of idolatry.

But we have in the fourth chapter of Galatians a very remarkable passage, and one which speaks in most impressive accents to the professing church. The Galatians had, like all other Gentiles, worshiped idols; but, on the reception of the gospel, had turned from idols to serve the living and true God. The Judaizing teachers, however, had come among them and taught them that unless they were circumcised and kept the law, they could not be saved.

Now this, the blessed apostle unhesitatingly pronounces to be idolatry—a going back to the grossness and moral degradation of their former days, and all this after having professed to receive the glorious gospel of Christ. Hence the moral force of the apostle's inquiry, "Howbeit then, when ye knew not God, ye did service unto them which by nature are no gods. *But now*, after that ye have known God, or rather are known of God, how *turn ye again* to the weak and beggarly elements, whereunto ye desire *again* to be in bondage? Ye observe days, and months, and times, and years. I am afraid of you, lest I have bestowed upon you labor in vain."

This is peculiarly striking. The Galatians were not outwardly going back to the worship of idols. It is not improbable that they would have indignantly repudiated any such idea. But, for all that, the inspired apostle asks them, "How turn ye again?" What does this inquiry mean if they were not going back to idolatry? and what are we now to learn from the whole passage? Simply this, that circumcision, and getting under the law, and observing days, and months, and times, and years—that all this, though apparently so different, was nothing more or less than going back to their old idolatry. The observance of days and the worship of false gods were both a turning away from the living and true God, from His Son Jesus Christ, from the Holy Ghost, from that brilliant cluster of dignities and glories which belong to Christianity.

All this is peculiarly solemn for professing Christians. We question if the full import of Galatians iv. 8-10 is really apprehended by the great majority of those who profess to believe the Bible. We solemnly press this whole subject upon the attention of all whom it may concern. We pray God to use it for the purpose of stirring up the hearts and consciences of His people every where to consider their position, their habits, ways, and associations; and to inquire how far they are really following the example of the assemblies of Galatia, in the observance of saints' days and such like, which can only lead away from Christ and His glorious salvation. There is a day coming which will open the eyes of thousands to the reality of these things, and then they will see what they now refuse to see, that the very darkest and grossest forms of paganism may be reproduced under the name of Christianity, and in connection with the very highest truths that ever shone on the human understanding.

But however slow we may be to admit our tendency to fall into the sin of idolatry, it is very plain, in Israel's case, that Moses, as taught and inspired of God, felt the deep need of warning them against it, in the most solemn and affecting terms. He appeals to them on every possible ground, and reiterates his counsels and admonitions in a manner so impressive as to leave them, assuredly, without any excuse. They never could say that they fell into idolatry from the want of warning, or of the most gracious and affectionate entreaty. Take such words as the following: "But the Lord hath taken you, and brought you forth out of the iron furnace, even out of Egypt, to be unto Him a people of inheritance, as ye are this day." (Ver. 20.)

Could any thing be more affecting than this? Jehovah, in His rich and sovereign grace, and by His mighty hand, brought them forth from the land of death and darkness, a redeemed and delivered people. He had brought them to Himself, that they might be to Him a peculiar treasure, above all the people upon earth. How, then, could they turn away from Him, from His holy covenant, and from His precious commandments?

Alas! alas! they could and did. "They *made* a calf, and said, 'These be thy gods, O Israel, which have brought thee up out of the land of Egypt.'" Think of this! A calf, made by their own hands—an image, graven by art and man's device, had brought them up out of Egypt! A thing made out of the women's earrings had redeemed and delivered them! And this has been written for our admonition. But why should it be written for us if we are not capable of and liable to the very same sin? We must either admit that God the Holy Ghost has penned an unnecessary sentence, or admit our need of an admonition against the sin of idolatry; and assuredly, our needing the admonition proves our tendency to the sin.

Are we better than Israel? In no wise. We have brighter light and higher privileges, but, so far as we are concerned, we are made of the same material, have the same capabilities and the same tendencies, as they. Our idolatry may take a different shape from theirs; but idolatry is idolatry, be the shape what it may; and the higher our privileges, the the greater our sin. We may perhaps feel disposed to wonder how a rational people could be guilty of such egregious folly as to make a calf and bow down to it, and this, too, after having had such a display of the majesty, power, and glory of God. Let us remember that their folly is recorded for our admonition; and that we, with all our light, all our knowledge, all our privileges, are warned to "flee from idolatry."

Let us deeply ponder all this and seek to profit by it. May every chamber of our hearts be filled with Christ, and then we shall have no room for idols. This is our only safeguard. If we slip away the breadth of a hair from our precious Saviour and Shepherd, we are capable of plunging into the darkest forms of error and moral evil. Light, knowledge, spiritual privileges, church position, sacramental benefits, are no security for the soul. They are very good in their right place and if rightly used, but in themselves they only increase our moral danger.

Nothing can keep us safe, right, and happy but having Christ dwelling in our hearts by faith. Abiding in Him and He in us, that wicked one toucheth us not. But if personal communion be not diligently maintained, the higher our position, the greater our danger and the more disastrous our fall. There was not a nation beneath the canopy of heaven more favored and exalted than Israel when they gathered around Mount Horeb to hear the word of God: there was not a nation on the face of the earth more degraded or more guilty than they when they bowed before the golden calf—an image of their own formation.

We must now give our attention to a fact of very deep interest, presented at verse 21 of our chapter, and that is, that Moses, for the third time, reminds the congregation of God's judicial dealing with himself. He had spoken of it, as we have seen, in chapter i. 37, and again at chapter iii. 26, and here, again, he says to them, "Furthermore *the Lord was angry with me for your sakes*, and sware that I should not go over Jordan, and that I should not go in unto that good land which the Lord thy God giveth thee for an inheritance; but I must die in this land, I must not go over Jordan; but ye shall go over and possess that good land."

Now, we may ask, Why this threefold reference to the same fact? and why the special mention, in each instance, of the circumstance that Jehovah was angry with him on their account? One thing is certain, it was not for the purpose of throwing the blame over upon the people, or of exculpating himself. No one but an infidel could think this. We believe the simple object was, to give increased moral force to his appeal, more solemnity to his warning voice. If Jehovah was angry with such an one as Moses—if he, for his unadvised speaking at the waters of Meribah, was forbidden to enter the promised land (much as he desired it), how needful for them to take heed! It is a serious thing to have to do with God—blessed, no doubt, beyond all human expression or thought, but most serious, as the lawgiver himself was called to prove in his own person.

That this is the correct view of this interesting question seems evident from the following words: *"Take heed unto yourselves,* lest ye forget the covenant of the Lord your God, which He made with you, and make you a graven image, or the likeness of any thing which the Lord thy God hath forbidden thee. For the Lord thy God is a consuming fire, even a jealous God."

This is peculiarly solemn. We must allow this statement to have its full, moral weight with our souls. We must not attempt to turn aside its sharp edge by any false notions about grace. We sometimes hear it said that "God is a consuming fire to the world." By and by He will be so, no doubt; but now He is dealing in grace, patience, and long-suffering mercy with the world. He is not dealing in judgment with the world now; but, as the apostle Peter tells us, "the time is come that judgment must begin at the house of God; and if it first begin at us, what shall the end be of them that obey not the gospel of God?" So also, in Hebrews xii, we read, "For *our* God *is* a consuming fire." He is not speaking of what God will be to the world, but of what He is to us. Neither is it, as some put it, "God is a consuming fire out of Christ." We know nothing of God out of Christ. He could not be *"our* God" out of Christ.

No, reader; Scripture does not need such twistings and turnings: it must be taken as it stands. It is clear and distinct, and all we have to do is to hearken and obey. "Our God is a consuming fire," "a jealous God," not to consume us, blessed be His holy name, but to consume the evil in us and in our ways. He is intolerant of every thing in us that is contrary to Himself— contrary to His holiness, and therefore contrary to our true happiness, our real, solid blessing. As the "Holy Father," He keeps us in a way worthy of Himself, and He chastens us in order to make us partakers of His holiness. He allows the world to go on its way for the present, not interfering publicly with it; but He judges His house, and He chastens His children, in order that they may more fully answer to His mind and be the expression of His moral image.

And is not this an immense privilege? Yes, verily; it is a privilege of the very highest order—a privilege flowing from the infinite grace of our God, who condescends to interest Himself in us, and occupy Himself even with our infirmities, our failures, and our sins, in order to deliver us from them, and make us partakers of His holiness.

There is a very fine passage bearing upon this subject in the opening of Hebrews xii, which, because of its immense practical importance, we must quote for the reader.—"My son, despise not thou the chastening of the Lord, nor faint when thou art rebuked of Him; for *whom the Lord loveth*

He chasteneth, and *scourgeth every son* whom He receiveth. If ye endure chastening, God dealeth with you as with sons; for *what son* is he whom the Father chasteneth not? But if ye be *without chastisement*, whereof all are partakers, then are ye *bastards* and *not sons*. Furthermore, we have had fathers of our flesh which corrected us, and we gave them reverence; shall we not much rather be in subjection unto the Father of spirits, and live? For they verily for a few days chastened us after their own pleasure; *but He for our profit, that we might be partakers of His holiness*. Now no chastening for the present *seemeth* to be joyous, but grievous; nevertheless afterward it yieldeth the peaceable fruit of righteousness unto them which are exercised thereby. Wherefore lift up the hands which hang down, and the feeble knees."

There are three ways of meeting divine chastening: We may *"despise"* it, as something commonplace—something that may happen to any one; we do not see *the hand of God* in it. Again, we may *"faint"* under it, as something too heavy for us to bear—something entirely beyond endurance; we do not see *the Father's heart* in it, or recognize His gracious object in it, namely, to make us partakers of His holiness. Lastly, we may be *"exercised"* by it. This is the way to reap "the peaceable fruit of righteousness afterward." We dare not *"despise"* a thing in which we trace the hand of God: we need not *"faint"* under a trial in which we plainly discern the heart of a loving Father, who will not suffer us to be tried above what we are able, but will with the trial make an issue, that we may be able to bear it, and who also graciously explains to us His object in the discipline, and assures us that every stroke of His rod is a proof of His love, and a direct response to the prayer of Christ in John xvii. 11, wherein He commends us to the care of the "Holy Father," to be kept according to that name and all that name involves.

Furthermore, there are three distinct attitudes of heart in reference to divine chastening, namely, subjection, acquiescence, and rejoicing. When the will is broken, there is subjection; when the understanding is enlightened as to the object of the chastening, there is calm acquiescence; and when the affections are engaged with the Father's heart, there is rejoicing, and we can go forth with glad hearts to reap a golden harvest of the peaceable fruit of righteousness, to the praise of Him who, in His painstaking love, undertakes to care for us and to deal with us in holy government, and concentrate His care upon each one as though there were but that one to attend to.

How wonderful is all this! and how the thought of it should help us in all our trials and exercises! We are in the hands of One whose love is infinite, whose wisdom is unerring, whose power is omnipotent, whose resources are inexhaustible. Why, then, should we ever be cast down? If He chastens us, it is because He loves us and seeks our real good. We may think the chastening grievous—we may feel disposed to wonder, at times, how love can inflict pain and sickness upon us; but we must remember that divine love is wise and faithful, and only inflicts the pain, the sickness, or the sorrow for our profit and blessing. We must not always judge of love by the form in which it clothes itself. Look at that fond and tender mother applying a blister to her child whom she loves as her own soul. She knows full well that the blister will cause her child real pain and suffering, and yet she unhesitatingly applies it, though her heart feels keenly at having to do it. But she knows it is absolutely necessary; she believes that, humanly and medically speaking, the child's life depends upon it; she feels that a few moments' pain may, with the blessing of God, restore the health of her precious child. Thus, while the child is only occupied with the transient suffering, the mother is thinking of the permanent good; and if the child could but think with the mother, the blister would not seem so hard to bear.

Now, it is just thus in the matter of our Father's disciplinary dealings with us; and the remembrance of this would greatly help us to endure whatever His chastening hand may lay upon us. It may perhaps be said that there is a very wide difference between a blister laid on for a few minutes, and years of intense bodily suffering. No doubt there is; but there is also a very wide difference between the result reached in each case. It is only with the principle of the thing we have to do. When we see a beloved child of God, or servant of Christ, called to pass through years of intense suffering, we may feel disposed to wonder why it is; and perhaps the beloved sufferer may also feel disposed to wonder, and at times be ready to faint under the weight of his long-protracted affliction. He may feel led to cry out, Why am I thus? Can this be love? can this be the expression of a Father's tender care? "Yes, verily," is Faith's bright and decided reply. "It is all love— all divinely right. I would not have it otherwise for worlds. I know this transient suffering is working out eternal blessing. I know my loving Father has put me into this furnace to purge away my dross and bring out in me the expression of His own image. I know that divine love will always do the very best for its object, and therefore this intense suffering is the very best thing for me. Of course, I feel it, for I am not a stick or a stone. My Father means me to feel it, just as the mother means the blister to rise, for it would do no good otherwise. But I bless Him, with my whole heart, for the grace that shines in the wondrous fact of His occupying Himself with me, in this way, to correct what He sees to be wrong in me. I praise Him for putting me into the furnace; and how can I but praise Him, when I see Himself, in infinite grace and patience, sitting over the furnace to watch the process, and lift me out the moment the work is done?"

This, beloved Christian reader, is the true way, and this the right spirit in which to pass through chastening of any kind, be it bodily affliction, sore bereavement, loss of property, or pressure of circumstances. We have to trace the hand of God, to read a Father's heart, to recognize the divine object in it all. This will enable us to vindicate, justify, and glorify God in the furnace of affliction. It will correct every murmuring thought, and hush every fretful utterance; it will fill our hearts with sweetest peace and our mouths with praise.

We must now turn, for a few moments, to the remaining verses of our chapter, in which we shall find some most touching and powerful appeals to the heart and conscience of the congregation. The lawgiver, in the deep, true, and fervent love of his heart, makes use of the most solemn warnings, the most earnest admonition, and the most tender entreaties, in order to move the people to the one grand and all-important point of obedience. If he speaks to them of the iron furnace of Egypt, out of which Jehovah, in His sovereign grace, had delivered them; if he dwells upon the mighty signs and wonders wrought on their behalf; if he holds up to their view the glories of that land on which they were about to plant their foot; or if he recounts the marvelous dealings of God with them in the wilderness, it is all for the purpose of strengthening the moral basis of Jehovah's claim upon their loving and reverent obedience. The past, the present, and the future are all brought to bear upon them—all made to furnish powerful arguments in favor of their whole-hearted consecration of themselves to the service of their gracious and almighty Deliverer. In short, there was every reason why they should obey, and no possible excuse for disobedience. All the facts of their history, from first to last, were eminently calculated to give moral force to the exhortation and warning of the following passage:—

"Take heed unto yourselves, lest ye forget the covenant of the Lord your God, which He made with you, and make you a graven image, or the likeness of any thing, which the Lord thy God hath forbidden thee. For the Lord thy God is a consuming fire, even a jealous God. When thou shalt beget children, and children's children, and ye shall have remained long in the land, and shall corrupt yourselves, and make a graven image, or the likeness of any thing, and shall do evil in the sight of the Lord thy God, to provoke Him to anger; I call heaven and earth to witness against you this day, that ye shall soon utterly perish from off the land whereunto ye go over Jordan to possess it; ye shall not prolong your days upon it, but shall utterly be destroyed. And the Lord shall scatter you among the nations, and ye shall be left few in number among the heathen, whither the Lord shall lead you. And there ye shall serve gods, the work of men's hands, wood and stone, which neither see, nor hear, nor eat, nor smell."

How solemn is all this! What faithful warnings are here! Heaven and earth are summoned to witness. Alas! how soon and how completely all this was forgotten! and how literally all those heavy denunciations have been fulfilled in the history of the nation!

But, thank God, there is a bright side of the picture—there is mercy as well as judgment, and our God (blessed forever be His holy name) is something more than "a consuming fire and a jealous God." True, He is a consuming fire, because He is holy; He is intolerant of evil, and must consume our dross. Moreover, He is jealous, because He cannot suffer any rival to have a place in the hearts of those He loves. He must have the whole heart, because He alone is worthy of it, as He alone can fill and satisfy it forever. And if His people turn away from Him and go after idols of their own making, they must be left to reap the bitter fruit of their own doings, and to prove, by sad and terrible experience, the truth of these words: "Their sorrows shall be multiplied that hasten after another."

But mark how touchingly Moses presents to the people the bright side of things—a brightness springing from the eternal stability of the grace of God, and the perfect provision which that grace has made for all His people's need, from first to last. "*But,*" he says—and oh, how lovely are some of the "buts" of holy Scripture!—"if from thence thou shalt seek the Lord thy God, thou shalt find Him, if thou seek Him with all thy heart and with all thy soul." Exquisite grace! "When thou art in tribulation"—that is the time to find what our God is,—"and all these things are come upon thee, even in the latter days, if thou turn to the Lord thy God, and shalt be obedient unto His voice;"—what then? "A consuming fire"? Nay; but "the Lord *thy God* is a merciful God; He will not forsake thee, neither destroy thee, nor forget the covenant of thy fathers which He sware unto them."

Here we have a remarkable onlook into Israel's future, their departure from God and consequent dispersion among the nations, the complete breaking up of their polity, and the passing away of their national glory. But, blessed forever be the God of all grace, there is something beyond all this failure and sin and ruin and judgment. When we get to the far end of Israel's melancholy history—a history which may truly be summed up in that one brief but comprehensive sentence, "O Israel, thou hast destroyed thyself," we are met by the magnificent display of the grace, mercy, and faithfulness of Jehovah, the God of their fathers, whose heart of love tells itself out in that added sentence, "In Me is thy help." Yes; the whole matter is wrapped up in these two vigorous sentences, "Thou hast destroyed thyself," "But in Me is thy help." In the former, we have the sharp arrow for Israel's conscience; in the latter, the soothing balm for Israel's broken heart.

In thinking of the nation of Israel, there are two pages which we have to study, namely, the historic and the prophetic. The page of history records, with unerring faithfulness, their utter ruin: the page of prophecy unfolds, in accents of matchless grace, God's remedy. Israel's past has been dark and gloomy: Israel's future will be bright and glorious. In the former, we see the miserable actings of man; in the latter, the blessed ways of God. That gives the forcible illustration of what man is; this, the bright display of what God is. We must look at both if we would understand aright the history of this remarkable people—"a people terrible from their beginning hitherto," and, we may truly add, a people wonderful to the end of time.

We do not, of course, attempt to adduce, in this place, proofs of our statement as to Israel's past and Israel's future. To do so would, we may say, without any exaggeration, demand a volume, inasmuch as it would simply be to quote a very large portion of the historical books of the Bible on the one hand, and of the prophetic books on the other. This, we need hardly say, is out of the question; but we feel bound to press upon the reader's attention the precious teaching contained in the quotation given above. It embodies, in its brief compass, the whole truth as to Israel's past, present, and future. Mark how their past is vividly portrayed in these few words: "When thou shalt beget children, and children's children, and ye shall have remained long in the land, and shall corrupt yourselves, and make a graven image, or the likeness of any thing, and shall do evil in the sight of the Lord thy God, to provoke Him to anger."

Is not this precisely what they have done? Is it not here, as it were, in a nutshell? They have done evil in the sight of Jehovah their God, to provoke Him to anger. That one word, "*evil*" takes all in, from the calf at Horeb to the cross at Calvary. Such is Israel's past.

And now, what of their present? Are they not a standing monument of the imperishable truth of God? Has a single jot or tittle failed of all that God has spoken? Hearken to these glowing words: "I call heaven and earth to witness against you this day, that ye shall soon utterly perish from off the land whereunto ye go over Jordan to possess it; ye shall not prolong your days upon it, but shall utterly be destroyed. And the Lord shall scatter you among the nations, and ye shall be left few in number among the heathen, whither the Lord shall lead you."

Has not all this been fulfilled to the letter? Who can question it? Israel's past and Israel's present alike attest the truth of God's Word. And are we not justified in declaring that inasmuch as the past and the present are a literal accomplishment of the truth of God, so shall the future? Assuredly. The page of history and the page of prophecy were both indited by the same Spirit, and therefore they are both alike true; and as the history records Israel's sin and Israel's dispersion, so doth the prophecy predict Israel's repentance and Israel's restoration. The one is as true to faith as the other. As surely as Israel sinned in the past and are scattered at the present, so surely shall they repent and be restored in the future.

This, we conceive, is beyond all question; and we rejoice to think of it. There is not one of the prophets, from Isaiah to Malachi, that does not most distinctly set forth, in accents of sweetest grace and most tender mercy, the future blessings, pre-eminence, and glory of the seed of Abraham.[11] It would be simply delightful to quote some of the sublime passages bearing upon this most interesting subject; but we must leave the reader to search them out for himself, especially commending to his notice the precious passages contained in the closing chapters of Isaiah, in which he will find a perfect feast, as well as the fullest confirmation of the apostle's statement that "all Israel shall be saved." All the prophets, "from Samuel and those that follow after," agree as to this. The teachings of the New Testament harmonize with the voices of the prophets, and hence to call in question the truth of Israel's restoration to their own land, and final blessing there, under the rule of their own Messiah, is simply to ignore or deny the testimony of prophets and apostles, speaking and writing by the direct inspiration of God the Holy Ghost; it is to set aside a body of Scripture evidence perfectly overwhelming.

It seems passing strange that any true lover of Christ should seek to do this; yet so it is, and so it has been, through religious prejudice, theological bias, and various other causes. But, notwithstanding all this, the glorious truth of Israel's restoration and pre-eminence in the earth shines with undimmed lustre on the prophetic page, and all who seek to set it aside, or interfere with it in any way, are not only flying in the face of holy Scripture—contradicting the unanimous voice of apostles and prophets, but also seeking to tamper (ignorantly and unwittingly, no doubt) with the counsel, purpose, and promise of the Lord God of Israel, and to nullify His covenant with Abraham, Isaac, and Jacob.

This is serious work for any one to engage in, and we believe many are doing it without being aware of it; for we must understand that any one who applies the promises made to the Old-Testament fathers to the New-Testament Church is, in reality, doing the serious work of which we speak. We maintain that no one has the slightest warrant to alienate the promises made to the fathers. We may learn from those promises, delight in them, draw comfort and encouragement from their eternal stability and direct literal application—all this is blessedly true; but it is another thing altogether for men, under the influence of a system of interpretation falsely called spiritual, to apply to the Church, or to believers of the New-Testament times, prophecies which, as simply and plainly as words can indicate, apply to Israel—to the literal seed of Abraham.

This is what we consider so very serious. We believe we have very little idea of how thoroughly opposed all this is to the mind and heart of God. He loves Israel—loves them for the fathers' sake, and we may rest assured He will not sanction our interference with their place, their portion, or their prospect. We are all familiar with the words of the inspired apostle in Romans xi, however we may have missed or forgotten their true import and moral force.

Speaking of Israel, in connection with the olive-tree of promise, he says, "And they also, if they abide not still in unbelief, shall be graffed in; for" the most simple, solid, and blessed of all reasons—"*God is able,*" as He is most surely willing, "to graff them in again. For if thou wert cut out of the olive-tree which is wild by nature, and wert graffed contrary to nature into a good olive-tree; how much more shall these, which be the natural branches, be graffed into their own olive-tree? For I would not, brethren, that ye should be ignorant of this mystery, lest ye should be wise in your own conceits; that blindness *in part* is happened to Israel, until the fullness of the Gentiles be come in.[12] And so all Israel shall be saved: as it is written, 'There shall come out of Sion the Deliverer, and shall turn away ungodliness from Jacob: *for this is My covenant unto them,* when I shall take away their sins.' As concerning the gospel, they are enemies for your sakes; but as touching the election, they are beloved for the fathers' sakes. For the gifts and calling of God are without repentance. For as ye in times past have not believed God, yet have now obtained mercy through their unbelief; even so have these also now not believed in your mercy [or, mercy to you. *See Greek.*] that they also may obtain mercy." That is, that instead of coming in on the ground of law, or fleshly descent, they should come in simply on the ground of sovereign mercy, just as the Gentiles. "For God hath concluded them all in unbelief, that He might have *mercy upon all.*"

Here ends the section bearing upon our immediate subject, but we cannot refrain from quoting the splendid doxology which bursts forth from the overflowing heart of the inspired apostle as he closes the grand dispensational division of his epistle—"O the depth of the riches both of the wisdom and knowledge of God! how unsearchable are His judgments, and His ways past finding out! For who hath known the mind of the Lord? or who hath been His counselor? or who hath first given to Him, and it shall be recompensed unto him again? For *of* Him," as the source, "and *through* Him," as the channel, "and *to* Him," as the object, "are all things: to whom be glory forever. Amen."

The foregoing splendid passage, as indeed all Scripture, is in perfect keeping with the teaching of the fourth chapter of our book. Israel's present condition is the fruit of their dark unbelief: Israel's future glory will be the fruit of God's rich sovereign mercy.—"The Lord thy God is a merciful God, He will not forsake thee, neither destroy thee, nor forget the covenant of thy fathers which He sware unto them. For ask now of the days that are past, which were before thee, since the day that God created man upon the earth, and ask from the one side of heaven unto the other"—The utmost bounds of time and space were to be appealed to, to see—"whether there hath been any such thing as this great thing is, or hath been heard like it? Did ever people hear the voice of God speaking out of the midst of the fire, as thou hast heard, and live? Or hath God assayed to go and take Him a nation from the midst of another nation, by temptations, by signs, and by wonders, and by war, and by a mighty hand, and by a stretched-out arm, and by great terrors, according to all that the Lord your God did for you in Egypt before your eyes? Unto thee it was showed, that thou mightest know that the Lord He is God; there is none else beside Him. Out of heaven He made thee to hear His voice, that He might instruct thee, and upon earth He showed thee His great fire; and thou heardest His words out of the midst of the fire."

Here we have set forth, with singular moral power, the grand object of all the divine actings on Israel's behalf. It was that they might know that Jehovah was the one true and living God, and that there was and could be none beside Him. In a word, it was the purpose of God that Israel should be a witness for Him on the earth; and so they most assuredly shall, though hitherto they have signally failed and caused His great and holy name to be blasphemed among the nations. Nothing can hinder the purpose of God. His covenant shall stand forever. Israel shall yet be a blessed and effective witness for God on the earth, and a channel of rich and everlasting blessing to all nations. Jehovah has pledged His word as to this, and not all the powers of earth and hell—men and devils combined can hinder the full accomplishment of all that He has spoken. His glory is involved in Israel's future, and if a single jot or tittle of His word were to fail, it would be a dishonor cast upon His great name, and an occasion for the enemy, which is utterly impossible. Israel's future blessing and Jehovah's glory are bound together by a link which can never be snapped. If this be not clearly seen, we can neither understand Israel's past nor Israel's future. Nay, more; we may assert, with all possible confidence, that unless this blessed fact be fully grasped, our system of prophetic interpretation must be utterly false.

But there is another truth set forth in our chapter—a truth of peculiar interest and preciousness. It is not merely that the glory of Jehovah is involved in Israel's future restoration and blessedness; the love of His heart is also engaged. This comes out with touching sweetness in the following words: "And because He loved thy fathers, therefore He chose their seed after them, and brought thee out in His sight with His mighty power out of Egypt; to drive out nations from before thee greater and mightier than thou art, to bring thee in, to give thee their land for an inheritance, as it is this day."

Thus the truth of God's word, the glory of His great name, and the love of His heart are all involved in His dealings with the seed of Abraham His friend; and albeit they have broken the law, dishonored His name, despised His mercy, rejected His prophets, crucified His Son, and resisted His Spirit— although they have done all this, and, in consequence thereof, are scattered and peeled and broken, and shall yet pass through unexampled tribulation, yet will the God of Abraham, Isaac, and Jacob glorify His name, make good His word, and manifest the changeless love of His heart in the future history of His earthly people. "Nothing changeth God's affection." Whom He loves and as He loves He loves unto the end.

If we deny this in reference to Israel, we have not so much as a single inch of solid standing-ground for ourselves: if we touch the truth of God in one department, we have no security as to any thing. "Scripture cannot be broken." "All the promises of God in Him are yea, and in Him Amen, unto the glory of God." God has pledged Himself to the seed of Abraham; He has promised to give them the land of Canaan, *forever*. "His gifts and calling are without repentance." He never repents of His gift or His call; and therefore for any one to attempt to alienate His promises and His gifts, or to interfere in any way with their application to their true and proper object, must be a grievous offense to Him. It mars the integrity of divine truth, deprives us of all certainty in the interpretation of holy Scripture, and plunges the soul in darkness, doubt, and perplexity.

The teaching of Scripture is clear, definite, and distinct. The Holy Ghost, who indited the sacred Volume, means what He says and says what He means. If He speaks of Israel, He means Israel—of Zion, He means Zion—of Jerusalem, He means Jerusalem. To apply any one of these names to the New-Testament Church is to confound things that differ, and introduce a method of interpreting Scripture which, from its vagueness and looseness, can only lead to the most disastrous consequences. If we handle the Word of God in such a loose and careless manner, it is utterly impossible to realize its divine authority over our conscience, or exhibit its formative power in our course, conduct, and character.

We must now look, for a moment, at the powerful appeal with which Moses sums up his address in our chapter: it demands our profound and reverent attention.—"Know *therefore* this day, and *consider it in thine heart,* that the Lord He is God in heaven above, and upon the earth beneath; there is none else. Thou shalt keep *therefore* His statutes, and His commandments, which I command thee this day, that it may go well with thee, and with thy children after thee, and that thou mayest prolong thy days upon the earth, which the Lord thy God giveth thee, forever." (Ver. 39, 40.)

Here we see that the moral claim upon their hearty obedience is grounded upon the revealed character of God, and His marvelous actings on their behalf. In a word, they were bound to obey—bound by every argument that could possibly act on the heart, the conscience, and the understanding. The One who had brought them out of the land of Egypt, with a mighty hand and outstretched arm; who had made that land to tremble to its very centre, by stroke after stroke of His judicial rod; who had opened up a pathway for them through the sea; who had sent them bread from heaven, and brought forth water for them out of the flinty rock; and all this for the glory of His great name, and because He loved their fathers—surely He was entitled to their whole-hearted obedience.

This is the grand argument, so eminently characteristic of this blessed book of Deuteronomy. And surely this is full of instruction for Christians now. If Israel were morally bound to obey, how much more are we! If their motives and objects were powerful, how much more so are ours! Do we feel their power? do we consider them in our hearts? Do we ponder the claims of Christ upon us? Do we remember that we are not our own, but bought with a price, even the infinitely precious price of the blood of Christ? Do we realize this? Are we seeking to live for Him? Is His glory our ruling object?—His love our constraining motive? or are we living for ourselves? Are we seeking to get on in the world—that world that crucified our blessed Lord and Saviour? Are we seeking to make money? do we love it in our hearts, either for its own sake or for the sake of what it can procure? does money *govern* us? Are we seeking a place in the world, either for ourselves or for our children? Let us honestly challenge our hearts, as in the divine presence, in the light of God's truth, what is our object—our real, governing, cherished, heart-sought object?

Reader, these are searching questions. Let us not put them aside: let us really weigh them in the very light of the judgment-seat of Christ. We believe they are wholesome, much-needed questions. We live in very solemn times. There is a fearful amount of sham on every side, and in nothing is this sham so awfully apparent as in so-called religion.

The very days in which our lot is cast have been sketched by a pen that never colors—never exaggerates, but always presents men and things precisely as they are.—"This know also, that in *the last days*"—quite distinct from "*the latter times*" of 1 Timothy iv.—far in advance, more pronounced, more closely defined, more strongly marked, these last days in which "perilous [or difficult] times shall come. For men shall be *lovers of their own selves*, covetous, *boasters*, proud, blasphemers, *disobedient to parents*, unthankful, unholy, *without natural affection*, truce-breakers, *false accusers*, incontinent, fierce, despisers of those that are good, traitors, heady, high-minded, *lovers of pleasures more* [or rather] *than lovers of God.*" And then mark the crown which the inspired apostle puts upon this appalling superstructure!—"Having a form of godliness, but denying the power thereof." (2 Tim. iii. 1-5.)

What a terrible picture! We have here, in a few glowing, weighty sentences, *infidel* christendom, just as in 1 Timothy iv. we have *superstitious* christendom. In the latter, we see popery; in the former, infidelity. Both elements are at work around us, but the latter will yet rise into prominence— indeed, even now it is advancing with rapid strides. The very leaders and teachers of christendom are not ashamed or afraid to attack the foundations of Christianity. A so-called Christian bishop is not ashamed or afraid to call in question the integrity of the five books of Moses, and, with them, of the whole Bible; for, most assuredly, if Moses was not the inspired writer of the Pentateuch, the entire edifice of holy Scripture is swept from beneath our feet. The writings of Moses are so intimately bound up with all the other grand divisions of the divine Volume, that if they are touched, all is gone. We boldly affirm that if the Holy Ghost did not inspire Moses, the servant of God, to write the first five books of our English Bible, we have not an inch of solid ground to stand upon; we are positively left without a single atom of divine authority on which to rest our souls; the very pillars of our glorious Christianity are swept away, and we are left to grope our way, in hopeless perplexity, amid the conflicting opinions and theories of infidel doctors, without so much as a single ray from Inspiration's heavenly lamp.

Does this appear too strong for the reader? Does he believe that we can listen, for a moment, to the infidel denier of Moses, and yet believe in the inspiration of the psalms, the prophets, and the New Testament? If he does, let him be well assured he is under the power of a fatal delusion. Let him take such passages as the following, and ask himself, What do they mean, and what is wrapped up in them? Our Lord, in speaking to the Jews—who, by the way, would not have agreed with a Christian bishop in denying the authenticity of Moses—says, "Do not think that I will accuse you to the Father; there is one that accuseth you, even Moses, in whom ye trust. For had ye believed Moses, ye would have believed Me; for he wrote of Me.

But if ye believe not his writings, how shall ye believe My words?" (John v. 45-47.)

Think of this: The man that does not believe in the writings of Moses—does not receive every line of his as divinely inspired, does not believe in Christ's words, and therefore cannot have any divinely wrought faith in Christ Himself—cannot be a Christian at all. This makes it a very serious matter for any one to deny the divine inspiration of the Pentateuch, and equally serious for any one to listen to him or sympathize with him. It is all very well to talk of Christian charity and liberality of spirit; but we have yet to learn that it is charity or liberality to sanction, in any way, a man who has the audacity to sweep from beneath our feet the very foundations of our faith. To speak of him as a Christian bishop, or a Christian minister of any kind, is only to make the matter a thousand times worse. We can understand a Voltaire or a Paine attacking the Bible—we do not look for any thing else from them; but when those who assume to be the recognized and ordained ministers of religion, and the guardians of the faith of God's elect—those who consider themselves alone entitled to teach and preach Jesus Christ, and feed and tend the Church of God—when they actually call in question the inspiration of the five books of Moses, may we not well ask, Where are we? What has the professing church come to?

But let us take another passage. It is the powerful appeal of the risen Saviour to the two bewildered disciples on their way to Emmaus—"'O fools, and slow of heart to believe all that the prophets have spoken; ought not Christ to have suffered these things, and to enter into His glory?' And *beginning at Moses* and all the prophets, He expounded unto them in all the scriptures the things concerning Himself." And again, to the eleven and others with them, He says, "These are the words which I spake unto you, while I was yet with you, that all things must be fulfilled, which were written *in the law of Moses*, and in the prophets, and in the psalms, concerning Me." (Luke xxiv. 25-27, 44.)

Here we find that our Lord, in the most distinct and positive manner, recognizes the law of Moses as an integral part of the canon of inspiration, and binds it up with all the other grand divisions of the divine Volume in such a way that it is utterly impossible to touch one without destroying the integrity of the whole. If Moses is not to be trusted, neither are the prophets, nor the psalms. They stand or fall together. And not only so, but we must either admit the divine authenticity of the Pentateuch or draw the blasphemous inference that our adorable Lord and Saviour gave the sanction of His authority to a set of spurious documents, by quoting as the writings of Moses what Moses never wrote at all! There is positively not a single inch of consistent standing-ground between these two conclusions.

Again, take the following most weighty and important passage at the close of the parable of the rich man and Lazarus: "Abraham saith unto him, 'They have *Moses and the prophets; let them hear them.*' And he said, 'Nay, father Abraham; but if one went unto them from the dead, they will repent.' And he said unto him, 'If they hear not Moses and the prophets, neither will they be persuaded though one rose from the dead.'" (Luke xvi. 29-31.)

Finally, if we add to all this the fact that our Lord, in His conflict with Satan in the wilderness, quotes only from the writings of Moses, we have a body of evidence quite sufficient, not only to establish, beyond all question, the divine inspiration of Moses, but also to prove that the man who calls in question the authenticity of the first five books of the Bible, can really have no Bible, no divine revelation, no authority, no solid foundation for his faith. He may call himself, or be called by others, a Christian bishop or a Christian minister; but, in solemn fact, he is a skeptic, and should be treated as such by all who believe and know the truth. We cannot understand how any one with a spark of divine life in his soul could be guilty of the awful sin of denying the inspiration of a large portion of the Word of God, or asserting that our Lord Christ could quote from spurious documents.

We may be deemed severe in thus writing. It seems the fashion nowadays to own as Christians those who deny the very foundations of Christianity. It is a very popular notion that, provided people are moral, amiable, benevolent, charitable, and philanthropic, it is of very small consequence what they believe. Life is better than creed or dogma, we are told. All this sounds very plausible: but the reader may rest assured that the direct tendency of all this manner of speech and line of argument is to get rid of the Bible—rid of the Holy Ghost—rid of Christ—rid of God—rid of all that the Bible reveals to our souls. Let him bear this in mind, and seek to keep close to the precious Word of God; let him treasure that Word in his heart, and give himself more and more to the prayerful study of it. Thus he will be preserved from the withering influence of skepticism and infidelity, in every shape and form; his soul will be fed and nourished by the sincere milk of the Word, and his whole moral being be kept in the shelter of the divine presence continually. This is what is needed: nothing else will do.

We must now close our meditations on this marvelous chapter which has been engaging our attention; but ere doing so, we would glance for a moment at the remarkable notice of the three cities of refuge. It might, to a cursory reader, seem abrupt; but, so far from that, it is, as we might expect, in perfect and beautiful moral order. Scripture is always divinely perfect, and if we do not see and appreciate its beauties and moral glories, it is simply owing to our blindness and insensibility.

"Then Moses severed three cities on this side Jordan toward the sunrising; that the slayer might flee thither, which should kill his neighbor unawares, and hated him not in times past; and that fleeing unto one of those cities he might live; namely, Bezer in the wilderness, in the plain country, of the Reubenites; and Ramoth in Gilead, of the Gadites; and Golan in Bashan, of the Manassites."

Here we have a lovely display of the grace of God rising, as it ever does, above human weakness and failure. The two tribes and a half, in choosing their inheritance on this side Jordan, were manifestly stopping short of the proper portion of the Israel of God, which lay on the other side of the river of death; but, notwithstanding this failure, God, in His abounding grace, would not leave the poor slayer without a refuge in the day of his distress. If man cannot come up to the height of God's thoughts, God can come down to the depths of man's need; and so blessedly does He do so in this case, that the two tribes and a half were to have as many cities of refuge on this side Jordan as the nine tribes and a half had in the land of Canaan.

This, truly, was grace abounding. How unlike the manner of man! How far above mere law or legal righteousness! It might, in a legal way, have been said to the two tribes and a half, If you are going to choose your inheritance short of the divine mark—if you are content with less than Canaan, the land of promise, you must not expect to enjoy the privileges and blessings of that land. The institutions of Canaan must be confined to Canaan, and hence your manslayer must try and make his way across the Jordan and find refuge there.

Law might speak thus, but Grace spoke differently. God's thoughts are not ours, nor His ways as ours. We might deem it marvelous grace to provide even one city for the two and a half tribes; but our God does exceeding abundantly above all that we ask or think, and hence the comparatively small district on this side Jordan was furnished with as full a provision of grace as the entire land of Canaan.

Does this prove that the two and a half tribes were right? Nay; but it proves that God was good, and that He must ever act like Himself, spite of all our weakness and folly. Could He leave a poor slayer without a place of refuge in the land of Gilead, though Gilead was not Canaan? Surely not. This would not be worthy of the One who says, "I bring near My righteousness." He took care to bring the city of refuge "near" to the slayer. He would cause His rich and precious grace to flow over and meet the needy one just where he was. Such is the way of our God, blessed be His holy name for evermore!

"And this is the law which Moses set before the children of Israel: these are the testimonies, and the statutes, and the judgments, which Moses spake unto the children of Israel, after they came forth out of Egypt, on this side Jordan, in the valley over against Beth-peor, in the land of Sihon king of the Amorites, who dwelt at Heshbon, whom Moses and the children of Israel smote, after they were come forth out of Egypt: and they possessed his land, and the land of Og king of Bashan, two kings of the Amorites, which were on this side Jordan toward the sunrising; from Aroer, which is by the bank of the river Arnon, even unto Mount Sion, which is Hermon, and all the plain on this side Jordan eastward, even unto the sea of the plain, under the springs of Pisgah."

Here closes this marvelous discourse. The Spirit of God delights to trace the boundaries of the people, and dwell on the most minute details connected with their history. He takes a lively and loving interest in all that concerns them—their conflicts, their victories, their possessions, all their landmarks; every thing about them is dwelt upon with a minuteness which, by its touching grace and condescension, fill the heart with wonder, love, and praise. Man, in his contemptible self-importance, thinks it beneath his dignity to enter upon minute details; but *our* God counts the hairs of our heads, puts our tears into His bottle, takes knowledge of our every care, our every sorrow, our every need. There is nothing too small for His love, as there is nothing too great for His power. He concentrates His loving care upon each one of His people as though He had only that one to attend to; and there is not a single circumstance in our private history, from day to day, however trivial, in which He does not take a loving interest.

Let us ever remember this, for our comfort; and may we learn to trust Him better, and use, with a more artless faith, His fatherly love and care. He tells us to cast *all* our care upon Him, in the assurance that He careth for us. He would have our hearts as free from care as our conscience is free from guilt. "Be careful for *nothing*; but in every thing by prayer and supplication with thanksgiving let your requests be made known unto God. And the peace of God, which passeth *all* understanding, shall keep your hearts and minds through Christ Jesus." (Phil. iv. 6, 7.)

It is to be feared that the great majority of us know but little of the real depth, meaning, and power of such words as these. We read them and hear them, but we do not take them in and make our own of them—we do not digest them and reduce them to practice. How little do we really enter into the blessed truth that our Father is interested in all our little cares and sorrows, and that we may go to Him with all our little wants and difficulties. We imagine that such things are beneath the notice of the high and mighty One who inhabiteth eternity and sitteth upon the circle of the earth. This is a serious mistake, and one that robs us of incalculable blessing in our daily history. We should ever remember that there is nothing great or small with our God: all things are alike to Him who sustains the vast universe by the word of His power, and takes notice of a falling sparrow. It is quite as easy to Him to create a world as to provide a breakfast for some poor widow. The greatness of His power, the moral grandeur of His government, and the minuteness of His tender care, do all alike command the wonder and the worship of our hearts.

Christian reader, see that you make your own of all these things. Seek to live nearer to God in your daily walk. Lean more upon Him. Use Him more. Go to Him in all your need, and you will never have to tell your need to a poor fellow-mortal. "My God shall supply *all* your need, according to His riches in glory by Christ Jesus." What a source—"God"! What a standard—"His riches in glory"! What a channel—"Christ Jesus"! It is your sweet privilege to place all *your need* over against *His riches*, and lose sight of the former in the presence of the latter. His exhaustless treasury is thrown open to you, in all the love of His heart; go and draw upon it, in the artless simplicity of faith, and you will never have occasion to look to a creature-stream or lean on a creature-prop.

CHAPTER V

"And Moses called all Israel, and said unto them, 'Hear, O Israel, the statutes and judgments which I speak in your ears this day, that ye may learn them, and keep and do them.'"

Let us carefully note these four words, so specially characteristic of the book of Deuteronomy, and so seasonable for the Lord's people at all times and in all places: "*Hear*," "*Learn*," "*Keep*," "*Do*." These are words of unspeakable preciousness to every truly pious soul—to every one who honestly desires to walk in that narrow path of practical righteousness so pleasing to God, and so safe and so happy for us.

The first of these words places the soul in the most blessed attitude in which any one can be found, namely, that of *hearing*. "Faith cometh by *hearing*, and hearing by the Word of God." "I will *hear* what God the Lord will speak." "*Hear*, and your soul shall live." The hearing ear lies at the very foundation of all true, practical Christian life. It places the soul in the only true and proper attitude for the creature. It is the real secret of all peace and blessedness.

It can scarcely be needful to remind the reader that when we speak of the soul in the attitude of hearing, it is assumed that what is heard is simply the Word of God. Israel had to hearken to "the statutes and judgments" of Jehovah, and to nothing else. It was not to the commandments, traditions, and doctrines of men they were to give ear, but to the very words of the living God, who had redeemed and delivered them from the land of Egypt—the place of bondage, darkness, and death.

It is well to bear this in mind. It will preserve the soul from many a snare, many a difficulty. We hear a good deal, in certain quarters, about obedience, and about the moral fitness of surrendering our own will and submitting ourselves to authority. All this sounds very well, and has great weight with a large class of very religious and morally excellent people; but when men speak to us about obedience, we must ask the question, Obedience to what? when they speak to us about surrendering our own will, we must inquire of them, To whom are we to surrender it? when they speak to us about submitting to authority, we must insist upon their telling us the source or foundation of the authority.

This is of the deepest possible moment to every member of the household of faith. There are many very sincere and very earnest people who deem it very delightful to be saved the trouble of thinking for themselves, and to have their sphere of action and line of service laid out for them by wiser heads than their own. It seems a very restful and very pleasing thing to have each day's work laid out for us by some master-hand. It relieves the heart of a great load of responsibility, and it looks like humility and self-distrust to submit ourselves to some authority.

But we are bound, before God, to look well to the basis of the authority to which we surrender ourselves, else we may find ourselves in an utterly false position. Take, for example, a monk, or a nun, or a member of a sisterhood. A monk obeys his abbot, a nun obeys her mother-abbess, "a sister" obeys her "lady-superior;" but the position and relationship of each is utterly false. There is not a shadow of authority in the New Testament for monasteries, convents, or sisterhoods; on the contrary, the teaching of holy Scripture, as well as the voice of nature, is utterly opposed to every one of them, inasmuch as they take men and women out of the place and out of the relationship in which God has set them, and in which they are designed and fitted to move, and form them into societies which are utterly destructive of natural affection, and subversive of all true Christian obedience.

We feel it right to call the attention of the Christian reader to this subject just now, seeing that the enemy is making a vigorous effort to revive the monastic system in our midst under various forms. Indeed some have had the temerity to tell us that monastic life is the only true form of Christianity. Surely, when such monstrous statements are made and listened to, it becomes us to look at the whole subject in the light of Scripture, and to call upon the advocates and adherents of monasticism to show us the foundations of the system in the Word of God. Where, within the covers of the New Testament, is there any thing, in the most remote degree, like a monastery, a convent, or a sisterhood? Where can we find an authority for any such office as that of an abbot, an abbess, or a lady-superior? There is absolutely no such thing, nor the shadow of it; and hence we have no hesitation in pronouncing the whole system, from foundation to top-stone, a fabric of superstition, alike opposed to the voice of nature and the voice of God: nor can we understand how any one, in his sober senses, could presume to tell us that a monk or a nun is the only true exponent of Christian life. Yet there are those who thus speak, and there are those who listen to them, and that, too, in this day when the full, clear light of our glorious Christianity is shining upon us from the pages of the New Testament.[13]

But, blessed be God, we are called to obedience. We are called to "hear"—called to bow down, in holy and reverent submission, to authority.

And here we join issue with infidelity and its lofty pretensions. The path of the devout and lowly Christian is alike removed from superstition on the one hand and from infidelity on the other. Peter's noble reply to the council, in Acts v, embodies, in its brief compass, a complete answer to both.—"We ought to obey God rather than men." We meet infidelity, in all its phases, in all its stages, and in its very deepest roots, with this one weighty sentence, "We ought to *obey*;" and we meet superstition, in every garb in which it clothes itself, with the all-important clause, "We ought to *obey God*."

Here we have set forth, in the most simple form, the duty of every true Christian. He is to obey God. The infidel may smile contemptuously at a monk or a nun, and marvel how any rational being can so completely surrender his reason and his understanding to the authority of a fellow-mortal, or submit himself to rules and practices so absurd, so degrading, and so contrary to nature. The infidel glories in his fancied intellectual freedom, and imagines that his own reason is quite a sufficient guide for him. He does not see that he is further from God than the poor monk or nun whom he so despises. He does not know that, while priding himself in his self-will, he is really led captive by Satan—the prince and god of this world. Man is formed to obey—formed to look up to some one above him. The Christian is sanctified unto the obedience of Jesus Christ, that is, to the very same character of obedience as that which was rendered by our adorable Lord and Saviour Himself.

This is of the deepest possible moment to every one who really desires to know what true Christian obedience is. To understand this is the real secret of deliverance from the self-will of the infidel and the false obedience of superstition. It can never be right to do our own will: it may be quite wrong to do the will of our fellow: it must always be right to do the will of God. This was what Jesus came to do, and what He always did.—"Lo, I come to do Thy will, O God."—"I delight to do Thy will, O My God; yea, Thy law is within My heart."

Now, we are called and set apart to this blessed character of obedience, as we learn from the inspired apostle Peter, in the opening of his first epistle, where he speaks of believers as "elect according to the foreknowledge of God the Father, through sanctification of the Spirit, unto obedience and sprinkling of the blood of Jesus Christ."

This is an immense privilege, and at the same time a most holy and solemn responsibility. We must never forget for a moment that God has elected us, and the Holy Spirit has set us apart, not only to the sprinkling of the blood of Jesus Christ, but also to His obedience. Such is the obvious meaning and moral force of the words just quoted—words of unspeakable preciousness to every lover of holiness—words which effectually deliver us from self-will, from legality, and from superstition. Blessed deliverance!

But it may be that the pious reader feels disposed to call our attention to the exhortation in Hebrews xiii.—"Obey them that have the rule over you, and submit yourselves; for they watch for your souls, as they that must give account; that they may do it with joy and not with grief; for that is unprofitable for you."

A deeply important word, most surely, with which we should also connect a passage in 1 Thessalonians—"And we beseech you, brethren, to know them that labor among you, and are over you in the Lord, and admonish you, and to esteem them very highly in love for their work's sakes." (Chap. v. 12, 13.) And again, in 1 Corinthians xvi. 15, 16—"I beseech you, brethren, (ye know the house of Stephanas, that it is the first-fruits of Achaia, and that they have addicted themselves to the ministry [or service] of the saints,) that ye submit yourselves unto such, and to every one that helpeth with us and laboreth." To all these we must add another very lovely passage from the first epistle of Peter—"The elders which are among you I exhort, who am also an elder, and a witness of the sufferings of Christ, and also a partaker of the glory that shall be revealed: feed the flock of God which is among you, taking the oversight thereof, not by constraint, but willingly; not for filthy lucre, but of a ready mind; neither as being lords over God's heritage, but being ensamples to the flock. And when the chief Shepherd shall appear, ye shall receive a crown of glory that fadeth not away." (Chap. v. 1-4.)

We may be asked, Do not the above passages set forth the principle of obedience to certain men? and if so, why object to human authority? The answer is very simple. Wherever Christ imparts a spiritual gift, whether it be the gift of teaching, the gift of rule, or the gift of pastorship, it is the bounden duty and privilege of Christians to recognize and appreciate such gifts. Not to do so would be to forsake our own mercies. But then we must bear in mind that in all such cases the gift must be a reality—a plain, palpable, *bona-fide*, divinely given thing. It is not a man assuming a certain office or position, or being appointed by his fellow to any so-called ministry. All this is perfectly worthless, and worse than worthless; it is a daring intrusion upon a sacred domain which must, sooner or later, bring down the judgment of God.

All true ministry is of God, and based upon the possession of a positive gift from the Head of the Church; so that we may truly say, No gift, no ministry. In all the passages quoted above, we see positive gift possessed, and actual work done. Moreover, we see a true heart for the lambs and sheep of the flock of Christ; we see divine grace and power. The word in Hebrews xiii. is, "Obey them that guide you [ἡγουμένοις]." Now, it is essential to a true guide that he should go before you in the way. It would be the height of folly for any one to assume the title of guide if he were ignorant of the way, and neither able nor willing to go in it. Who would think of obeying such?

So also when the apostle exhorts the Thessalonians to "know" and "esteem" certain persons, on what does he found his exhortation? Is it upon the mere assumption of a title, an office, or a position? Nothing of the kind. He grounds his appeal upon the actual, well-known fact that these persons were "over them, *in the Lord*," and that they admonished them. And why were they to "esteem them very highly in love"? Was it for their office or their title? No; but "for their work's sake." And why were the Corinthians exhorted to submit themselves to the household of Stephanas? Was it because of an empty title or assumed office? By no means; but because "they addicted themselves to the ministry of the saints." They were actually in the work. They had received gift and grace from Christ, and they had a heart for His people. They were not boasting of their office or insisting upon their title, but giving themselves devotedly to the service of Christ, in the persons of His dear people.

Now this is the true principle of ministry. It is not human authority at all, but divine gift and spiritual power communicated by Christ to His servants, exercised by them, in responsibility to Him, and thankfully recognized by His saints. A man may set up to be a teacher or a pastor, or he may be appointed by his fellows to the office or title of a pastor; but unless he possesses a positive gift from the Head of the Church, it is all the merest sham, a hollow assumption, an empty conceit; and his voice will be the voice of a stranger, which the true sheep of Christ do not know and ought not to recognize.[14]

But, on the other hand, where there is the divinely gifted teacher, the true, loving, wise, faithful, laborious pastor, watching for souls, weeping over them, waiting upon them, like a gentle, tender nurse, able to say to them, "Now we live, if ye stand fast in the Lord"—where these things are found, there will not be much difficulty in recognizing and appreciating them. How do we know a good dentist? Is it by seeing his name on a brass plate? No; but by his work. A man may call himself a dentist ten thousand times over, but if he be only an unskillful operator, who would think of employing him?

Thus it is in all human affairs, and thus it is in the matter of ministry. If a man has a gift, he is a minister; if he has not, all the appointment, authority, and ordination in the world could not make him a minister of Christ. It may make him a minister of religion; but a minister of religion and a minister of Christ—a minister in christendom and a minister in the Church of God, are two totally different things. All true ministry has its source in God; it rests on divine authority, and its object is to bring the soul into His presence, and link it on to Him. False ministry, on the contrary, has its source in man; it rests on human authority, and its object is to link the soul on to itself. This marks the immense difference between the two. The former leads to God; the latter leads away from Him: that feeds, nourishes, and strengthens the new life; this hinders its progress, in every way, and plunges it in doubt and darkness. In a word, we may say, true ministry is of God, through Him, and to Him: false ministry is of man, through him, and to him. The former we prize more than we can say; the latter we reject with all the energy of our moral being.

We trust sufficient has been said to satisfy the mind of the reader in reference to the matter of obedience to those whom the Lord may see fit to call to the work of the ministry. We are bound, in every case, to judge by the Word of God, and to be assured that it is a divine reality and not a human sham—a positive gift from the Head of the Church, and not an empty title conferred by men. In all cases where there is real gift and grace, it is a sweet privilege to obey and submit ourselves, inasmuch as we discern Christ in the person and ministry of His beloved servants.

There is no difficulty, to a spiritual mind, in owning real grace and power. We can easily tell whether a man is seeking, in true love, to feed our souls with the bread of life, and lead us on in the ways of God, or whether he is seeking to exalt himself, and promote his own interests. Those who are living near the Lord can readily discern between true power and hollow assumption. Moreover, we never find Christ's true ministers parading their authority, or vaunting themselves of their office; they do the work and leave it to speak for itself. In the case of the blessed apostle Paul, we find him referring again and again to the plain proofs of his ministry— the unquestionable evidence afforded in the conversion and blessing of souls. He could say to the poor misguided Corinthians, when, under the influence of some self-exalting pretender, they foolishly called in question his apostleship, "Since ye seek a proof of Christ speaking in me ... examine yourselves."

This was close, pointed dealing with them. They themselves were the living proofs of his ministry. If his ministry was not of God, what and where were they? But it was of God, and this was his joy, his comfort, and his strength. He was "an apostle, not of men, neither by man, but by Jesus Christ, and God the Father, who raised Him from the dead." He gloried in the source of his ministry; and as to its character, he had but to appeal to a body of evidence quite sufficient to carry conviction to any right mind. In his case, it could be truly said, it was not the speech, but the power.

Thus it must be, in measure, in every case. We must look for the power: we must have reality. Mere titles are nothing. Men may undertake to confer titles and appoint to offices, but they have no more authority to do so than they have to appoint admirals in her majesty's fleet or generals in her army. If we were to see a man assuming the style and title of an admiral or a general, without her majesty's commission, we should pronounce him an idiot or a lunatic. This is but a feeble illustration to set forth the folly of men taking upon them the title of ministers of Christ without one atom of spiritual gift or divine authority.

Shall we be told, We must not judge? We are bound to judge. "Beware of false prophets." How can we beware if we are not to judge? But how are we to judge? "By their fruits ye shall know them." Can the Lord's people not tell the difference between a man who comes to them in the power of the Spirit, gifted by the Head of the Church, full of love to their souls, earnestly desiring their true blessing, seeking not theirs but them—a holy, gracious, humble, self-emptied servant of Christ; and a man who comes with a self-assumed or a humanly conferred title, without a single trace of any thing divine or heavenly either in his ministry or in his life? Of course they can; no one in his senses would think of calling in question a fact so obvious.

But further, we may ask, What mean those words of the venerable apostle John—"Beloved, believe not every spirit, but try the spirits whether they are of God; because many false prophets are gone out into the world"? How are we to try the spirits, or how are we to discern between the true and the false, if we are not to judge? Again, the same apostle, writing to "the elect lady," gives her the following most solemn admonition: "If there come any unto you, and bring not this doctrine, receive him not into your house, neither bid him Godspeed; for he that biddeth him Godspeed is partaker of his evil deeds." Was she not responsible to act on this admonition? Assuredly. But how could she if we are not to judge? And what had she to judge? Was it as to whether those who came to her house were ordained, authorized, or licensed by any man or body of men? Nothing of the kind. The one great and all-important question for her was as to the doctrine. If they brought the true, the divine doctrine of Christ—the doctrine of Jesus Christ come in the flesh, she was to receive them; if not, she was to shut her door, with a firm hand, against them, no matter who they were or where they came from. If they had all the credentials that man could bestow upon them, yet if they brought not *the truth*, she was to reject them with stern decision. This might seem very harsh, very narrow-minded, very bigoted; but with this she had nothing whatever to do. She had just to be as broad and as narrow as the truth. Her door and her heart were to be wide enough to admit all who brought Christ, and no wider. Was she to pay compliments at the expense of her Lord? was she to seek a name for largeness of heart or breadth of mind by receiving to her house and to her table the teachers of a false Christ? The very thought is absolutely horrible.

But finally, in the second chapter of Revelation, we find the church at Ephesus commended for having tried those who said they were apostles and were not. How could this be if we are not to judge? Is it not most evident to the reader that an utterly false use is made of our Lord's words in Matthew vii. 1—"Judge not, that ye be not judged," and also of the apostle's words in 1 Corinthians iv. 5—"Therefore judge nothing before the time"? It is impossible that Scripture can contradict itself; and hence, whatever be the true meaning of our Lord's "Judge not," or the apostle's "Judge nothing," it is perfectly certain that they do not, in the most remote way, interfere with the solemn responsibility of all Christians to judge the gift, the doctrine, and the life of all who take the place of preachers, teachers, and pastors in the Church of God.

And then, if we be asked as to the meaning of "Judge not" and "Judge nothing," we believe the words simply forbid our judging motives, or hidden springs of action. With these we have nothing whatever to do. We cannot penetrate below the surface, and, thanks be to God, we are not asked to do so—yea, we are positively forbidden. We cannot read the counsels of the heart; it is the province and prerogative of God alone to do this: but to say that we are not to judge the doctrine, the gift, or the manner of life of those who take the place of preachers, teachers, and pastors in the Church of God, is simply to fly in the face of holy Scripture, and to ignore the very instincts of the divine nature implanted in us by the Holy Ghost.

Hence, therefore, we can return, with increased clearness and decision, to our thesis of Christian obedience. It seems perfectly plain that the fullest recognition of all true ministry in the Church, and the most gracious submission of ourselves to all those whom our Lord Christ may see fit to raise up as pastors, teachers, and guides in our midst, can never, in the smallest degree, interfere with the grand fundamental principle set forth in Peter's magnificent reply to the council—"We ought to obey God rather than men."

It will ever be the aim and object of all true ministers of Christ to lead those to whom they minister in the true path of obedience to the Word of God. The chapter which lies open before us, as indeed the entire book of Deuteronomy, shows us very plainly how Moses, that eminent servant of God, ever sought and diligently labored to press upon the congregation of

Israel the urgent necessity of the most implicit obedience to all the statutes and judgments of God. He did not seek any place of authority for himself: he never lorded it over God's heritage. His one grand theme, from first to last, was obedience. This was the burden of all his discourses—obedience, not to him, but to his and their Lord. He rightly judged that this was the true secret of their happiness, their moral security, their dignity, and their strength. He knew that an obedient people must also, of necessity, be an invincible and invulnerable people. No weapon formed against them could prosper so long as they were governed by the word of God. In a word, he knew and believed that Israel's province was to obey Jehovah, as it was Jehovah's province to bless Israel. It was their one simple business to "hear," "learn," "keep," and "do" the revealed will of God; and so doing, they might count on Him, with all possible confidence, to be their shield, their strength, their safeguard, their refuge, their resource, their all in all. The only true and proper path for the Israel of God is that narrow path of obedience on which the light of God's approving countenance ever shines, and all who, through grace, tread that path will find Him "a guide, a glory, a defense, to save from every fear."

This, surely, is quite enough. We have nothing to do with consequences: these we may, in simple confidence, leave to Him whose we are and whom we are responsible to serve. "The name of the Lord is a strong tower; the righteous runneth into it and is safe." If we are doing His will, we shall ever find His name a strong tower; but, on the other hand, if we are not walking in a path of practical righteousness—if we are doing our own will—if we are living in the habitual neglect of the plain Word of God, then, verily, it is utterly vain for us to think that the name of the Lord will be a strong tower to us; rather would His name be a reproof to us, leading us to judge our ways and to return to the path of righteousness from which we have wandered.

Blessed be His name, His grace will ever meet us, in all its precious fullness and freeness, in the place of self-judgment and confession, however we may have failed and wandered; but this is a totally different thing. We may have to say, with the Psalmist, "Out of the depths have I cried unto Thee, O Lord. Lord, hear my voice; let Thine ears be attentive to the voice of my supplications. If Thou, Lord, shouldest mark iniquities, O Lord, who shall stand? But there is forgiveness with Thee, that Thou mayest be feared." But then, a soul crying to God from the depths, and getting forgiveness, is one thing; and a soul looking to Him in the path of practical righteousness is quite another. We must carefully distinguish between these two things. Confessing our sins and finding pardon must never be confounded with walking uprightly and counting on God. Both are blessedly true, but they are not the same thing.

We shall now proceed with our chapter.

At the second verse, Moses reminds the people of their covenant-relationship with Jehovah. He says, "The Lord *our* God made a covenant with us in Horeb. The Lord made not this covenant with our fathers, but with us, even us, who are all of us here alive this day. The Lord talked with you face to face, in the mount, out of the midst of the fire, (I stood between the Lord and you at that time, to show you the word of the Lord; for ye were afraid by reason of the fire, and went not up into the mount) saying," etc.

The reader must distinguish and thoroughly understand the difference between the covenant made at Horeb and the covenant made with Abraham, Isaac, and Jacob. They are essentially different. The former was a covenant of works, in which the people undertook to do all that the Lord had spoken: the latter was a covenant of pure grace, in which God pledged Himself with an oath to do all which He promised.

Human language would utterly fail us to set forth the immense difference, in every respect, between these two covenants. In their basis, in their character, in their accompaniments, and in their practical result, they are as different as any two things could possibly be. The Horeb covenant rested upon human competency for the fulfillment of its terms, and this one fact is quite sufficient to account for the total failure of the whole thing. The Abrahamic covenant rested upon divine competency for the fulfillment of its terms, and hence the utter impossibility of its failure in a single jot or tittle.

Having in our "Notes on the Book of Exodus" gone somewhat fully into the subject of the law, and endeavored to set forth the divine object in giving it, and, further, the utter impossibility of any one getting life or righteousness by keeping it, we must refer the reader to what we have there advanced on this profoundly interesting subject.

It seems strange, to one taught exclusively by Scripture, that such confusion of thought should prevail amongst professing Christians in reference to a question so distinctly and definitively settled by the Holy Ghost. Were it merely a question of the divine authority of Exodus xx. or Deuteronomy v. as inspired portions of the Bible, we should not have a word to say. We most fully believe that these chapters are as much inspired as the seventeenth of John or the eighth of Romans.

But this is not the point. All true Christians receive, with devout thankfulness, the precious statement that "all Scripture is given by inspiration of God;" and, further, they rejoice in the assurance that "whatsoever things were written aforetime were written for our learning; that we through patience and comfort of the Scriptures might have hope;" and, finally, they believe that the morality of the law is of abiding and universal application. Murder, adultery, theft, false witness, covetousness, are wrong—always wrong—every-where wrong: to honor our parents is right—always and every-where right. We read, in the fourth chapter of Ephesians, "Let him that stole steal no more;" and again, in chapter vi, we read, "Honor thy father and mother; which is the first commandment with promise; that it may be well with thee, and thou mayest live long on the earth."

All this is so divinely plain and settled that discussion is definitively closed; but when we come to look at the law as a ground of relationship with God, we get into an entirely different region of thought. Scripture, in manifold places, and in the clearest possible manner, teaches us that, as Christians, as children of God, we are not on that ground at all. The Jew was on that ground, but he could not stand there with God. It was death and condemnation. "They could not endure that which was commanded, 'And if so much as a beast touch the mountain, it shall be stoned, or thrust through with a dart;' and so terrible was the sight, that Moses said, 'I exceedingly fear and quake.'" The Jew found the law to be a bed on which he could not stretch himself, and a covering in which he could not wrap himself.

As to the Gentile, he was never, by any one branch of the divine economy, placed under law. His condition is expressly declared, in the opening of the epistle to the Romans, to be "without law [ἀνόμως]."—"For when the Gentiles, which have not the law," etc., and, "As many as have sinned without law shall perish without law; and as many as have sinned in the law shall be judged by the law."

Here the two classes are brought into sharp and vivid contrast, in the matter of their dispensational position. The Jew, under law; the Gentile, without law,—nothing can be more distinct. The Gentile was placed under government, in the person of Noah; but never under law. Should any one feel disposed to call this in question, let him produce a single line of Scripture to prove that God ever placed the Gentiles under the law. Let him search and see. It is of no possible use to argue and reason and object,—it is utterly vain to say, "We think" this or that: the question is, "What saith the Scripture?" If it says that the Gentiles were put under the law, let the passage be produced. We solemnly declare it says nothing of the kind, but the very reverse. It describes the condition and the position of the Gentile as "without law"—"having not the law."

In Acts x, we see God opening the kingdom of heaven to the Gentile; in Acts xiv. 27, we see Him opening "the door of faith" to the Gentile; in Acts xxviii. 28, we see Him sending His salvation to the Gentile: but we search in vain, from cover to cover of the blessed Book, for a passage in which He places the Gentile under the law.

We would very earnestly entreat the Christian reader to give this deeply interesting and important question his calm attention. Let him lay aside all his preconceived thoughts, and examine the matter simply in the light of holy Scripture. We are quite aware that our statements on this subject will be regarded by thousands as novel, if not actually heretical; but this does not move us, in the smallest degree. It is our one grand desire to be taught absolutely and exclusively by Scripture. The opinions, commandments, and doctrines of men have no weight whatever with us. The dogmas of the various schools of divinity must just go for what they are worth. We demand Scripture. A single line of inspiration is amply sufficient to settle this question, and close all discussion, forever. Let us be shown from the Word of God that the Gentiles were ever put under the law, and we shall at once bow; but inasmuch as we cannot find it there, we reject the notion altogether, and we would have the reader to do the same. The invariable language of Scripture, in describing the position of the Jew, is, "under law;" and, in describing the position of the Gentile, is, "without law." This is so obvious that we cannot but marvel how any reader of the Bible can fail to see it.[15]

If the reader will turn, for a few moments, to the fifteenth chapter of the Acts of the Apostles, he will see how the first attempt to put Gentile converts under the law was met by the apostles and the whole church at Jerusalem. The question was raised at Antioch; and God, in His infinite goodness and wisdom, so ordered that it should not be settled there, but that Paul and Barnabas should go up to Jerusalem and have the matter fully and freely discussed, and definitively settled by the unanimous voice of the twelve apostles and the whole church.

How we can bless our God for this! We can at once see that the decision of a local assembly, such as Antioch, even though approved by Paul and Barnabas, would not carry the same weight as that of the twelve apostles assembled in council at Jerusalem. But the Lord, blessed be His name, took care that the enemy should be completely confounded, and that the law-teachers of that day, and of every other day, should be distinctly and authoritatively taught that it was not according to His mind that Christians should be put under law, for any object whatsoever.

The subject is so deeply important that we cannot forbear quoting a few passages for the reader. We believe it will refresh both the reader and the writer to refer to the soul-stirring addresses delivered at the most remarkable and interesting council that ever sat.

"And certain men which came down from Judæa taught the brethren, 'Except ye be circumcised after the manner of Moses, ye cannot be saved.'" How awful! How terribly chilling! What a death-knell to ring in the ears of those who had been converted under Paul's splendid address in the synagogue at Antioch!—"Be it known unto you therefore, men and brethren, that *through this Man*"—without circumcision or works of law of any kind whatsoever—"is preached unto you the forgiveness of sins; and *by Him* all that believe"—irrespective altogether of circumcision—"are justified *from all things*, from which ye could not be justified by the law of Moses.... And when the Jews were gone out of the synagogue, the Gentiles besought that these words might be preached to them the next Sabbath."

Such was the glorious message sent to the Gentiles by the lips of the apostle Paul—a message of free, full, immediate, and perfect salvation—full remission of sins and perfect justification, through faith in our Lord Jesus Christ. But according to the teaching of the "certain men which came down from Judæa," all this was insufficient—Christ was not enough, without circumcision and the law of Moses. Poor Gentiles, who had never heard of circumcision or the law of Moses, must add to Christ and His glorious salvation the keeping of the whole law.

How must Paul's heart have burned within him to have the beloved Gentile converts brought under such monstrous teaching as this! He saw in it nothing short of the complete surrender of Christianity. If circumcision must be added to the cross of Christ—if the law of Moses must supplement the grace of God, then verily all was gone.

But, blessed forever be the God of all grace, He caused a noble stand to be made against such deadly teaching. When the enemy came in like a flood, the Spirit of the Lord raised up a standard against him. "When therefore Paul and Barnabas had no small dissension and disputation with them, they determined that Paul and Barnabas, and certain other of them, should go up to Jerusalem, unto the apostles and elders about this question. And being brought on their way by the church, they passed through Phenice and Samaria, declaring," not the circumcision, but "the conversion of the Gentiles; and they caused great joy unto all the brethren."

The brethren were in the current of the mind of Christ, and in sweet communion with the heart of God; and hence they rejoiced to hear of the conversion and salvation of the Gentiles. We may rest assured it would have afforded them no joy to hear of the heavy yoke of circumcision and the law of Moses being put upon the necks of those beloved disciples who had just been brought into the glorious liberty of the gospel. But to hear of their conversion to God, their salvation by Christ, their being sealed by the Holy Ghost, filled their hearts with a joy which was in lovely harmony with the mind of heaven.

"And when they were come to Jerusalem, they were received of the church, and of the apostles and elders, and they declared all things that God had done with them. But there rose up certain of the sect of the Pharisees which believed, saying that it was needful to circumcise them, and to command them to keep the law of Moses."

Who made it "needful"? Not God, surely; inasmuch as He had, in His infinite grace, opened the door of faith to them without circumcision or any command to keep the law of Moses. No; it was "certain men" who presumed to speak of such things as needful—men who have troubled the Church of God from that day to the present—men "desiring to be teachers of the law, knowing neither what they say nor whereof they affirm." Law-teachers never know what is involved in their dark and dismal teaching. They have not the most distant idea of how thoroughly hateful their teaching is to the God of all grace, the Father of mercies.

But, thanks be to God, the chapter from which We are now quoting affords the very clearest and most forcible evidence that could be given as to the divine mind on the subject. It proves, beyond all question, that it was not of God to put Gentile believers under the law.

"And the apostles and elders came together for to consider of this matter. And when there had been much disputing" (alas! how soon it began!) "Peter rose up and said unto them, Men and brethren, ye know how that a good while ago God made choice among us, that the Gentiles by my mouth should hear," not the law of Moses or circumcision, but "the word of the gospel, and believe. And God which knoweth the hearts, bare them witness, giving them the Holy Ghost, even as unto us. *And put no difference between us and them,* purifying their hearts by faith. Now therefore *why tempt ye God,* to put a yoke upon the neck of the disciples, which neither our fathers nor we were able to bear?"

Mark this, reader. The law had proved an intolerable yoke to those who were under it, that is, the Jews; and, further, it was nothing short of tempting God to put that yoke upon the neck of Gentile Christians. Would that all the law-teachers throughout the length and breadth of christendom would but open their eyes to this grand fact! and not only so, but that all the Lord's beloved people every where were given to see that it is in positive opposition to the will of God that they should be put under the law for any object whatsoever. "But," adds the blessed apostle of the circumcision, "we believe that through the grace of the Lord Jesus Christ," and not by law in any shape or form, "*we shall be saved even as they.*"

This is uncommonly fine, coming from the lips of the apostle of the circumcision. He does not say, They shall be saved even as we; but, "We shall be saved even as they." The Jew is well content to come down from his lofty dispensational position, and be saved after the pattern of the poor uncircumcised Gentile. Surely, those noble utterances must have fallen in stunning force upon the ears of the law-party. They left them, as we say, not a leg to stand upon.

"Then all the multitude kept silence, and gave audience to Barnabas and Paul, declaring what miracles and wonders God had wrought among the Gentiles by them." The inspiring Spirit has not thought good to tell us what Paul and Barnabas said on this memorable occasion, and we can see His wisdom in this. It is evidently His object to give prominence to Peter and James, as men whose words would, of necessity, have more weight with the law-teachers than those of the apostle to the Gentiles and his companion.

"And after they had held their peace, James answered, saying, Men and brethren, hearken unto me: Simeon hath declared how God at the first did visit the Gentiles," not to convert them all, but "to take out of them a people for His name. And to this agree the words of the prophets;" (here he brings an overwhelming tide of evidence from the Old Testament to bear down upon the Judaizers,) "as it is written, After this I will return, and will build again the tabernacle of David, which is fallen down; and I will build again the ruins thereof, and I will set it up: that the residue of men might seek after the Lord, and *all the Gentiles,*" without the slightest reference to circumcision or the law of Moses, but "upon whom My name is called, saith the Lord, who doeth all these things. Known unto God are all His works from the beginning of the world. Wherefore my sentence is, that we trouble not them, which from among the Gentiles are turned to God."

Here, then, we have this great question definitively settled by the Holy Ghost, the twelve apostles, and the whole Church; and we cannot but be struck with the fact that, at this most important council, none spoke more emphatically, more distinctly, or more decidedly than Peter and James; the former, the apostle of the circumcision, and the latter, the one who specially addressed the twelve tribes, and whose position and ministry were calculated to give great weight to his words, in the judgment of all who were still, in any measure, occupying Jewish or legal ground. Both these eminent apostles were clear and decided in their judgment that the Gentile converts were not to be "troubled" or burdened with the law. They proved, in their powerful addresses, that to place the Gentile Christians under the law was directly contrary to the Word, the will, and the ways of God.

Who can fail to see the marvelous wisdom of God in this? The words of Paul and Barnabas are not recorded. We are simply told that they rehearsed what things God had wrought among the Gentiles. That they should be utterly opposed to putting the Gentiles under the law was only what might be expected; but to find Peter and James so decided would carry great weight with all parties.

But if the reader would have a clear view of Paul's thoughts on the question of the law, he should study the epistle to the Galatians. There this blessed apostle, under the direct inspiration of the Holy Ghost, pours out his heart to the Gentile converts in words of glowing earnestness and commanding power. It is perfectly amazing how any one can read this wonderful epistle and yet maintain that Christians are under the law, in any way or for any purpose. Hardly has the apostle got through his brief opening address when he plunges, with his characteristic energy, into the subject with which his large, loving, though grieved and troubled heart is full to overflowing. "I marvel," he says—and well he might—"that ye are so soon removed from Him that called you into"—what? The law of Moses? Nay, but "the grace of Christ into a different gospel which is not another [ἕτερον εὐαγγέλιον ὃ οὐκ ἔστιν ἄλλο]; but there be some that trouble you, and would pervert the gospel of Christ. But though we or an angel from heaven preach any other gospel unto you than that which we have preached unto you, let him be accursed. As we said before, so say I now again, If any man preach any other gospel unto you than that ye have received, let him be accursed."

Let all law-teachers ponder these burning words. Do they seem strong and severe? Let us remember that they are the very words of God the Holy Ghost. Yes, reader, God the Holy Ghost hurls His awful anathema at any one who presumes to add the law of Moses to the gospel of Christ—any one who attempts to place Christians under the law. How is it that men are not afraid, in the face of such words, to contend for the law? Are they not afraid of coming under the solemn curse of God the Holy Ghost?

Some, however, seek to meet this question by telling us that they do not take the law for justification, but as a rule of life; but this is neither reasonable nor intelligent, inasmuch as we may very lawfully inquire, Who gave us authority to decide as to the use we are to make of the law? We are either under the law or we are not. If we are under it at all, it is not a question of how we take it, but how it takes us.

This makes all the difference. The law knows no such distinctions as those which some theologians contend for. If we are under it for any object whatsoever, we are under the curse; for it is written, "Cursed is every one that continueth not in *all* things which are written in the book of the law to do them." To say that I am born again, I am a Christian, will not meet the case at all; for what has the law to do with the question of new birth, or of Christianity? Nothing whatever. The law is addressed to man, as a responsible being. It demands perfect obedience, and pronounces its curse upon every one who fails to render it.

Moreover, it will not do to say that though we have failed to keep the law, yet Christ has fulfilled it in our room and stead. The law knows nothing of obedience by proxy. Its language is, "The man that doeth them shall live in them."

Nor is it merely on the man who fails to keep the law that the curse is pronounced, but, as if to put the principle in the clearest possible light before us, we read that "as many as are of works of law are under the curse." (See Greek.) That is, as many as take their stand on legal ground—as many as are on that principle—in a word, as many as have to do with works of law, are, of necessity, under the curse. Hence we may see at a glance the terrible inconsistency of a Christian's maintaining the idea of being under the law as a rule of life and yet not being under the curse. It is simply flying in the face of the very plainest statements of holy Scripture. Blessed be the God of all grace, the Christian is not under the curse. But why? Is it because the law has lost its power, its majesty, its dignity, its holy stringency? By no means. To say so were to blaspheme the law. To say that any "man," call him what you please—Christian, Jew, or heathen—can be under the law, can stand on that ground, and yet not be under the curse, is to say that he perfectly fulfills the law or that the law is abrogated—it is to make it null and void. Who will dare to say this? Woe be to all who do so.

But how comes it to pass that the Christian is not under the curse? Because he is not under the law. And how has he passed from under the law? Is it by another having fulfilled it in his stead? Nay; we repeat the statement, there is no such idea throughout the entire legal economy as obedience by proxy. How is it, then? Here it is, in all its moral force, fullness, and beauty: "*I* through law am dead to law, that I might live unto God."[16]

Now, if it be true, and the apostle says it is, that we are *dead to law*, how can the law, by any possibility, be a rule of life to us? It proved *only* a rule of death, curse, and condemnation to those who were under it—those who had received it by the disposition of angels. Can it prove to be aught else to us? Did the law ever produce a single cluster of living fruit, or of the fruits of righteousness, in the history of any son or daughter of Adam? Hear the apostle's reply—"When we were in the flesh," that is, when we were viewed as men in our fallen nature, "the motions of sins, which were by the law, did work in our members to bring forth fruit unto death."

It is very important for the reader to understand the real force of the expression, "in the flesh." It does not, in this passage, mean "in the body." It simply sets forth the condition of unconverted men and women responsible to keep the law. Now, in this condition, all that was or ever could be produced was "fruit unto death"—"motions of sins." No life, no righteousness, no holiness, nothing for God, nothing right at all.[17]

But where are we now, as Christians? Hear the reply—"I through law am dead to law, that I might live unto God. I am crucified with Christ: nevertheless I live; yet not I, but Christ liveth in me; and the life which I now live in the flesh" (here it means in the body) "I live"—how? By the law, as a rule of life? Not a hint at such a thing, but "by the faith of the Son of God, who loved me, and gave Himself for me."

This, and nothing else, is Christianity. Do we understand it? do we enter into it? are we in the power of it? There are two distinct evils from which we are completely delivered by the precious death of Christ, namely, legality on the one hand and licentiousness on the other. Instead of those terrible evils, it introduces us into the holy liberty of grace—liberty to serve God—liberty to "mortify our members which are upon the earth"—liberty to deny "ungodliness and worldly lusts"—liberty to "live soberly, righteously, and godly"—liberty to "keep under the body and bring it into subjection."

Yes, beloved Christian reader, let us remember this; let us deeply ponder the words, "I am crucified with Christ: nevertheless I live; yet not I, but Christ liveth in me." The old "I" dead—crucified, buried: the new "I" alive in Christ. Let us not mistake this. We know of nothing more awful, nothing more dangerous, than for the old "I" to assume the new ground; or, in other words, the glorious doctrines of Christianity taken up in the flesh—unconverted people talking of being free from the law, and turning the grace of God into lasciviousness. We must confess we would rather, a thousand times, have legality than licentiousness. It is this latter that many of us have to watch against with all possible earnestness. It is growing around us with appalling rapidity, and paving the way for that dark and desolating tide of infidelity which shall, ere long, roll over the length and breadth of christendom.

To talk of being free from the law in any way save by being dead to it, and alive to God, is not Christianity at all, but licentiousness, from which every pious soul must shrink with holy horror. If we are dead to the law, we are dead to sin also; and hence we are not to do our own will, which is only another name for sin; but the will of God, which is true practical holiness.

Further, let us ever bear in mind that if we are dead to the law, we are dead to this present evil world also, and linked with a risen, ascended, and glorified Christ. Hence, we are not of the world, even as Christ is not of the world. To contend for position in the world is to deny that we are dead to the law; for we cannot be alive to the one and dead to the other. The death of Christ has delivered us from the law, from the power of sin, from this present evil world, and from the fear of death. But then all these things hang together, and we cannot be delivered from one without being delivered from all. To assert our freedom from the law, while pursuing a course of carnality, self-indulgence, and worldliness, is one of the darkest and deadliest evils of the last days.

The Christian is called to prove, in his daily life, that grace can produce results that law could never reach. It is one of the moral glories of Christianity to enable a man to surrender self and live for others. Law never could do this. It occupied a man with himself. Under its rule, every man had to do the best he could for himself. If he tried to love his neighbor, it was to work out a righteousness for himself. Under grace, all is blessedly and gloriously reversed—self is set aside as a thing crucified, dead, and buried; the old "I" is gone, and the new "I" is before God in all the acceptability and preciousness of Christ; He is our life, our righteousness, our holiness, our object, our model, our all; He is in us and we are in Him, and our daily practical life is to be simply Christ reproduced in us by the power of the Holy Ghost. Hence, we are not only called to love our neighbor, but our enemy; and this, not to work out a righteousness, for we have become the righteousness of God in Christ: it is simply the outflow of the life which we possess—which is in us, and this life is Christ. A Christian is a man who should live Christ. He is neither a Jew "under law" nor a Gentile "without law," but "a man in Christ," standing in grace, called to the same character of obedience as that which was rendered by the Lord Jesus Himself.

We shall not pursue this subject further here, but we earnestly entreat the Christian reader to study attentively the fifteenth chapter of Acts and the epistle to the Galatians. Let him drink in the blessed teaching of these scriptures, and we feel assured he will arrive at a clear understanding of the great question of the law. He will see that the Christian is not under the law for any purpose whatsoever; that his life, his righteousness, his holiness, are on a different ground or principle altogether; that to place the Christian under law in any way is to deny the very foundations of Christianity and contradict the plainest statements of the Word. He will learn, from the third chapter of Galatians, that to put ourselves under the law is to give up Christ, to give up the Holy Ghost, to give up faith, to give up the promises.

Tremendous consequences! But there they are, plainly set forth before our eyes; and truly, when we contemplate the state of the professing church, we cannot but see how terribly those consequences are being realized.

May God the Holy Ghost open the eyes of all Christians to the truth of these things. May He lead them to study the Scriptures, and to submit themselves to their holy authority in all things. This is the special need of this our day. We do not study Scripture sufficiently; we are not governed by it; we do not see the absolute necessity of testing every thing by the light of Scripture, and rejecting all that will not stand the test; we go on with a quantity of things that have no foundation whatever in the Word—yea, that are positively opposed to it.

What must be the end of all this? We tremble to think of it. We know, blessed be God, that our Lord Jesus Christ will soon come and take His own beloved and blood-bought people home to the prepared place in the Father's house, to be forever with Himself, in the ineffable blessedness of that bright home; but what of those who shall be left behind? what of that vast mass of baptized worldly profession? These are solemn questions, which must be weighed in the immediate presence of God, in order to have the true, the divine answer. Let the reader ponder them there, in all tenderness of heart and teachableness of spirit, and the Holy Ghost will lead him to the true answer.

Having sought to set forth, from various parts of Scripture, the glorious truth that believers are not under law, but under grace, we may now pursue our study of this fifth chapter of Deuteronomy. In it we have the ten commandments, but not exactly as we have them in the twentieth chapter of Exodus. There are some characteristic touches which demand the reader's attention.

In Exodus xx, we have history; in Deuteronomy v, we have not only history, but commentary. In the latter, the lawgiver presents moral motives, and makes appeals which would be wholly out of place in the former. In the one, we have naked facts; in the other, facts and comments—facts and their practical application. In a word, there is not the slightest ground for imagining that Deuteronomy v. is intended to be a literal repetition of Exodus xx; and hence the miserable arguments which infidels ground upon their apparent divergence just crumble into dust beneath our feet. They are simply baseless, and utterly contemptible.

Let us, for instance, compare the two scriptures in reference to the subject of the Sabbath. In Exodus xx, we read, "Remember the Sabbath day, to keep it holy. Six days shalt thou labor, and do all thy work; but the seventh day is the Sabbath of the Lord thy God; in it thou shalt not do any work, thou, nor thy son, nor thy daughter, thy man-servant, nor thy maid-servant, nor thy cattle, nor thy stranger that is within thy gates: *for in six days the Lord made heaven and earth, the sea, and all that in them is,* and rested the seventh day; wherefore the Lord blessed the Sabbath day, and hallowed it."

In Deuteronomy v, we read, "Keep the Sabbath day to sanctify it, *as the Lord thy God hath commanded thee.* Six days thou shalt labor, and do all thy work; but the seventh day is the Sabbath of the Lord thy God; in it thou shalt not do any work, thou, nor thy son, nor thy daughter, nor thy man-servant, nor thy maid-servant, *nor thine ox, nor thine ass,* nor any of thy cattle, nor thy stranger that is within thy gates; that thy man-servant and thy maid-servant may rest as well as thou. *And remember that thou wast a servant in the land of Egypt, and that the Lord thy God brought thee out thence, through a mighty hand and by a stretched-out arm; therefore the Lord thy God commanded thee to keep the Sabbath day.*" (Ver. 12-15.)

Now, the reader can see at a glance the difference between the two passages. In Exodus xx, the command to keep the Sabbath is grounded on *creation*; in Deuteronomy v, it is grounded on *redemption,* without any allusion to creation at all. In short, the points of difference arise out of the distinct character of each book, and are perfectly plain to every spiritual mind.

With regard to the institution of the Sabbath, we must remember that it rests wholly upon the direct authority of the word of God. Other commandments set forth plain moral duties. Every man knows it to be morally wrong to kill or steal; but as to the observance of the Sabbath, no one could possibly recognize it as a duty had it not been distinctly appointed by divine authority. Hence its immense importance and interest. Both in our chapter and in Exodus xx. it stands side by side with all those great moral duties which are universally recognized by the human conscience.

And not only so, but we find, in various other scriptures, that the Sabbath is singled out and presented, with special prominence, as a precious link between Jehovah and Israel, a seal of His covenant with them, and a powerful test of their devotedness to Him. Every one could recognize the moral wrong of theft and murder; only those who loved Jehovah and His word would love and honor His Sabbath.

Thus, in the sixteenth chapter of Exodus, in connection with the giving of the manna, we read, "And it came to pass, that on the sixth day they gathered twice as much bread, two omers for one man; and all the rulers of the congregation came and told Moses. And he said unto them, 'This is that which the Lord hath said, To-morrow is *the rest of the holy Sabbath unto the Lord*: bake that which ye will bake to-day, and seethe that ye will seethe; and that which remaineth over lay up for you, to be kept until the morning.' ... And Moses said, 'Eat that to-day; for to-day is *a Sabbath unto the Lord*; to-day ye shall not find it in the field. Six days ye shall gather it; but on the seventh day, which is the Sabbath, in it there shall be none.' And it came to pass,"—so little were they capable of appreciating the high and holy privilege of keeping Jehovah's Sabbath—"that there went out some of the people on the seventh day for to gather, and they found none. And the Lord said unto Moses, 'How long refuse ye to keep My commandments and My laws?'" Their neglect of the Sabbath proved their moral condition to be all wrong—proved them to be astray as to all the commandments and laws of God. The Sabbath was the great touchstone—the measure and gauge of the real state of their hearts toward Jehovah. "See, for that the Lord hath *given you* the Sabbath, therefore He giveth you on the sixth day the bread of two days; abide ye every man in his place; let no man go out of his place on the seventh day. So the people rested on the seventh day." They found rest and food on the holy Sabbath.

Again, at the close of chapter xxxi, we have a very remarkable passage in proof of the importance and interest attaching to the Sabbath in the mind of Jehovah. A full description of the tabernacle and its furniture had been given to Moses, and he was about to receive the two tables of testimony from the hand of Jehovah; but, as if to prove the prominent place which the holy Sabbath held in the divine mind, we read, "And the Lord spake unto Moses, saying, 'Speak thou also unto the children of Israel, saying, Verily My Sabbaths ye shall keep: *for it is a sign between Me and you throughout your generations*; that ye may know that I am the Lord that doth sanctify you. Ye shall keep the Sabbath therefore; for it is holy unto you: every one that defileth it shall surely be put to death; for whosoever doeth any work therein, that soul shall be cut off from among his people. Six days may work be done; but in the seventh is the Sabbath of rest, holy to the Lord: whosoever doeth any work in the Sabbath day, he shall surely be put to death. Wherefore the children of Israel shall keep the Sabbath, to observe the Sabbath throughout their generations, *for a perpetual covenant. It is a sign between Me and the children of Israel forever*: for in six days the Lord made heaven and earth, and on the seventh day He rested, and was refreshed." (Exod. xxxi. 12-17.)

Now, this is a very important passage. It proves very distinctly the abiding character of the Sabbath. The terms in which it is spoken of are quite sufficient to show that it was no mere temporary institution.—"A sign between Me and you throughout your generations." — "A perpetual covenant." — "A sign forever."

Let the reader carefully mark these words. They prove, beyond all question, first, that the Sabbath was for Israel; secondly, that the Sabbath is, in the mind of God, a permanent institution. It is needful to bear these things in mind in order to avoid all vagueness of thought and looseness of expression on this deeply interesting subject.

The Sabbath was distinctly and exclusively for the Jewish nation. It is spoken of emphatically as a sign between Jehovah and His people Israel. There is not the most remote hint of its being intended for the Gentiles. We shall see, further on, that it is a lovely type of the times of the restitution of all things, of which God has spoken by the mouth of all His holy prophets since the world began; but this in no wise touches the fact of its being an exclusively Jewish institution. There is not so much as a single sentence of Scripture to show that the Sabbath had any reference whatever to the Gentiles.

Some would teach us that inasmuch as we read of the Sabbath day in the second chapter of Genesis, it must, of necessity, have a wider range than the Jewish nation. But let us turn to the passage and see what it says. — "And on the seventh day God ended His work which He had made; and He rested on the seventh day from all His work which He had made. And God blessed the seventh day, and sanctified it; because that in it He had rested from all His work which God created and made."

This is simple enough. There is no mention here of man at all. We are not told that man rested on the seventh day. Men may infer, conclude, or imagine that he did so; but the second of Genesis says nothing about it. And not only so, but we look in vain for any allusion to the Sabbath throughout the entire book of Genesis. The very first notice we have of the Sabbath in connection with man, is in the sixteenth of Exodus, a passage already quoted; and there we see, most distinctly, that it was given to Israel, as a people in recognized covenant-relationship with Jehovah. That they did not understand or appreciate it is perfectly plain; that they never entered into it is equally plain, according to psalm xcv. and Hebrews iv. But we are now speaking of what it was in the mind of God; and He tells us it was a sign between Him and His people Israel, and a powerful test of their moral condition and of the state of their heart as to Him. It was not only an integral part of the law, as given by Moses to the congregation of Israel, but it is specially referred to and singled out, again and again, as an institution holding a very peculiar place in the mind of God.

Thus, in the book of the prophet Isaiah, we read, "Blessed is the man that doeth this, and the son of man that layeth hold on it; that keepeth the Sabbath from polluting it, and keepeth his hand from doing any evil. Neither let the son of the stranger, that hath joined himself to the Lord, speak, saying, The Lord hath utterly separated me from His people; neither let the eunuch say, Behold I am a dry tree. For thus saith the Lord unto the eunuchs that keep My Sabbaths, and choose the things that please Me, and take hold of My covenant; even unto them will I give in Mine house, and within My walls, a place and a name better than of sons and of daughters: I will give them an everlasting name that shall not be cut off. Also the sons of the stranger," (here, of course, viewed in connection with Israel, as in Numbers xv. and other scriptures,) "that join themselves to the Lord, to serve Him, and to love the name of the Lord, to be His servants, every one that keepeth the Sabbath from polluting it, and taketh hold of My covenant; even them will I bring to My holy mountain, and make them joyful in My house of prayer: their burnt-offerings and their sacrifices shall be accepted upon Mine altar; for Mine house shall be called a house of prayer for all people."

Again, "If thou turn away thy foot from the Sabbath, from doing thy pleasure on My holy day; and call the Sabbath a delight, the holy of the Lord, honorable; and shalt honor Him, not doing thine own ways, nor finding thine own pleasure, nor speaking thine own words: then shalt thou delight thyself in the Lord; and I will cause thee to ride upon the high places of the earth, and feed thee with the heritage of Jacob thy father; for the mouth of the Lord hath spoken it." (Isaiah lviii. 13, 14.)

The foregoing quotations are amply sufficient to show the place which the Sabbath holds in the mind of God. It is needless to multiply passages, but there is just one to which we must refer the reader, in connection with our present subject, namely, Leviticus xxiii.—"And the Lord spake unto Moses, saying, 'Speak unto the children of Israel, and say unto them, Concerning the feasts of the Lord, which ye shall proclaim to be holy convocations, even these are My feasts. Six days shall work be done; but the seventh day is the Sabbath of rest, a holy convocation; ye shall do no work therein: it is the Sabbath of the Lord in all your dwellings." (Ver. 1-3.)

Here it stands at the head of all the feasts given in this marvelous chapter, in which we have foreshadowed the entire history of God's dealings with His people Israel. The Sabbath is the expression of God's eternal rest, into which it is His purpose yet to bring His people, when all their toils and sorrows, their trials and tribulations, shall have passed away—that blessed "Sabbath-keeping [σαββατισμός]" which "remaineth for the people of God." In various ways He sought to keep this glorious rest before the hearts of His people; the seventh day, the seventh year, the year of jubilee—all these lovely sabbatic seasons were designed to set forth that blessed time when Israel shall be gathered back to their own beloved land, when the Sabbath shall be kept, in all its deep, divine blessedness, as it never has been kept yet.

And this leads us, naturally, to the second point in connection with the Sabbath, namely, its permanency. This is plainly proved by such expressions as, "perpetual," "a sign forever," "throughout your generations." Such words would never be applied to any merely temporary institution. True it is, alas! that Israel never really kept the Sabbath according to God; they never understood its meaning, never entered into its blessedness, never drank into its spirit. They made it a badge of their own righteousness; they boasted in it as a national institution, and used it for self-exaltation; but they never celebrated it in communion with God.

We speak of the nation as a whole. We doubt not there were precious souls who, in secret, enjoyed the Sabbath, and entered into the thoughts of God about it; but as a nation, Israel never kept the Sabbath according to God. Hear what Isaiah says, "Bring no more vain oblations; incense is an abomination unto Me; the new moons and *Sabbaths*, the calling of assemblies, I cannot away with; it is iniquity, even the solemn meeting." (Chap. i. 13.)

Here we see that the precious and beautiful institution of the Sabbath which God had given as a sign of His covenant with His people, had, in their hands, become a positive abomination, perfectly intolerable to Him. And when we open the pages of the New Testament, we find the leaders and heads of the Jewish people continually at issue with our Lord Jesus Christ in reference to the Sabbath. Look, for example, at the opening verses of Luke vi.—"And it came to pass on the second Sabbath after the first, that He went through the corn-fields; and His disciples plucked the ears of corn, and did eat, rubbing them in their hands. And certain of the Pharisees said unto them, 'Why do ye that which is not lawful to do on the Sabbath days?' And Jesus answering them said, 'Have ye not read so much as this, what David did, when himself was a hungred, and they which were with him; how he went into the house of God, and did take and eat the show-bread, and gave also to them that were with him; which it is not lawful to eat, but for the priests alone?' And He said unto them that the Son of Man is Lord also of the Sabbath."

And again, we read, "It came to pass also on another Sabbath, that He entered into the synagogue and taught; and there was a man whose right hand was withered. And the scribes and Pharisees *watched Him*, whether He would heal on the Sabbath day, that they might find an accusation against

Him." (Only conceive, an accusation for healing a poor, afflicted fellow-mortal!) "But He knew their thoughts"—yes, He read their hearts through to their very centre, "and said to the man which had the withered hand, 'Rise up, and stand forth in the midst.' And he arose and stood forth. Then said Jesus unto them, 'I will ask you one thing, Is it lawful on the Sabbath day to do good, or to do evil? to save life, or to destroy it?' And looking round about upon them all, He said unto the man, 'Stretch forth thine hand.' And he did so; and his hand was restored whole as the other. And they were filled with madness; and communed one with another what they might do to Jesus."

What an insight we have here into the hollowness and worthlessness of man's Sabbath-keeping! Those religious guides would rather let the disciples starve than have *their* Sabbath interfered with; they would allow the man to carry his withered hand to the grave rather than have him healed on *their* Sabbath. Alas! alas! it was indeed their Sabbath, and not God's. His rest could never comport with hunger and withered hands. They had never read aright the record of David's act in eating the show-bread. They did not understand that legal institutions must give way in the presence of divine grace meeting human need. Grace rises, in its magnificence, above all legal barriers, and faith rejoices in its lustre; but mere religiousness is offended by the activities of grace and the boldness of faith. The Pharisees did not see that the man with the withered hand was a striking commentary upon the nation's moral condition, a living proof of the fact that they were far away from God. If they were as they ought to be, there would have been no withered hands to heal; but they were not, and hence their Sabbath was an empty formality—a powerless, worthless ordinance—a hideous anomaly, hateful to God, and utterly inconsistent with the condition of man.

Take another instance, in Luke xiii.—"And He was teaching in one of the synagogues on the Sabbath." (Assuredly, the Sabbath was no day of rest to Him.) "And, behold, there was a woman which had a spirit of infirmity eighteen years, and was bowed together, and could in no wise lift up herself. And when Jesus saw her, He called her to Him, and said unto her, 'Woman, thou art loosed from thine infirmity.' And He laid His hands on her, and *immediately she was made straight, and glorified God.*" Beautiful illustration of the work of grace in the soul, and the practical result, in every case. All on whom Christ lays His blessed hands are "immediately made straight," and enabled to glorify God.

But man's Sabbath was touched. "The ruler of the synagogue answered with indignation, because that Jesus had healed on the Sabbath day." He was indignant at the gracious work of healing, though quite indifferent as to the humiliating case of infirmity; and he "said unto the people, 'There are six days in which men ought to work: in them therefore come and be healed, and not on the Sabbath day.'" How little this poor hollow religionist knew that he was in the very presence of the Lord of the true Sabbath! How utterly insensible he was to the moral inconsistency of attempting to keep a Sabbath while man's condition called aloud for divine work! "The Lord then answered him, and said, 'Thou hypocrite, doth not each one of you on the Sabbath loose his ox or his ass from the stall, and lead him away to watering? And ought not this woman, being a daughter of Abraham, whom Satan hath bound, lo, these eighteen years, be loosed from this bond on the Sabbath day?'"

What a withering rebuke! What an opening up of the hollowness and utter wretchedness of their whole system of Judaism! Only think of the glaring incongruity of a Sabbath and a daughter of Abraham bound by the cruel hand of Satan for eighteen years! There is nothing in all this world so blinding to the mind, so hardening to the heart, so deadening to the conscience, so demoralizing to the whole being, as religion without Christ. Its deceiving and degrading power can only be thoroughly judged in the light of the divine presence. For aught that the ruler of the synagogue cared, that poor woman might have gone on to the end of her days bowed together and unable to lift up herself. He would have been well content to let her go on as a sad witness of the power of Satan, provided he could keep his Sabbath. His religious indignation was excited, not by the power of Satan as seen in the woman's condition, but by the power of Christ as seen in her complete deliverance.

But the Lord gave him his answer. "And when He had said these things, all His adversaries were ashamed" (as well they might); "and all the people rejoiced for all the glorious things that were done by Him." What a striking contrast! The advocates of a powerless, heartless, worthless religion unmasked and covered with shame and confusion on the one hand, and on the other, all the people rejoicing in the glorious actings of the Son of God, who had come into their midst to deliver them from the crushing power of Satan, and fill their hearts with the joy of God's salvation, and their mouths with His praise!

We must now ask the reader to turn to the gospel of John for further illustration of our subject. We earnestly desire that this vexed question of the Sabbath should be thoroughly examined in the light of Scripture. We are convinced that there is very much more involved in it than many professing Christians are aware.

At the opening of John v, we are introduced to a scene strikingly indicative of Israel's condition. We do not here attempt to go fully into the passage, we merely refer to it in connection with the subject before us.

The pool of Bethesda, or "house of mercy"—while it was undoubtedly the expression of the mercy of God toward His people—afforded abundant evidence of the miserable condition of man in general, and of Israel in particular. Its five porches were thronged with "a great multitude of impotent folk, of blind, halt, withered, waiting for the moving of the water." What a sample of the whole human family, and of the nation of Israel! What a striking illustration of their moral and spiritual condition as viewed from a divine stand-point. "Blind, halt, withered"—such is man's real state, if he only knew it.

But there was one man in the midst of this impotent throng so far gone—so feeble and helpless, that the pool of Bethesda could not meet his case. "A certain man was there, which had an infirmity thirty and eight years. When Jesus saw him lie, and knew that he had been now a long time in that case, He saith unto him, 'Wilt thou *be made* whole?'" What grace and power in this question! It went far beyond the utmost stretch of the impotent man's thoughts. He thought only of human help, or of his own ability to get into the pool. He knew not that the speaker was above and beyond the pool, with its occasional movement—beyond angelic ministry— beyond all human help and effort, the Possessor of all power in heaven and on earth. "The impotent man answered Him, 'Sir, I have no man, when the water is troubled, to put me into the pool; but while I am coming, another steppeth down before me.'" What a true picture of all those who are seeking salvation by ordinances! Each one doing the best he could for himself. No care for others. No thought of helping them. "Jesus saith unto him, 'Rise, take up thy bed, and walk.' And immediately the man was made whole, and took up his bed, and walked: *and on the same day was the Sabbath.*"

Here we have man's Sabbath again. It certainly was not God's Sabbath. The miserable multitude gathered around the pool proved that God's full rest had not yet come—that His glorious antitype of the Sabbath had not yet dawned on this sin-stricken earth. When that bright day comes, there will be no blind, halt, and withered folk thronging the porches of the pool of Bethesda. God's Sabbath and human misery are wholly incompatible.

But it was man's Sabbath. It was no longer the seal of Jehovah's covenant with the seed of Abraham (as it was once, and will be again), but the badge of man's self-righteousness. "The Jews therefore said unto him that was cured, 'It is the Sabbath day; it is not lawful for thee to carry thy bed.'" It was no doubt lawful enough for him to lie on that bed, week after week, month after month, year after year, while they were going on with their empty, worthless, hollow attempt at Sabbath-keeping. If they had had one ray of spiritual light, they would have seen the flagrant inconsistency of attempting to maintain their traditionary notions respecting the Sabbath in the presence of human misery, disease, and degradation. But they were utterly blind, and hence when the glorious fruits of Christ's ministry were being displayed, they had the temerity to pronounce them unlawful.

Nor this only; but "therefore did the Jews persecute Jesus, and sought to slay Him, because He had done these things on the Sabbath day." What a spectacle! Religious people—yea, the leaders and teachers of religion—the guides of the professed people of God, seeking to slay the Lord of the Sabbath because He had made a man every whit whole on the Sabbath day!

But mark our Lord's reply.—"My Father *worketh* hitherto, and I work." This brief but comprehensive statement gives us the root of the whole matter. It opens up to us the real condition of mankind in general, and of Israel in particular; and, in the most affecting manner, presents the grand secret of our Lord's life and ministry. Blessed be His name, He had not come into this world to rest. How could He rest? how could He keep a Sabbath in the midst of human need and misery? Ought not that impotent, blind, halt, and withered multitude which thronged the porches of the pool of Bethesda have taught "the Jews" the folly of their notions about the Sabbath? For what was that multitude but a sample of the condition of the nation of Israel, and of the whole human family? and how could divine love rest in the midst of such a condition of things? Utterly impossible. Love can only be a worker in a scene of sin and sorrow. From the moment of man's fall, the Father had been working; then the Son appeared to carry on the work; and now, the Holy Ghost is working. Work, and not rest, is the divine order in a world like this. "There remaineth therefore a rest to the people of God."

The blessed Lord Jesus went about doing good on the Sabbath day as well as on every other day; and finally, having accomplished the glorious work of redemption, He spent the Sabbath in the grave, and rose on the first day of the week, as the First-begotten from the dead, and Head of the new creation, in which all things are of God, and to which, we may surely add, the question of "days and months and times and years" can have no possible application. No one who thoroughly understands the meaning of death and resurrection could sanction for a moment the observance of days. The death of Christ put an end to all that order of things, and His resurrection introduces us into another sphere entirely, where it is our high privilege to walk in the light and power of those eternal realities which are ours in Christ, and which stand in vivid contrast with the superstitious observances of a carnal and worldly religiousness.

But here we approach a very interesting point in our subject, namely, the difference between the Sabbath and the Lord's day, or first day of the week. These two are often confounded. We frequently hear, from the lips of truly pious people, the phrase, "Christian Sabbath," an expression no where to be found in the New Testament. It may be that some who make use of it mean a right thing; but we should not only mean right, but also seek to express ourselves according to the teaching of holy Scripture.

We are persuaded that the enemy of God and of His Christ has had a great deal more to do with the conventionalisms of christendom than many of us are aware; and this it is which makes the matter so very serious. The reader may perhaps feel disposed to pronounce it mere hair-splitting to find any fault with the term "Christian Sabbath;" but he may rest assured it is nothing of the sort: on the contrary, if he will only calmly examine the matter in the light of the New Testament, he will find that it involves questions not only interesting, but also weighty and important. It is a common saying, "There is nothing in a name;" but in the matter now before us, there is much in a name.

We have already remarked that our Lord spent the Sabbath in the grave. Is not this a telling and deeply significant fact? We cannot doubt it. We read in it, at least, the setting aside of the old condition of things, and the utter impossibility of keeping a Sabbath in a world of sin and death. Love could not rest in a world like this; it could only labor and die. This is the inscription which we read on the tomb where the Lord of the Sabbath lay buried.

But what of the first day of the week? Is not it the Sabbath on a new footing—the Christian Sabbath? It is never so called in the New Testament. There is not so much as a hint of any thing of the kind. If we look through the Acts of the Apostles, we shall find the two days spoken of in the most distinct way. On the Sabbath, we find the Jews assembled in their synagogues for the reading of the law and the prophets: on the first day of the week, we find the Christians assembled to break bread. The two days were as distinct as Judaism and Christianity; nor is there so much as a shadow of Scripture foundation for the idea that the Sabbath was merged in the first day of the week. Where is the slightest authority for the assertion that the Sabbath is changed from the seventh day to the eighth, or first, day of the week? Surely, if there be any, nothing is easier than to produce it; but there is absolutely none.

And be it remembered that the Sabbath is not merely *a* seventh day, but *the* seventh day. It is well to note this, inasmuch as some entertain the idea that provided a seventh portion of time be given to rest and the public ordinances of religion, it is quite sufficient, and it does not matter what you call it; and thus different nations and different religious systems have their Sabbath day. But this can never satisfy any one who desires to be taught exclusively by Scripture. The Sabbath of Eden was *the* seventh day: the Sabbath for Israel was *the* seventh day. But the eighth day leads our thoughts onward into eternity; and, in the New Testament, it is called "the first day of the week," as indicating the beginning: of that new order of things of which the cross is the imperishable foundation, and a risen Christ the glorious Head and Centre. To call this day the "Christian Sabbath" is simply to confound things earthly and heavenly; it is to bring the Christian down from his elevated position as associated with a risen and glorified Head in the heavens, and occupy him with the superstitious observance of days, the very thing which made the blessed apostle stand in doubt of the assemblies in Galatia.

In short, the more deeply we ponder the phrase "Christian Sabbath," the more we are convinced that its tendency is, like many other formularies of christendom, to rob the Christian of all those grand distinctive truths of the New Testament which mark off the Church of God from all that went before and all that is to follow after. The Church, though on the earth, is not of this world, even as Christ is not of this world. It is heavenly in its origin, heavenly in its character, heavenly in its principles, walk, and hope. It stands between the cross and the glory. The boundaries of its existence on earth are, the day of Pentecost, when the Holy Ghost came down to form it, and the coming of Christ to receive it to Himself.

Nothing can be more strongly marked than this; and hence, for any one to attempt to enjoin upon the Church of God the legal or superstitious observance of "days and months and times and years," is to falsify the entire Christian position, mar the integrity of divine revelation, and rob the Christian of the place and portion which belong to him through the infinite grace of God and the accomplished atonement of Christ.

Does the reader deem this statement unwarrantably strong? If so, let him ponder the following splendid passage from Paul's epistle to the Colossians—a passage which ought to be written in letters of gold: "As ye have therefore received Christ Jesus the Lord, so walk ye in Him; rooted and built up in Him, and stablished in the faith, as ye have been taught, abounding therein with thanksgiving. Beware lest any man spoil [or make a prey of] you through *philosophy and vain deceit*"—mark the combination! not very flattering to philosophy—"after the tradition of men, after the rudiments of the world, and not after Christ. For in Him dwelleth *all the fullness of the Godhead* [Θεότης, deity] bodily. And ye are complete in Him, which is the head of all principality and power." What more can we possibly want? "In whom also ye are circumcised with the circumcision *made without hands*, in putting off the body of the sins of the flesh by the circumcision of Christ: buried with Him in baptism, wherein also ye are risen with Him through the faith of the operation of God, who hath raised Him from the dead. And you, being dead in your sins and the uncircumcision of your flesh, hath He quickened together with Him, *having forgiven you all trespasses*; blotting out the handwriting of ordinances that was against us, which was contrary to us, and took it out of the way, nailing it to His cross; and having spoiled principalities and powers, He made a show of them openly, triumphing over them in it."

Magnificent victory! A victory gained single-handed—gained for us! Universal and eternal homage to His peerless name! What remains? "Let no man *therefore* judge you in meat, or in drink, or in respect of a holy day, or of the new moon, or of the Sabbath: which are a shadow of things to come; but the body is of Christ."

What can one who is complete and accepted in a risen and glorified Christ have to do with meats, drinks, or holy days? what can philosophy, tradition, or human religiousness do for him? What can passing shadows add to one who has grasped, by faith, the eternal substance? Surely nothing; and hence the blessed apostle proceeds—"Let no man beguile you of your reward, in a voluntary humility, and worshiping of angels, intruding into those things which he hath not seen, vainly puffed up by his fleshly mind, and *not holding the Head*, from which all the body by joints and bands having nourishment ministered, and knit together, increaseth with the increase of God. Wherefore *if ye be dead with Christ* from the rudiments of the world, why, *as though living in the world*, are ye subject to ordinances, [such as,] 'Touch not [this],' 'Taste not [that],' 'Handle not [the other]'; which all are to perish with the using; after the commandments and doctrines of men? Which things have indeed a show of wisdom in will-worship, and humility, and neglecting of the body; not in any honor to the satisfying of the flesh;" that is, not giving the measure of honor to the body which is due to it as God's vessel, but puffing up the flesh with religious pride, fed by a hollow and worthless sanctimoniousness. (Col. ii. 6-23.)

We do not dare to offer any apology for this lengthened quotation. An apology for quoting Scripture! Far be the thought! It is not possible for any one to understand this marvelous passage and not have a complete settlement, not only of the Sabbath question, but also of that entire system of things with which this question stands connected. The Christian who understands his position, is done forever with all questions of meats and drinks, days and months and times and years. He knows nothing of holy seasons and holy places. He is dead with Christ from the rudiments of the world, and as such, is delivered from all the ordinances of a traditionary religion. He belongs to heaven, where new moons, holy days, and Sabbaths have no place. He is in the new creation, where all things are of God; and hence he can see no moral force in such words as "Touch not, taste not, handle not." They have no possible application to him. He lives in a region where the clouds, vapors, and mists of monasticism and asceticism are never seen. He has given up all the worthless forms of mere fleshly pietism, and got, in exchange, the solid realities of Christian life. His ear has been opened to hear, and his heart to understand, the powerful exhortation of the inspired apostle, "If ye then be risen with Christ, seek those things which are above, where Christ sitteth on the right hand of God. Set your affection on things above, not on things on the earth. For *ye are dead*, and your life is hid with Christ in God. When Christ, our life, shall appear, then shall ye also appear with Him in glory. Mortify therefore your members which are upon the earth."

Here we have unfolded before our eyes some of the glories of true, practical, vital Christianity, in striking contrast with all the barren and dreary forms of carnal and worldly religiousness. Christian life does not consist in the observance of certain rules, commandments, or traditions of men. It is a divine reality. It is Christ in the heart, and Christ reproduced in the daily life, by the power of the Holy Ghost. It is the new man, formed on the model of Christ Himself, and displaying itself in all the most minute details of our daily history—in the family, in the business, in all our intercourse with our fellow-men, in our temper, spirit, style, deportment, all. It is not a matter of mere profession, or of dogma, or of opinion, or of sentiment; it is an unmistakable, living reality. It is the kingdom of God, set up in the heart, asserting its blessed sway over the whole moral being, and shedding its genial influence upon the entire sphere in which we are called to move from day to day. It is the Christian walking in the blessed footsteps of Him who went about doing good; meeting, so far as in him lies, every form of human need; living not for himself, but for others; finding his delight in serving and giving; ready to soothe and sympathize wherever he finds a crushed spirit or a bereaved and desolate heart.

This is Christianity. And oh, how it differs from all the forms in which legality and superstition clothe themselves! How different from the unintelligent and unmeaning observance of days and months and times and years, abstaining from meats, forbidding to marry, and such like! How different from the vaporings of the mystic, the gloom of the ascetic, and the austerities of the monk! How totally different from all these! Yes, reader; and we may add, how different from the unsightly union of high profession and low practice—lofty truths held in the intellect, professed, taught, and discussed, and worldliness, self-indulgence, and unsubduedness! The Christianity of the New Testament differs alike from all these things. It is the divine, the heavenly, and the spiritual, displayed amid the human, the earthly, and the natural. May it be the holy purpose of the writer and the reader of these lines to be satisfied with nothing short of that morally glorious Christianity revealed in the pages of the New Testament.

It is needless, we trust, to add more on the question of the Sabbath. If the reader has at all seized the import of those scriptures which have passed before us, he will have little difficulty in seeing the place which the Sabbath holds in the dispensational ways of God. He will see that it has direct reference to Israel and the earth—that it was a sign of the covenant between Jehovah and His earthly people, and a powerful test of their moral condition.

Furthermore, he will see that Israel never really kept the Sabbath, never understood its import, never appreciated its value. This was made manifest in the life, ministry, and death of our Lord Jesus Christ; who performed many of His works of healing on the Sabbath day, and, at the end, spent that day in the tomb.

Finally, he will clearly understand the difference between the Jewish Sabbath and the first day of the week, or the Lord's day; that the latter is never once called the Sabbath in the New Testament, but on the contrary, is constantly presented in its own proper distinctness: it is not the Sabbath changed or transferred, but a new day altogether, having its own special basis and its own peculiar range of thought, leaving the Sabbath wholly untouched, as a suspended institution, to be resumed by and by, when the seed of Abraham shall be restored to their own land. (See Ezek. xlvi. 1, 12.)

But we cannot happily turn from this interesting subject without a few words on the place assigned, in the New Testament, to the Lord's day, or first day of the week. Though it is not the Sabbath; and though it has nothing to do with holy days, or new moons, or "days and months and times and years;" yet it has its own unique place in Christianity, as is evident from manifold passages in the scriptures of the New Testament.

Our Lord rose from the dead on that day; He met His disciples again and again on that day; the apostle and the brethren at Troas came together to break bread on that day (Acts xx. 7.); the apostle instructs the Corinthians, and all that in every place call on the name of our Lord Jesus Christ, to lay by their offerings on that day; thus teaching us, distinctly, that the first day of the week was *the* special day for the Lord's people to assemble for the Lord's supper, and the worship, communion, and ministry connected with that most precious institution. The blessed apostle John expressly tells us that he was in the Spirit on that day, and received that marvelous revelation which closes the Divine Volume.[18]

Thus, then, we have a body of Scripture evidence before us amply sufficient to prove to every pious mind that the Lord's day must not be reduced to the level of ordinary days. It is, to the true Christian, neither the Jewish Sabbath on the one hand, nor the Gentile Sunday on the other; but the Lord's day, on which His people gladly and thankfully assemble around His table, to keep that precious feast by which they show forth His death until He come.

Now, it is needless to say that there is not a shade of legal bondage or of superstition connected with the first day of the week. To say so, or to think so, would be to deny the entire circle of truths with which that day stands connected. We have no direct commandment respecting the observance of the day, but the passages already referred to are amply sufficient for every spiritual mind; and further, we may say that the instincts of the divine nature would lead every true Christian to honor and love the Lord's day, and to set it apart, in the most reverent manner, for the worship and service of God. The very thought of any one professing to love Christ engaging in business or unnecessary traveling on the Lord's day, would, in our judgment, be revolting to every pious feeling. We believe it to be a hallowed privilege to retire, as much as possible, from all the distractions of natural things, and to devote the hours of the Lord's day to Himself and to His service.

It will perhaps be said that the Christian ought to devote every day to the Lord. Most surely; we are the Lord's, in the very fullest and highest sense. All we have and all we are belongs to Him; this we fully, gladly own. We are called to do every thing in His name and to His glory. It is our high privilege to buy and sell, eat and drink, yea, to carry on all our business, under His eye, and in the fear and love of His holy name. We should not put our hand to any thing, on any day in the week, on which we could not, with the fullest confidence, ask the Lord's blessing.

All this is most fully admitted. Every true Christian joyfully owns it. But, at the same time, we deem it impossible to read the New Testament and not see that the Lord's day gets a unique place; that it is marked off for us, in the most distinct way; that it has a significance and an importance which cannot, with justice, be claimed for any other day in the week. Indeed, so fully are we convinced of the truth of all this, that even though it were not the law of England that the Lord's day should be observed, we should deem it to be both our sacred duty and holy privilege to abstain from all business engagements, save such as were absolutely unavoidable.

Thanks be to God, it is the law of England that the Lord's day should be observed. This is a signal mercy to all who love the day for the Lord's sake. We cannot but own His great goodness in having wrested the day from the covetous grasp of the world, and bestowed it upon His people and His servants to be devoted to His worship and to His work.

What a boon is the Lord's day, with its profound retirement from worldly things! What should we do without it? What a blessed break in upon the week's toil! How refreshing its exercises to the spiritual mind! How precious the assembly around the Lord's table to remember Him, to show forth His death, and celebrate His praise! How delightful the varied services of the Lord's day, whether those of the evangelist, the pastor, the teacher, the Sunday-school worker, or the tract distributor! What human language can adequately set forth the value and interest of all these things? True it is that the Lord's day is any thing but a day of bodily rest to His servants; indeed, they are often more fatigued on that day than on any other day of the week. But oh! it is a blessed fatigue—a delightful fatigue—a fatigue which will meet its bright reward in the rest that remains for the people of God.

Once more, then, beloved Christian reader, let us lift up our hearts in a note of praise to our God for the blessed boon of the Lord's day. May He continue it to His Church until He come. May He countervail, by His almighty power, every effort of the infidel and the atheist to remove the barriers which English law has erected around the Lord's day. Truly, it will be a sad day for England when those barriers are removed.

It may perhaps be said by some that the Jewish Sabbath is done away, and is therefore no longer binding. A large number of professing Christians have taken this ground, and pleaded for the opening of the parks and places of public recreation on the Sunday. Alas! it is easily seen where such people are drifting to, and what they are seeking. They would set aside the law, in order to procure a license for fleshly indulgence. They do not understand that the only way in which any one can be free from the law is by being dead to it; and if dead to the law, we are also, of blessed necessity, dead to sin and dead to the world.

This makes it a different matter altogether. The Christian is, thank God, free from the law; but if he is, it is not that he may amuse and indulge himself, on the Lord's day or any other day, but that he may live to God. "I through law am dead to law, that I might live unto God." This is Christian ground, and it can only be occupied by those who are truly born of God. The world cannot understand it; neither can they understand the holy privileges and spiritual exercises of the Lord's day.

All this is true; but, at the same time, we are thoroughly convinced that were England to remove the barriers which surround the Lord's day, it would afford a melancholy proof of her abandonment of that profession of religion which has so long characterized her as a nation, and of her drifting away in the direction of infidelity and atheism. We must not lose sight of the weighty fact that England has taken the ground of being a Christian nation—a nation professing to be governed by the Word of God. She is therefore much more responsible than those nations wrapped in the dark shades of heathenism. We believe that nations, like individuals, will be held responsible for the profession they make; and hence those nations which profess and call themselves Christian shall be judged, not merely by the light of creation, nor by the law of Moses, but by the full-orbed light of that Christianity which they profess—by all the truth contained within the covers of that blessed book which they possess, and in which they make their boast. The heathen shall be judged on the ground of creation; the Jew, on the ground of the law; the nominal Christian, on the ground of the truth of Christianity.

Now this grave fact renders the position of England, and all other professing Christian nations, most serious. God will most assuredly deal with them on the ground of their profession. It is of no use to say they do not understand what they profess; for why profess what they do not understand and believe? The fact is, they profess to understand and believe; and by this fact they shall be judged. They make their boast in this familiar sentence, that "the Bible, and the Bible alone, is the religion of Protestants."

If this be so, how solemn is the thought of England judged by the standard of an open Bible! What will be her judgment?—what her end? Let all whom it may concern ponder the appalling answer.

We must now turn from the deeply interesting subject of the Sabbath and the Lord's day, and draw this section to a close by quoting for the reader the remarkable paragraph with which our chapter ends. It does not call for any lengthened comment, but we deem it profitable, in these "Notes on Deuteronomy," to furnish the reader with very full quotations from the book itself, in order that he may have before him the very words of the Holy Ghost, without even the trouble of laying aside the volume which he holds in his hand.

Having laid before the people the ten commandments, the lawgiver proceeds to remind them of the solemn circumstances which accompanied the giving of the law, together with their own feelings and utterances on the occasion.

"These words the Lord spake unto all your assembly in the mount out of the midst of the fire, of the cloud, and of the thick darkness, with a great voice; and He added no more. And He wrote them in two tables of stone, and delivered them unto me. And it came to pass, when ye heard the voice out of the midst of the darkness, (for the mountain did burn with fire,) that ye came near unto me, even all the heads of your tribes, and your elders; and ye said, 'Behold, the Lord our God hath showed us His glory and His greatness, and we have heard His voice out of the midst of the fire: we have seen this day that God doth talk with man, and he liveth. Now therefore why should we die? for this great fire will consume us: if we hear the voice of the Lord our God any more, then we shall die. For who is there of all flesh, that hath heard the voice of the living God speaking out of the midst of the fire, as we have, and lived? Go thou near, and hear all that the Lord our God shall say; and speak thou unto us all that the Lord our God shall speak unto thee, and *we will hear it and do it.*' And the Lord heard the voice of your words, when ye spake unto me; and the Lord said unto me, 'I have heard the voice of the words of this people, which they have spoken unto thee: they have well said all that they have spoken. O that there were such a heart in them, that they would fear Me, and keep *all* My commandments *always*, that it might be well with them, and with their children forever! Go say to them, Get you into your tents again. But as for thee, stand thou here by Me, and I will speak unto thee all the commandments, and the statutes, and the judgments, which thou shalt teach them, that they may do them in the land which I give them to possess it.' Ye shall observe to do therefore as the Lord your God hath commanded you: ye shall not turn aside either to the right hand or to the left. Ye shall walk in *all the ways* which the Lord your God hath commanded you, that ye may live, and that it may be well with you, and that ye may prolong your days in the land which ye shall possess."

Here the grand principle of the book of Deuteronomy shines out with uncommon lustre. It is embodied in those touching and forcible words which form the very heart's core of the splendid passage just quoted. —"O that there were *such a heart in them, that they would fear Me,* and keep all My commandments always, that it might be well with them, and with their children forever!"

Precious words! They set before us, most blessedly, the secret spring of that life which we, as Christians, are called to live from day to day—the life of simple, implicit, and unqualified obedience, namely, a heart fearing the Lord—fearing Him, not in a servile spirit, but with all that deep, true, adoring love which the Holy Ghost sheds abroad in our hearts. It is this that delights the heart of our loving Father. His word to us is, "My son, give Me thine heart." Where the heart is given, all follows, in lovely moral order. A loving heart finds its very deepest joy in obeying all God's commandments; and nothing is of any value to God but what springs from a loving heart. The heart is the source of all the issues of life; and hence, when it is governed by the love of God, there is a loving response to all His commandments.

We love His commandments because we love Him. Every word of His is precious to the heart that loves Him. Every precept, every statute, every judgment—in a word, His whole law is loved, reverenced, and obeyed, because it has His name and His authority attached to it.

The reader will find in psalm cxix. an uncommonly fine illustration of the special point now before us—a most striking example of one who blessedly answered to the words quoted above—"O that there were *such a heart* in them, that they would fear Me, and keep *all* My commandments *always!*" It is the lovely breathing of a soul who found its deep, unfailing, constant delight in the law of God. There are no less than one hundred and seventy allusions to that precious law, under some one title or another. We find scattered along the surface of this marvelous psalm, in rich profusion, such gems as the following:—

"Thy Word have I *hid* in mine *heart*, that I might not sin against Thee." "I have rejoiced in the way of Thy testimonies as much as in all riches." "I will meditate in Thy precepts, and have respect unto Thy ways." "*I will delight myself* in Thy statutes; I will not forget Thy Word." "My soul breaketh for the longing that it hath unto Thy judgments at all times." "*Thy testimonies* are also *my delight*, and my counselors." "*I have stuck* unto Thy testimonies." "Behold, *I have longed* after Thy precepts." "*I trust* in Thy Word." "*I have hoped* in Thy judgments." "*I seek* Thy precepts." "*I will delight myself* in Thy commandments, which *I have loved.*" "*I remembered* Thy judgments." "*Thy statutes* have been *my songs* in the house of my pilgrimage." "I turned *my feet* unto *Thy testimonies.*" "*I have believed* Thy commandments." "*The law of Thy mouth* is better unto me than thousands of gold and silver." "*I have hoped* in Thy Word." "*Thy law* is *my delight.*" "*Mine eyes* fail for *Thy Word.*" "All Thy commandments are faithful." "Forever, O Lord, Thy Word is settled in heaven." "*I will never forget* Thy precepts." "*I have sought* Thy precepts." "*I will consider* Thy testimonies." "Thy commandment is exceeding broad." "O how love I *Thy law*! it is *my meditation* all the day." "How sweet are *Thy words* unto *my taste*! yea, sweeter than honey to my mouth." "*Thy testimonies* have I taken as a *heritage forever*; for they are *the rejoicing of my heart.*" "I will have respect unto Thy statutes *continually.*" "I love Thy commandments above gold, yea, above find gold." "I esteem *all* Thy precepts concerning *all* things to be *right.*" "Thy testimonies are wonderful." "I opened my mouth and *panted*, for I *longed* for Thy commandments." "Upright are Thy judgments." "Thy testimonies ... are righteous, and very faithful." "Thy Word is very pure." "Thy law is the truth." "The righteousness of thy testimonies is everlasting." "All Thy commandments are truth." "Thy Word is *true from the beginning*; and every one of Thy righteous judgments *endureth forever.*" "*My heart* standeth *in awe* of Thy Word." "*I rejoice* at Thy Word, as one that findeth great spoil." "Great peace have they that love Thy law." "*My soul* hath kept *Thy testimonies*; and I love them exceedingly." "I have chosen Thy precepts." "Thy law is my delight."

Truly, it does the heart good, and refreshes the spirit, to transcribe such utterances as the foregoing, many of which are the suited utterances of our Lord Himself, in the days of His flesh. He ever lived upon the Word. It was the food of His soul, the authority of His path, the material of His ministry. By it He vanquished Satan; by it He silenced Sadducees, Pharisees, and Herodians; by it He taught His disciples; to it He commended His servants, as He was about to ascend into the heavens.

How important is all this for us! How intensely interesting! How deeply practical! What a place it gives the holy Scriptures! For we remember that it is, in very deed, the blessed Volume of inspiration which is brought before us in all those golden sentences culled from psalm cxix. How strengthening, refreshing, and encouraging for us to mark the way in which our Lord uses the holy Scriptures at all times, the place He gives them, and the dignity He puts upon them! He appeals to them on all occasions as a divine authority from which there can be no appeal. He, though Himself as God over all, the Author of the Volume, having taken His place as man on the earth, sets forth with all possible plainness what is man's bounden duty and high privilege, namely, to live by the Word of God, to bow down in reverent subjection to its divine authority.

And have we not here a very complete answer to the oft-raised question of infidelity, "How do we know that the Bible is the Word of God?" If indeed we believe in Christ—if we own Him to be the Son of God, God manifest in the flesh, very God and very man, we cannot fail to see the moral force of the fact that this divine Person constantly appeals to the Scriptures—to Moses, the prophets, and the psalms, as to a divine standard. Did He not know them to be the Word of God? Undoubtedly. As God, He had given them; as Man, He received them, lived by them, and owned their paramount authority, in all things.

What a weighty fact is here for the professing church! What a withering rebuke to all those so-called Christian doctors and writers who have presumed to tamper with the grand fundamental truth of the plenary inspiration of the holy Scriptures in general, and of the five books of Moses in particular! How terrible to think of the professed teachers of the Church of God daring to designate as spurious, writings which our Lord and Master received and owned as divine!

And yet we are told, and we are expected to believe that things are improving! Alas! alas! it is a miserable delusion. The degrading absurdities of ritualism, and the blasphemous reasonings of infidelity, are rapidly increasing around us; and where these influences are not actually dominant, we observe, for the most part, a cold indifference, carnal ease, self-indulgence, and worldliness—any thing and every thing, in short, but the evidence of improvement. If people are not led away by infidelity on the one hand, or by ritualism on the other, it is, for the most part, owing to the fact that they are too much occupied with pleasure and gain to think of any thing else. And as to the religion of the day, if you subtract money and music, you will have a lamentably trifling balance.

Hence, therefore, it is impossible to shake off the conviction that the combined testimony of observation and experience is directly opposed to the notion that things are improving. Indeed, for any one, in the face of such an array of evidence to the contrary, to cling to such a theory, can only be regarded as the fruit of a most unaccountable credulity.

But perhaps some may feel disposed to say that we must not judge by the sight of our eyes; we must be hopeful. True, provided only we have a divine warrant for our hopefulness. If a single line of Scripture can be produced to prove that the present system of things is to be marked by gradual improvement, religiously, politically, morally, or socially, then, by all means, be hopeful. Yes; hope against hope. A single clause of inspiration is quite sufficient to form the basis of a hope which will lift the heart above the very darkest and most depressing surroundings.

But where is such a clause to be found? Simply no where. The testimony of the Bible, from cover to cover; the distinct teaching of holy Scripture, from beginning to end; the voices of prophets and apostles, in unbroken harmony—all, without a single divergent note, go to prove, with a force and clearness perfectly unanswerable, that the present condition of things, so far from gradually improving, will rapidly grow worse; that ere the bright beams of millennial glory can gladden this groaning earth, the sword of judgment must do its appalling work. To quote the passages in proof of our assertion would literally fill a volume; it would simply be to transcribe a large portion of the prophetic scriptures of the Old and New Testament.

This, of course, we do not attempt. There is no need. The reader has his Bible before him; let him search it diligently. Let him lay aside all his preconceived ideas, all the conventionalisms of christendom, all the ordinary phraseology of the religious world, all the dogmas of the schools of divinity, and come, with the simplicity of a little child, to the pure fountain of holy Scripture, and drink in its heavenly teaching. If he will only do this, he will rise from the study with the clear and settled conviction that the world will, most assuredly, not be converted by the means now in operation—that it is not the gospel of peace, but the besom of destruction that shall prepare the earth for glory.

Is it, then, that we deny the good that is being done? Are we insensible to it? Far be the thought! We heartily bless God for every atom of it. We rejoice in every effort put forth to spread the precious gospel of the grace of God; we render thanks for every soul gathered within the blessed circle of God's salvation. We delight to think of eighty-five millions of Bibles scattered over the earth. What human mind can calculate the results of all these, yea, the results of a single copy? We earnestly wish Godspeed to every true-hearted missionary who goes forth with the glad tidings of salvation, whether into the lanes and court-yards of London, or to the most distant parts of the earth.

But, admitting all this, as we most heartily do, we nevertheless do not believe in the conversion of the world by the means now in operation. Scripture tells us that it is when the divine judgments are in the earth, the inhabitants of the world shall learn righteousness. This one clause of inspiration ought to be sufficient to prove that it is not by the gospel that the world is to be converted; and there are hundreds of clauses which speak the same language and teach the same truth. It is not by grace, but by judgment, that the inhabitants of the world shall learn righteousness.

What, then, is the object of the gospel? If it be not to convert the world, for what purpose is it preached? The apostle James, in his address at the memorable council at Jerusalem, gives an answer, direct and conclusive, to the question. He says, "Simeon hath declared how God at the first did visit the Gentiles." For what? To convert them all? The very reverse—"*To take out of them* a people for His name." Nothing can be more distinct than this. It sets before us that which ought to be the grand object of all missionary effort—that which every divinely sent and divinely taught missionary will keep before his mind in all his blessed labors. It is "to take out a people for His name."

How important to remember this! How needful to have ever before us a true object in all our work! Of what possible use can it be to work for a false object? Is it not much better to work with a direct view to what God is doing? Will it cripple the missionary's energies, or clip his wings, to keep before his eyes the divine purpose in his work? Surely not. Take the case of two missionaries going forth to some distant mission-field: the one has for his object the conversion of the world; the other, the gathering out of a people. Will the latter, by reason of his object, be less devoted, less energetic, less enthusiastic, than the former? We cannot believe it; on the contrary, the very fact of his being in the current of the divine mind will impart stability and consistency to his work, and, at the same time, encourage his heart in the face of the difficulties and hindrances which surround him.

But however this may be, it is perfectly plain that the apostles of our Lord and Saviour Jesus Christ had no such object, in going forth to their work, as the conversion of the world. "Go ye into all the world, and preach the gospel to every creature; he that believeth and is baptized shall be saved; but he that believeth not shall be damned."

This was to the twelve. The world was to be their sphere. The aspect of their message was, unto every creature; the application, to him that believeth. It was pre-eminently an individual thing. The conversion of the whole world was not to be their object; that will be effected by a different agency altogether, when God's present action by the gospel shall have resulted in the gathering out of a people for the heavens.[19] The Holy Ghost came down on the day of Pentecost, not to convert the world, but to "*convict* [ἐλέγξει]" it, or demonstrate its guilt in having rejected the Son of God.[20] The effect of His presence was to prove the world guilty; and as to the grand object of His mission, it was to form a body composed of believers from amongst both Jews and Gentiles. With this He has been occupied for the last eighteen hundred years. This is "the mystery" of which the apostle Paul was made a minister, and which he unfolds, so fully and blessedly, in his epistle to the Ephesians. It is impossible for any one to understand the truth set forth in this marvelous document, and not see that the conversion of the world and the formation of the body of Christ are two totally different things, which could not possibly go on together.

Let the reader ponder the following beautiful passage: "For this cause I Paul, the prisoner of Jesus Christ for you Gentiles, if ye have heard of the dispensation of the grace of God which is given me to you-ward: how that by revelation He made known unto me the mystery; (as I wrote afore in few words, whereby, when ye read, ye may understand my knowledge in the mystery of Christ) which in other ages was not made known unto the sons of men" —not made known in the scriptures of the Old Testament, nor revealed to the Old-Testament saints or prophets—"as it is now revealed unto His holy apostles and prophets" (that is, to the New-Testament prophets) "by the Spirit; that the Gentiles should be fellow-heirs, and of the same body, and partakers of His promise in Christ by the gospel: whereof I was made a minister according to the gift of the grace of God given unto me by the effectual working of His power. Unto me, who am less than the least of all saints, is this grace given, that I should preach among the Gentiles the unsearchable riches of Christ; and to make all men see what is the dispensation [οἰκονομία] of the mystery, which *from the beginning of the world* hath been *hid in God*, who created all things by Jesus Christ: to the intent that now unto the principalities and powers in the heavenlies might be known by the Church the manifold wisdom of God." (Eph. iii. 1-10.)

Take another passage from the epistle to the Colossians.—"If ye continue in the faith grounded and settled, and be not moved away from the hope of the gospel, which ye have heard, and which was preached to every creature which is under heaven, whereof I Paul am made a minister, who now rejoice in my sufferings for you, and fill up that which is behind of the afflictions of Christ in my flesh for His body's sake, which is the Church: whereof I am made a minister, according to the dispensation of God which is given to me for you, to complete the Word of God; even the mystery which hath been hid from ages and from generations, but now is made manifest to His saints: to whom God would make known what is the riches of the glory of this mystery among the Gentiles; which is Christ in you, the hope of glory: whom we preach, warning every man, and teaching every man in all wisdom; that we may present every man perfect in Christ Jesus: whereunto I also labor, striving according to His working, which worketh in me mightily." (Chap. i. 23-29.)

From these and numerous other passages, the reader may see the special object of Paul's ministry. Assuredly he had no such thought in his mind as the conversion of the world. True, he preached the gospel, in all its depth, fullness, and power—preached it "from Jerusalem and round about unto Illyricum"—"preached among the Gentiles the unsearchable riches of Christ," but with no thought of converting the world. He knew better. He knew and taught that the world was ripening for judgment—yes, ripening rapidly; that "evil men and seducers shall wax worse and worse;" that "in *the latter times* some shall depart from the faith, giving heed to seducing spirits, and doctrines of devils; speaking lies in hypocrisy; having their conscience seared with a hot iron; forbidding to marry, and commanding to abstain from meats, which God had created to be received with thanksgiving of them which believe and know the truth."

And further still, this faithful and divinely inspired witness taught that "in *the last days*" —far in advance of "the latter times" —"perilous [or difficult] times shall come. For men shall be lovers of their own selves, covetous, boasters, proud, blasphemers, disobedient to parents, unthankful, unholy, without natural affection, truce-breakers, false accusers, incontinent, fierce, despisers of those that are good, traitors, heady, high-minded, *lovers of pleasures rather than lovers of God*; having a form of godliness, but denying the power thereof." (Compare 1 Tim. iv. 1-3 with 2 Tim. iii. 1-5.)

What a picture! It brings us back to the close of the first of Romans, where the same inspired pen portrays for us the dark forms of heathenism;

but with this terrible difference, that in 2 Timothy it is not heathenism, but nominal Christianity—"a form of godliness."

And is this to be the end of the present condition of things? Is this the converted world of which we hear so much? Alas! alas! there are false prophets abroad; there are those who cry, Peace, peace, when there is no peace; there are those who attempt to daub the crumbling walls of christendom with untempered mortar.

But it will not do. Judgment is at the door. The professing church has utterly, shamefully failed; she has grievously departed from the Word of God, and revolted from the authority of her Lord. There is not a single ray of hope for christendom. It is the darkest moral blot in the wide universe of God, or on the page of history. The same blessed apostle from whose writings we have already so largely quoted, tells us that "the mystery of iniquity doth already work;" hence it has been working now for over eighteen centuries. "Only He that now hindereth will hinder until He be taken out of the way. And then shall that Wicked be revealed, whom the Lord shall consume with the spirit of His mouth, and shall destroy with the brightness of His coming: even him, whose coming is after the working of Satan with all power and signs and lying wonders, and with all deceivableness of unrighteousness in them that perish; because they received not the love of the truth, that they might be saved. And for this cause God shall send them strong delusion, that they should believe a lie: that they all might be damned who believed not the truth, but had pleasure in unrighteousness." (2 Thess. ii. 7-12.)

How awful is the doom of christendom! Strong delusion! Dark damnation! And all this in the face of the dreams of those false prophets who talk to the people about "the bright side of things." Thank God, there is a bright side for all those who belong to Christ. To them, the apostle can speak in bright and cheering accents.—"We are bound to give thanks alway to God for you, brethren beloved of the Lord, because God hath from the beginning chosen you to salvation through sanctification of the Spirit and belief of the truth: whereunto He called you by our gospel, to the obtaining of the glory of our Lord Jesus Christ." (2 Thess. ii. 13, 14.)

Here we have, most surely, the bright side of things—the bright and blessed hope of the Church of God—the hope of seeing "the bright and morning Star." All rightly instructed Christians are on the look-out, not for an improved or a converted world, but for their coming Lord and Saviour, who has gone to prepare a place for them in the Father's house, and is coming again to receive to Himself, that where He is, there they may be also. This is His own sweet promise, which may be fulfilled at any moment. He only waits, as Peter tells us, in long-suffering mercy, not willing that any should perish, but that all should come to repentance. But when the last member shall be incorporated, by the Holy Ghost, into the blessed body of Christ, then shall the voice of the archangel and the trump of God summon *all* the redeemed, from the beginning, to meet their descending Lord in the air, to be forever with Him.

This is the true and proper hope of the Church of God—a hope which He would have ever shining down into the hearts of all His beloved people, in its purifying and elevating power. Of this blessed hope the enemy has succeeded in robbing a large number of the Lord's people. Indeed, for centuries it was well-nigh blotted out from the Church's horizon; and it has only been partially recovered within the last fifty years. And, alas! how partially! Where do we hear of it, throughout the length and breadth of the professing church? Do the pulpits of christendom ring with the joyful sound, "Behold the Bridegroom cometh"? Far from it. Even the few beloved servants of Christ who are looking for His coming, hardly dare to preach it, because they fear it would be utterly rejected. And so it would. We are thoroughly persuaded that, in the vast majority of cases, men who should venture to preach the glorious truth that the Lord is coming for His Church, would speedily have to vacate their pulpits.

What a solemn and striking proof of Satan's blinding power! He has robbed the Church of her divinely given hope, and instead thereof, he has given her a delusion—a lie. Instead of looking out for "the bright and morning Star," he has set her looking for a converted world—a millennium without Christ. He has succeeded in casting such a haze over the future, that the Church has completely lost her bearings. She does not know where she is. She is like a vessel tossed on the stormy ocean, having neither compass nor rudder, seeing neither sun nor stars. All is darkness and confusion.

And how is this? Simply because the Church has lost sight of the pure and precious word of her Lord, and accepted instead those bewildering creeds and confessions of men which so mar and mutilate the truth of God that Christians seem utterly at sea as to their proper standing and their proper hope.

And yet they have the Bible in their hands. True; but so had the Jews, and yet they rejected that blessed One who is the great theme of the Bible from beginning to end. This was the moral inconsistency with which our Lord charged them in John v.—"Ye search the Scriptures; for in them ye think ye have eternal life; and they are they which testify of Me; and ye will not come to Me, that ye might have life."[21]

And why was this? Simply because their minds were blinded by religious prejudice. They were under the influence of the doctrines and commandments of men. Hence, although they had the Scriptures, and boasted of having them, they were as ignorant of them, and as little governed by them, as the poor dark heathen around them. It is one thing to have the Bible in our hands, in our homes, and in our assemblies, and quite another thing to have the truths of the Bible acting on our hearts and consciences, and shining in our lives.

Take, for instance, the great subject now before us, and which has led us into this very lengthened digression. Can any thing be more plainly taught in the New Testament than this, namely, that the end of the present condition of things will be terrible apostasy from the truth, and open rebellion against God and the Lamb? The gospels, the epistles, and the Revelation all agree in setting forth this most solemn truth, with such distinctness and simplicity that a babe in Christ may see it.

And yet how few, comparatively, believe it! The vast majority believe the very reverse. They believe that by means of the various agencies now in operation all nations shall be converted. In vain we call attention to our Lord's parables in Matthew xiii.—the tares, the leaven, and the mustard-seed. How do these agree with the idea of a converted world? If the whole world is to be converted by a preached gospel, how is it that tares are found in the field at the end of the age? how is it that there are as many foolish virgins as wise ones when the Bridegroom comes? If the whole world is to be converted by the gospel, then on whom will "the day of the Lord so come as a thief in the night"? or what mean those awful words, "For when they shall say, Peace and safety; then sudden destruction cometh upon them, as travail upon a woman with child; and they shall not escape"? In view of a converted world, what would be the just application, what the moral force, of those most solemn words in the first of Revelation, "Behold, He cometh with clouds, and every eye shall see Him, and they also which pierced Him; and *all kindreds of the earth shall wail* because of Him"? Where are all those wailing kindreds to be found if the whole world is to be converted?

Reader, is it not as clear as a sunbeam that the two things cannot stand for a moment together? Is it not perfectly plain that the theory of a world converted by the gospel is diametrically opposed to the teaching of the entire New Testament? How is it, then, that the vast majority of professing Christians persist in holding it? There can be but the one reply, and that is, they do not bow to the authority of Scripture. It is most sorrowful and solemn to have to say it; but it is, alas! too true. The Bible is read in christendom, but the truths of the Bible are not believed—nay, they are persistently rejected; and all this in view of the oft-repeated boast that "the Bible, and the Bible alone, is the religion of Protestants."

But we shall not pursue this subject further here, much as we feel its weight and importance. We trust the reader may be led by the Spirit of God to feel its deep solemnity. We believe the Lord's people every where need to be thoroughly roused to a sense of how entirely the professing church has departed from the authority of Scripture. Here, we may rest assured, lies the real cause of all the confusion, all the error, all the evil, in our midst. We have departed from the Word of the Lord, and from Himself. Until this is seen, felt, and owned, we cannot be right. The Lord looks for true repentance, real brokenness of spirit, in His presence. *"To this man* will I look, even to him that is *poor*, and of a *contrite* spirit, and trembleth at My Word."

This always holds good. There is no limit to the blessing when the soul is in this truly blessed attitude. But it must be a reality. It will not do to talk of being "poor and contrite," we must be in the condition. It is an individual matter. *"To this man* will I look."

Oh may the Lord, in His infinite mercy, lead us, every one, into true self-judgment, under the action of His Word. May our ears be open to hear His voice. May there be a real turning of our hearts to Himself and to His Word. May we turn our backs, in holy decision, once and forever, upon every thing that will not stand the test of Scripture. This, we are persuaded, is what our Lord Christ looks for on the part of all who belong to Him, amid the terrible and hopeless *debris* of christendom.

CHAPTER VI

"Now these are the commandments, the statutes, and the judgments, which the Lord your God commanded to teach you, that ye might do them in the land whither ye go to possess it: that thou mightest fear the Lord thy God, to keep all His statutes and His commandments, which I command thee, thou, and thy son, and thy son's son, all the days of thy life; and that thy days may be prolonged. Hear therefore, O Israel, and observe to do it; that it may be well with thee, and that ye may increase mightily, as the Lord God of thy fathers hath promised thee, in the land that floweth with milk and honey. Hear, O Israel: The Lord our God is one Lord."

We have here presented to us that great cardinal truth which the nation of Israel was specially responsible to hold fast and confess, namely, the unity of the Godhead. This truth lay at the very foundation of the Jewish economy. It was the grand centre around which the people were to rally. So long as they maintained this, they were a happy, prosperous, fruitful people; but when it was let go, all was gone. It was their great national bulwark, and that which was to mark them off from all the nations of the earth. They were called to confess this glorious truth in the face of an idolatrous world, with "its gods many, and lords many." It was Israel's high privilege and holy responsibility to bear a steady witness to the truth contained in that one weighty sentence, "The Lord our God is one Lord," in marked opposition to the false gods innumerable of the heathen around. Their father Abraham had been called out from the very midst of heathen idolatry, to be a witness to the one true and living God, to trust Him, to walk with Him, to lean on Him, and to obey Him.

If the reader will turn to the last chapter of Joshua, he will find a very striking allusion to this fact, and a very important use made of it, in his closing address to the people.—"And Joshua gathered all the tribes of Israel to Shechem, and called for the elders of Israel, and for their heads, and for their judges, and for their officers; and they presented themselves before God. And Joshua said unto all the people, 'Thus saith the Lord God of Israel, Your fathers dwelt on the other side of the flood in old time, even Terah, the father of Abraham, and the father of Nachor; and *they served other gods.* And I took your father Abraham from the other side of the flood, and led him throughout all the land of Canaan, and multiplied his seed, and gave him Isaac.'"

Here Joshua reminds the people of the fact that their fathers had served other gods—a very solemn and weighty fact most surely, and one which they ought never to have forgotten, inasmuch as the remembrance of it would have taught them their deep need of watchfulness over themselves, lest by any means they should be drawn back into that gross and terrible evil out of which God, in His sovereign grace and electing love, had called their father Abraham. It would have been their wisdom to consider that the self-same evil in which their fathers had lived, in the olden time, was just the one into which they themselves were likely to fall.

Having presented this fact to the people, Joshua brings before them, with uncommon force and vividness, all the leading events of their history, from the birth of their father Isaac, down to the moment in which he was addressing them; and then sums up with the following telling appeal: "Now therefore fear the Lord, and serve Him in sincerity and in truth; and *put away the gods which your fathers served on the other side of the flood, and in Egypt*; and serve ye the Lord. And if it seem evil unto you to serve the Lord, choose you this day whom ye will serve; whether *the gods which your fathers served that were on the other side of the flood*, or the gods of the Amorites in whose land ye dwell; but as for me and my house, we will serve the Lord."

Mark the repeated allusion to the fact that their fathers had worshiped false gods; and further, that the land into which Jehovah had brought them had been polluted, from one end to the other, by the dark abominations of heathen idolatry.

Thus does this faithful servant of the Lord, evidently by the inspiration of the Holy Ghost, seek to set before the people their danger of giving up the grand central and foundation truth of the one true and living God, and falling back into the worship of idols. He urges upon them the absolute necessity of whole-hearted decision. "Choose you *this day* whom ye will serve." There is nothing like plain, out-and-out decision for God. It is due to Him always. He had proved Himself to be unmistakably for them in redeeming them from the bondage of Egypt, bringing them through the wilderness, and planting them in the land of Canaan; hence, therefore, that they should be wholly for Him was nothing more than their reasonable service.

How deeply Joshua felt all this for himself is evident from those very memorable words, "As for me and my house, we will serve the Lord." Lovely words! Precious decision! National religion might, and, alas! did, go to ruin; but personal and family religion could, by the grace of God, be maintained every where and at all times.

Thank God for this! May we never forget it. "Me and my house" is Faith's clear and delightful response to God's "Thou and thy house." Let the condition of the ostensible, professed people of God, at any given time, be what it may, it is the privilege of every true-hearted man of God to adopt and act upon this immortal decision: "As for me and my house, we will serve the Lord."

True, it is only by the grace of God, continually supplied, that this holy resolution can be carried out; but we may rest assured that where the bent of the heart is to follow the Lord fully, all needed grace will be ministered, day by day; for those encouraging words must ever hold good, "My grace is sufficient for *thee*; for My strength is made perfect in weakness."

Let us now look for a moment at the apparent effect of Joshua's soul-stirring appeal to the congregation. It seemed very promising. "The people answered and said, 'God forbid that we should forsake the Lord, to serve other gods; for the Lord our God, He it is that brought us up and our fathers out of the land of Egypt, from the house of bondage, and which did those great signs in our sight, and preserved us in all the way wherein we went, and among all the people through whom we passed: and the Lord drave out from before us all the people, even the Amorites which dwelt in the land; therefore will we also serve the Lord, for He is our God."

All this sounded very well, and looked very hopeful. They seemed to have a clear sense of the moral basis of Jehovah's claim upon them for implicit obedience. They could accurately recount all His mighty deeds on their behalf, and make very earnest and no doubt sincere protestations against idolatry, and promises of obedience to Jehovah, their God.

But it is very evident that Joshua was not particularly sanguine about all this profession, for he "said unto the people, 'Ye cannot serve the Lord: for He is a holy God; He is a jealous God; He will not forgive your transgressions nor your sins. If ye forsake the Lord, and serve strange gods, then He will turn and do you hurt, and consume you, after that He hath done you good.' And the people said unto Joshua, 'Nay; but we will serve the Lord.' And Joshua said unto the people, 'Ye are witnesses against yourselves that ye have chosen you the Lord, to serve Him.' And they said, 'We are witnesses.' 'Now therefore put away,' said he, '*the strange gods which are among you*, and *incline your heart unto the Lord God of Israel*.' And the people said unto Joshua, 'The Lord our God will we serve, and His voice will we obey.'"

We do not now stop to contemplate the aspect in which Joshua presents God to the congregation of Israel, inasmuch as our object in referring to the passage is to show the prominent place assigned, in Joshua's address, to the truth of the unity of the Godhead. This was the truth to which Israel was called to bear witness, in view of all the nations of the earth, and in which they were to find their moral safeguard against the ensnaring influences of idolatry.

But, alas! this very truth was *the* one as to which they most speedily and signally failed. The promises, vows, and resolutions made under the powerful influence of Joshua's appeal soon proved to be like the early dew and the morning cloud, that passeth away. "The people served the Lord all the days of Joshua, and all the days of the elders that outlived Joshua, who had seen all the great works of the Lord, that He did for Israel. And Joshua, the son of Nun, the servant of the Lord, died, being a hundred and ten years old.... And also all that generation were gathered unto their fathers; and there arose another generation after them, which knew not the Lord, nor yet the works which He had done for Israel. And the children of Israel did evil in the sight of the Lord, *and served Baalim*; and they forsook the Lord God of their fathers, which brought them out of the land of Egypt, *and followed* other gods, of the gods of the people that were round about them, *and bowed themselves unto them*, and provoked the Lord to anger. And they forsook the Lord, and served Baal and Ashtaroth." (Judges ii. 7-13.)

Reader, how admonitory is all this! how full of solemn warning to us all! The grand, all-important, special, and characteristic truth so soon abandoned! The one only true and living God given up for Baal and Ashtaroth! So long as Joshua and the elders lived, their presence and their influence kept Israel from open apostasy; but no sooner were those moral embankments removed than the dark tide of idolatry rolled in and swept away the very foundations of the national faith. Jehovah of Israel was displaced by Baal and Ashtaroth. Human influence is a poor prop, a feeble barrier. We must be sustained by the power of God, else we shall, sooner or later, give way. The faith that stands merely in the wisdom of men, and not in the power of God, must prove a poor, flimsy, worthless faith. It will not stand the day of trial; it will not bear the furnace; it will most assuredly break down.

It is well to remember this. Second-hand faith will never do. There must be a living link connecting the soul with God. We must have to do with God for ourselves individually, else we shall give way when the testing-time comes. Human example and human influence may be all very good in their place. It was all very well to look at Joshua and the elders, and see how they followed the Lord. It is quite true that "as iron sharpeneth iron, so doth the countenance of a man his friend." It is very encouraging to be surrounded by a number of truly devoted hearts—very delightful to be borne along upon the bosom of the tide of collective loyalty to Christ—to His Person and to His cause. But if this be all,—if there be not the deep spring of personal faith and personal knowledge,—if there be not the divinely formed and the divinely sustained link of individual relationship and communion, then when the human props are removed,—when the tide of human influence ebbs,—when general declension sets in, we shall be, in principle, like Israel following the Lord all the days of Joshua and the elders, and then giving up the confession of His name and returning to the follies and vanities of this present world—things no better, in reality, than Baal and Ashtaroth.

But, on the other hand, when the heart is thoroughly established in the truth and grace of God,—when we can say—as it is the privilege of each true believer to say—"I know *whom* I have believed, and am persuaded that He is able to keep that which I have committed unto Him against that day," then, although all should turn aside from the public confession of Christ,—although we should find ourselves left without the help of a human countenance or the support of a human arm, we shall find "the foundation of God" as sure as ever, and the path of obedience as plain before us as though thousands were treading it with holy decision and energy.

We must never lose sight of the fact that it is the divine purpose that the professing church of God should learn deep and holy lessons from the history of Israel. "Whatsoever things were written aforetime were written for our learning, that we through patience and comfort of the Scriptures might have hope." Nor is it by any means necessary, in order to our thus learning from the Old-Testament scriptures, that we should occupy ourselves in searching out fanciful analogies, curious theories, or far-fetched illustrations. Many, alas! have tried these things, and instead of finding "comfort" in the Scriptures, they have been led away into empty and foolish conceits, if not into deadly errors.

But our business is with the living facts recorded on the page of inspired history. These are to be our study; from these we are to draw our great practical lessons. Take, for example, the weighty and admonitory fact now before us—a fact standing out in characters deep and broad on the page of Israel's history from Joshua to Isaiah—the fact of Israel's lamentable departure from that very truth which they were specially called to hold and confess—the truth of the unity of the Godhead. The very first thing they did was to let go this grand and all-important truth, this key-stone of the arch, the foundation of the whole edifice, the very heart of their national existence, the living centre of their national polity. They gave it up, and turned back to the idolatry of their fathers on the other side of the flood, and of the heathen nations around them. They abandoned that most glorious and distinctive truth on the maintenance of which their very existence as a nation depended. Had they only held fast this truth, they would have been invincible; but in surrendering it, they surrendered all, and became much worse than the nations around them, inasmuch as they sinned against light and knowledge—sinned with their eyes open—sinned in the face of the most solemn warnings and earnest entreaties, and, we may add, in the face of the most vehement and oft-repeated promises and protestations of obedience.

Yes, reader, Israel gave up the worship of the one true and living God, Jehovah-Elohim, their covenant-God; not only their Creator, but their Redeemer—the One who had brought them up out of the land of Egypt, conducted them through the Red Sea, led them through the wilderness, brought them across the Jordan, and planted them in triumph in the inheritance which He had promised to Abraham their father—"a land flowing with milk and honey, which is the glory of all lands." They turned their backs upon Him, and gave themselves up to the worship of false gods; "they provoked Him to anger with their high places, and moved Him to jealousy with their graven images."

It seems perfectly wonderful that a people who had seen and known so much of the goodness and loving-kindness of God—His mighty acts, His faithfulness, His majesty, His glory, could ever bring themselves to bow down to the stock of a tree; but so it was. Their whole history, from the days of the calf at the foot of Mount Sinai, to the day in which Nebuchadnezzar reduced Jerusalem to ruins, is marked by an unconquerable spirit of idolatry. In vain did Jehovah, in His long-suffering mercy and abounding goodness, raise up deliverers for them, to lift them from beneath the terrible consequences of their sin and folly. Again and again, in His inexhaustable mercy and patience, He saved them from the hand of their enemies. He raised up an Othniel, an Ehud, a Barak, a Gideon, a Jephthah, a Samson— those instruments of His mercy and power—those witnesses of His deep and tender love and compassion toward His poor infatuated people. No sooner had each judge passed off the scene than back the nation plunged into their besetting sin of idolatry.

So, also, in the days of the kings; it is the same melancholy, heart-rending story. True, there were bright spots here and there—some brilliant stars shining out through the deep gloom of the nation's history; we have a David, an Asa, a Jehoshaphat, a Hezekiah, a Josiah—refreshing and blessed exceptions to the dark and dismal rule. But even men like these failed to eradicate from the heart of the nation the pernicious root of idolatry. Even amid the unexampled splendors of Solomon's reign, that root sent forth its bitter shoots, in the monstrous form of high places to Ashtaroth, the goddess of the Zidonians; Milcom, the abomination of the Ammonites; and Chemosh, the abomination of Moab.

Reader, only think of this. Pause for a moment, and contemplate the astounding fact of the writer of the Canticles, Ecclesiastes, and Proverbs bowing at the shrine of Molech! Only conceive, the wisest, the wealthiest, and the most glorious of Israel's monarchs burning incense and offering sacrifices upon the altar of Chemosh!

Truly, there is something here for us to ponder. It was written for our learning. The reign of Solomon affords one of the most striking and impressive evidences of the fact which is just now engaging our attention, namely, Israel's complete and hopeless apostasy from the grand truth of the unity of the Godhead—their unconquerable spirit of idolatry. The truth which they were specially called out to hold and confess was the very truth which they first of all and most persistently abandoned.

We shall not pursue the dark line of evidence further, neither shall we dwell upon the appalling picture of the nation's judgment in consequence of their idolatry. They are now in the condition of which the prophet Hosea speaks—"The children of Israel shall abide many days without a king, and without a prince, and without a sacrifice, and without an image, and without an ephod, and without teraphim." "The unclean spirit of idolatry has gone out of them," during these "many days," to return, by and by, with "seven other spirits more wicked than himself"—the very perfection of spiritual wickedness. And then will come days of unparalleled tribulation upon that long misguided and deeply revolted people—"the time of Jacob's trouble."

But deliverance will come, blessed be God! Bright days are in store for the restored nation—"days of heaven upon earth"—as the same prophet Hosea tells us, "Afterward shall the children of Israel return, and seek the Lord their God, and David their king; and shall fear the Lord and His goodness in the latter days." All the promises of God to Abraham, Isaac, Jacob, and David shall be blessedly accomplished; all the brilliant predictions of the prophets, from Isaiah to Malachi, shall be gloriously fulfilled. Yes, both promises and prophecies shall be literally and gloriously made good to restored Israel, in the land of Canaan; for "the Scripture cannot be broken." The long, dark, dreary night shall be followed by the brightest day that has ever shone upon this earth; the daughter of Zion shall bask in the bright and blessed beams of "the Sun of Righteousness;" and "the earth shall be filled with the knowledge of the Lord as the waters cover the sea."

It would indeed be a most delightful exercise to reproduce upon the pages of this volume those glowing passages from the prophets which speak of Israel's future; but this we cannot attempt; it is not needful; and we have a duty to fulfill which, if not so pleasing to us or so refreshing to the reader, will, we earnestly hope, prove not less profitable.

The duty is this: to press upon the attention of the reader (and upon the attention of the whole Church of God) the practical application of that solemn fact in Israel's history on which we have dwelt at such length—the fact of their having so speedily and so completely given up the great truth set forth in Deuteronomy vi. 4, "Hear, O Israel; the Lord our God is one Lord."

We may perhaps be asked, What bearing can this fact have upon the Church of God? We believe it has a most solemn bearing; and further, we believe we should be guilty of a very culpable shirking of our duty to Christ and to His Church if we failed to point it out. We know that all the great facts of Israel's history are full of instruction, full of admonition, full of warning, for us. It is our business, our bounden duty, to see that we profit by them—to take heed that we study them aright.

Now, in contemplating the history of the Church of God as a public witness for Christ on the earth, we find that hardly had it been set up, in all the fullness of blessing and privilege which marked the opening of its career, ere it began to slip away from those very truths which it was specially responsible to maintain and confess. Like Adam in the garden of Eden; like Noah in the restored earth; like Israel in Canaan; so the Church, as the responsible steward of the mysteries of God, was no sooner set in its place than it began to totter and fall. It almost immediately began to give up those grand truths which were characteristic of its very existence, and which were to mark off Christianity from all that had gone before. Even under the eyes of the apostles of our Lord and Saviour Jesus Christ, errors and evils had begun to work which sapped the very foundations of the Church's testimony.

Are we asked for proofs? Alas! we have them in melancholy abundance. Hear the words of that blessed apostle who shed more tears and heaved more sighs over the ruins of the Church than any man that ever lived. "I marvel," he says, and well he might, "that ye are *so soon* removed from Him that called you into the grace of Christ, unto another gospel: which is not another." "O foolish Galatians, who hath bewitched you, that ye should not obey the truth, before whose eyes Jesus Christ hath been evidently set forth, crucified among you?" "Howbeit then, when ye knew not God, ye did service to them which by nature are no gods. But now, after that ye have known God, or rather are known of God, how turn ye again to the weak and beggarly elements, whereunto ye desire again to be in bondage? Ye observe days and months and times and years;" Christian festivals, so called, very imposing and gratifying to religious nature; but, in the judgment of the apostle, the judgment of the Holy Ghost, it was simply giving up Christianity and going back to the worship of idols. "I am afraid of you" — and no wonder, when they could thus so speedily turn away from the grand characteristic truths of a heavenly Christianity, and occupy themselves with superstitious observances. "I am afraid of you, lest I have bestowed upon you labor in vain." "Ye did run well; who did hinder you, that ye should not obey the truth? This persuasion cometh not of Him that calleth you. A little leaven leaveneth the whole lump."

And all this in the apostle's own day. The departure was even more rapid than in Israel's case; for they served the Lord all the days of Joshua, and all the days of the elders that outlived Joshua; but in the Church's sad and humiliating history, the enemy succeeded almost immediately in introducing leaven into the meal, tares among the wheat. Ere the apostles themselves had left the scene, seed was sown which has been bearing its pernicious fruit ever since, and shall continue to bear till angelic reapers clear the field.

But we must give further proof from Scripture. Let us hearken to the same inspired witness, near the close of his ministry, pouring out his heart to his beloved son Timothy, in accents at once pathetic and solemn. "This thou knowest, that all they which are in Asia be turned away from me." Again, "Preach the Word; be instant in season, out of season; reprove, rebuke, exhort with all long-suffering and doctrine. For the time will come when they will not endure sound doctrine; but after their own lusts shall they heap to themselves teachers, having itching ears; and *they shall turn away their ears from the truth*, and shall be turned unto fables."

Here is the testimony of the man who, as a wise master-builder, had laid the foundation of the Church. And what was his own personal experience? He was, like his blessed Master, left alone, deserted by those who had once gathered around him in the freshness, bloom, and ardor of early days. His large loving heart was broken by Judaizing teachers, who sought to overturn the very foundations of Christianity, and to overthrow the faith of God's elect. He wept over the ways of many who, while they made a profession, were nevertheless "the enemies of the cross of Christ."

In a word, the apostle Paul, as he looked forth from his prison at Rome, saw the hopeless wreck and ruin of the professing body. He saw that it would happen to that body as it had happened to the ship in which he had made his last voyage—a voyage strikingly significant and illustrative of the Church's sad history in this world.

But here let us just remind the reader that we are dealing now only with the question of the Church as a responsible witness for Christ on the earth. This must be distinctly seen, else we shall greatly err in our thoughts on the subject. We must accurately distinguish between the Church as the body of Christ, and as His light-bearer or witness in the world. In the former character, failure is impossible; in the latter, the ruin is complete and hopeless.

The Church as the body of Christ, united to her living and glorified Head in the heavens, by the presence and indwelling of the Holy Ghost, can never, by any possibility, fail—never be smashed to pieces, like Paul's ship, by the storms and billows of this hostile world. It is as safe as Christ Himself. The Head and the body are one—indissolubly one. No power of earth or hell—men or devils can ever touch the feeblest and most obscure member of that blessed body. All stand before God, all are under His gracious eye, in the fullness, beauty, and acceptability of Christ Himself. As is the Head, so are the members—all the members together—each member in particular. All stand in the full eternal results of Christ's finished work on the cross. There is, there can be, no question of responsibility here. The Head made Himself responsible for the members. He perfectly met every claim, and discharged every liability. Nothing remains but love—love, deep as the heart of Christ, perfect as His work, unchanging as His throne. Every question that could possibly be raised against any one or all of the members of the Church of God was raised, gone into, and definitively settled, between God and His Christ, on the cross. All the sins, all the iniquities, all the transgressions, all the guilt, of each member in particular, and all the members together—yes, all, in the fullest and most absolute way, was laid on Christ and borne by Him. God, in His inflexible justice, in His infinite holiness, in His eternal righteousness, dealt with every thing that could ever, in any possible manner, stand in the way of the full salvation, perfect blessedness, and everlasting glory of every one of the members of the body of Christ—the assembly of God. Every member of the body is permeated by the life of the Head; every stone in the building is animated by the life of the Chief Corner-Stone. All are bound together in the power of a bond which can never—no, never be dissolved.

And furthermore, let it be distinctly understood that the unity of the body of Christ is absolutely indissoluble. This is a cardinal point which must be tenaciously held and faithfully confessed. But obviously it cannot be held and confessed unless it is understood and believed; and, judging from the expressions which one sometimes hears in speaking on the subject, it is very questionable indeed if people so expressing themselves have ever grasped in a divine way the glorious truth of the unity of the body of Christ—a unity maintained on earth by the indwelling of the Holy Ghost.

Thus, for example, we sometimes hear people speak of "rending the body of Christ." It is a complete mistake. Such a thing is utterly impossible. The Reformers were accused of rending the body of Christ when they turned their backs upon the Romish system. What a gross misconception! It simply amounted to the monstrous assumption that a vast mass of moral evil, doctrinal error, ecclesiastical corruption, and debasing superstition was to be owned as the body of Christ! How could any one with the New Testament in his hand regard the so-called church of Rome, with its numberless and nameless abominations, as the body of Christ? How could any one possessing the very faintest idea of the true Church of God ever think of bestowing that title upon the darkest mass of wickedness, the greatest masterpiece of Satan the world has ever beheld?

No, reader; we must never confound the ecclesiastical systems of this world—ancient, medieval, or modern; Greek, Latin, Anglican; national or popular, established or dissenting—with the true Church of God, the body of Christ. There is not, beneath the canopy of heaven, this day, nor ever was, a religious system, call it what you please, possessing the very smallest claim to be called "the Church of God," or "the body of Christ." And, as a consequence, it can never be rightly or intelligently called schism, or rending the body of Christ, to separate from such systems; nay, on the contrary, it is the bounden duty of every one who would faithfully maintain and confess the truth of the unity of the body to separate, with the most unqualified decision, from every thing falsely calling itself a church. It can only be viewed as schism to separate from those who are unmistakably and unquestionably gathered on the ground of the assembly of God.

No body of Christians can now lay claim to the title of the body of Christ, or Church of God. The members of that body are scattered every where; they are to be found in all the various religious organizations of the day, save such as deny the deity of our Lord Jesus Christ. We cannot admit the idea that any true Christian could continue to frequent a place where his Lord is blasphemed. But although no body of Christians can lay claim to the title of the assembly of God, all Christians are responsible to be gathered on the ground of that assembly, and on no other.

And if we be asked, How are we to know—where are we to find this ground? We reply, "If thine eye be single, thy whole body shall be full of light." "If any man *will do* His will, he shall know of the doctrine." "*There is a path*" (thanks be to God for it!) though "no fowl knoweth, and the vulture's eye hath not seen it. The lion's whelps have not trodden it, nor the fierce lion passed by it." Nature's keenest vision cannot see this path, nor its greatest strength tread it. Where is it, then? Here it is: *"Unto man"* —to the reader and to the writer, to each, to all—"He said, 'Behold, *the fear of the Lord*, that is wisdom; and *to depart from evil* is understanding.'" (Job xxviii.)

But there is another expression which we not unfrequently hear from persons from whom we might expect more intelligence, namely, "Cutting off the members of the body of Christ."[22] This, too, blessed be God, is impossible. Not a single member of the body of Christ can ever be severed from the Head, or ever disturbed from the place into which he has been incorporated by the Holy Ghost, in pursuance of the eternal purpose of God, and in virtue of the accomplished atonement of our Lord Jesus Christ. The divine Three in One are pledged for the eternal security of the very feeblest member of the body, and for the maintenance of the indissoluble unity of the whole.

In a word, then, it is as true to-day as it was when the inspired apostle penned the fourth chapter of his epistle to the Ephesians, that "there is one body," of which Christ is Head, of which the Holy Ghost is the formative power, and of which all true believers are members. This body has been on earth since the day of Pentecost, is on earth now, and shall continue on earth until that moment, so rapidly approaching, when Christ shall come and take it to His Father's house. It is the same body, with a continual succession of members, just as we speak of a certain regiment of her majesty's army having been at Waterloo, and now quartered at Aldershot, though not a man in the regiment of to-day appeared at the memorable battle of 1815.

Does the reader feel any difficulty as to all this? It may be that he finds it hard, in the present broken and scattered condition of the members, to believe and confess the unbroken unity of the whole. He may feel disposed, perhaps, to limit the application of Ephesians iv. 4 to the day in which the apostle penned the words, when Christians were manifestly one, and when there was no such thing thought of as being a member of this church or a member of that church, because all believers were members of *the* one Church.[23]

In reply, we must protest against the very idea of limiting the Word of God. What possible right have we to single out one clause from Ephesians iv. 4-6, and say it only applied to the days of the apostles? If one clause is to be so limited, why not all? Are there not still "one Spirit, one Lord, one faith, one baptism, one God and Father of all"? Will any question this? Surely not. Well, then, it follows that there is as surely one body as there is one Spirit, one Lord, one God. All are intimately bound up together, and you cannot touch one without touching all. We have no more right to deny the existence of the one body than we have to deny the existence of God, inasmuch as the self-same passage that declares to us the one declares to us the other also.

But some will doubtless inquire, Where is this one body to be seen? Is it not an absurdity to speak of such a thing, in the face of the almost numberless denominations of christendom? Our answer is this: We are not going to surrender the truth of God because man has so signally failed to carry it out. Did not Israel utterly fail to maintain, confess, and carry out the truth of the unity of the Godhead? and was that glorious truth, in the smallest degree, touched by their failure? Was it not as true that there was one God, though there were as many idolatrous altars as streets in Jerusalem, and every housetop sent up a cloud of incense to the queen of heaven, as when Moses sounded forth, in the ears of the whole congregation, those sublime words, "Hear, O Israel, the Lord our God is one Lord"? Blessed be God, His truth does not depend upon the faithless, foolish ways of men. It stands in its own divine integrity; it shines in its own heavenly, undimmed lustre, spite of the grossest human failure. Were it not so, what should we do? whither should we turn? or what would become of us? In fact, it comes to this: if we were only to believe the measure of truth which we see practically carried out in the ways of men, we might give up in despair, and be of all men most miserable.

But how is the truth of the one body to be practically carried out? By refusing to own any other principle of Christian fellowship—any other ground of meeting. All true believers should meet on the simple ground of membership of the body of Christ, and on no other. They should assemble, on the first day of the week, around the Lord's table, and break bread, as members of the one body, as we read in 1 Corinthians x, "For we, being many, are one loaf, one body; for we are all partakers of that one loaf." This is as true and as practical to-day as it was when the apostle addressed the assembly at Corinth. True, there were divisions at Corinth as there are divisions in christendom; but that did not in any wise touch the truth of God. The apostle rebuked the divisions—pronounced them carnal. He had no sympathy with the poor, low idea which one sometimes hears advocated, that divisions are good things, as superinducing emulation. He believed they were very bad things—the fruit of the flesh, the work of Satan.

Neither, we feel persuaded, would the apostle have accepted the popular illustration that divisions in the Church are like so many regiments, with different facings, all fighting under the same commander-in-chief. It would not hold good for a moment; indeed, it has no application whatever, but rather gives a flat contradiction to that distinct and emphatic statement, "There is one body."

Reader, this is a most glorious truth. Let us ponder it deeply. Let us look at christendom in the light of it. Let us judge our own position and ways by it. Are we acting on it? Do we give expression to it, at the Lord's table, every Lord's day? Be assured it is our sacred duty and high privilege so to do. Say not there are difficulties of all sorts, many stumbling-blocks in the way, much to dishearten us in the conduct of those who profess to meet on this very ground of which we speak.

All this is, alas! but too true. We must be quite prepared for it. The devil will leave no stone unturned to cast dust in our eyes, so that we may not see God's blessed way for His people. But we must not give heed to his suggestions or be snared by his devices. There always have been, and there always will be difficulties in the way of carrying out the precious truth of God; and perhaps one of the greatest difficulties is found in the inconsistent conduct of those who profess to act upon it.

But then we must ever distinguish between the truth and those who profess it—between the ground and the conduct of those who occupy it. Of course, they ought to harmonize, but they do not; and hence we are imperatively called to judge the conduct by the ground, not the ground by the conduct. If we saw a man farming on a principle which we knew to be thoroughly sound, but he was a bad farmer, what should we do? Of course, we should reject his mode of working, but hold the principle all the same.

Not otherwise is it in reference to the truth now before us. There were heresies at Corinth, schisms, errors, evils of all sorts. What then? Was the truth of God to be surrendered as a myth, as something wholly impracticable? was it all to be given up? Were the Corinthians to meet on some other principle? were they to organize themselves on some new ground? were they to gather around some fresh centre? No, thank God! His truth was not to be surrendered for a moment, although Corinth was split up into ten thousand sects, and its horizon darkened by ten thousand heresies. The body of Christ is one; and the apostle simply displays in their view the banner with this blessed inscription: "Ye are the body of Christ, and members in particular."

Now, these words were addressed, not merely "unto the church at Corinth," but also "to all that in every place call upon the name of Jesus Christ our Lord, both theirs and ours." Hence, the truth of the one body is abiding and universal. Every true Christian is bound to recognize it and to act on it, and every assembly of Christians, wherever convened, should be the local expression of this grand and all-important truth.

Some might perhaps feel disposed to ask how it could be said to any one assembly, "Ye are the body of Christ." Were there not saints at Ephesus,

Colosse, and Philippi? No doubt; and had the apostle been addressing them on the same subject, he could have said to them likewise, "Ye are the body of Christ," inasmuch as they were the local expression of the body; and not only so, but, in addressing them, he had before his mind all saints, to the end of the Church's earthly career.

But we must bear in mind that the apostle could not possibly address such words to any human organization, ancient or modern. No; nor if all such organizations, call them what you please, were amalgamated into one, could he speak of it as "the body of Christ." That body, let it be distinctly understood, consists of all true believers on the face of the earth. That they are not gathered on that only divine ground, is their serious loss and their Lord's dishonor. The precious truth holds good all the same—"There is one body," and this is the divine standard by which to measure every ecclesiastical association and every religious system under the sun.

We deem it needful to go somewhat fully into the divine side of the question of the Church, in order to guard the truth of God from the results of misapprehension, and also that the reader may clearly understand that in speaking of the utter failure and ruin of the Church, we are looking at the human side of the subject. To this latter we must return for a moment.

It is impossible to read the New Testament with a calm and unprejudiced mind and not see that the Church as a responsible witness for Christ on the earth has most signally and shamefully failed. To quote all the passages in proof of this statement would literally fill a small volume; but let us glance at the second and third chapters of the book of Revelation, where the Church is seen under judgment. We have, in these solemn chapters, what we may call a divine Church-history. Seven assemblies are taken up, as illustrative of the various phases of the Church's history, from the day in which it was set up, in responsibility, on the earth, until it shall be spued out of the Lord's mouth, as something utterly intolerable. If we do not see that these two chapters are prophetic, as well as historic, we shall deprive ourselves of a vast field of most valuable instruction. For ourselves, we can only assure the reader that no human language could adequately set forth what we have gathered from Revelation ii. and iii., in their prophetic aspect.

However, we are only referring to them now as the last of a series of Scripture proofs of our present thesis. Take the address to Ephesus, the self-same church to which the apostle Paul wrote his marvelous epistle, opening up so blessedly the heavenly side of things, God's eternal purpose respecting the Church—the position and portion of the Church, as accepted in Christ and blessed with all spiritual blessings in the heavenlies in Him. No failure here; no thought of such a thing; no possibility of it. All is in God's hands here. The counsel is His; the work His. It is His grace, His glory, His mighty power, His good pleasure; and all founded upon the blood of Christ. There is no question of responsibility here. The Church was "dead in trespasses and sins;" but Christ died for her; He placed Himself judicially where she was morally; and God, in His sovereign grace, entered the scene and raised up Christ from the dead, and the Church in Him. Glorious fact! Here all is sure and settled. It is the Church in the heavenlies *in* Christ, not the Church on earth *for* Christ,—it is *the body "accepted,"* not *the candlestick judged.* If we do not see both sides of this great question, we have much to learn.

But there is the earthly side as well as the heavenly—the human as well as the divine—the candlestick as well as the body. Hence it is that in the judicial address in Revelation ii. we read such solemn words as these: "*I have against thee, that thou hast left thy first love.*"

How very distinct! Nothing like this in Ephesians; nothing against the body, nothing against the bride; but there is something against the candlestick. The light had even already become dim. Hardly had it been lighted ere the snuffers were needed.

Thus, at the very outset, symptoms of decline showed themselves, unmistakably, to the penetrating eye of Him who walked amongst the seven golden candlesticks; and when we reach the close, and contemplate the last phase of the Church's condition—the last stage of its earthly history, as illustrated by the assembly at Laodicea—there is not a single redeeming feature. The case is almost hopeless. The Lord is outside the door.— "Behold, I stand at the door, and knock." It is not here as at Ephesus, "I have somewhat against thee." The whole condition is bad. The whole professing body is about to be given up.—"I will spue thee out of My mouth." He still lingers, blessed be His name, for He is ever slow to leave the place of mercy, or enter the place of judgment. It reminds us of the departure of the glory, in the opening of Ezekiel. It moved with a slow and measured pace, loth to leave the house, the people, and the land. "Then the glory of the Lord went up from the cherub, and stood over the threshold of the house; and the house was filled with the cloud, and the court was full of the brightness of the Lord's glory." "Then the glory of the Lord departed from off the threshold of the house, and stood over the cherubim." And finally, "the glory of the Lord went up from the midst of the city, and stood upon the mountain which is on the east side of the city." (Ezek. x. 4, 18; xi. 23.)

This is deeply affecting. How striking the contrast between this slow departure of the glory and its speedy entrance, in the day of Solomon's dedication of the house in 2 Chronicles vii. 1. Jehovah was quick to enter His abode in the midst of His people; slow to leave it. He was, to speak after the manner of men, forced away by the sins and hopeless impenitence of His infatuated people.

So also with the Church. We see in the second of Acts His rapid entrance into His spiritual house. He came like a rushing mighty wind to fill the house with His glory. But in the third of Revelation, see His attitude: He is outside. Yes; but He is knocking. He lingers, not indeed with any hope of corporate restoration, but if haply *"any man"* would hear His voice and open the door." The fact of His being outside shows what the church is. The fact of His knocking shows what He is.

Christian reader, see that you thoroughly understand this whole subject: it is of the very last importance that you should. We are surrounded on all sides with false notions as to the present condition and future destiny of the professing church. We must fling these all behind our backs, with holy decision, and listen, with circumcised ear and reverent mind, to the teaching of holy Scripture. That teaching is as clear as noonday. The professing church is a hopeless ruin, and judgment is at the door. Read the epistle of Jude; read 2 Peter ii. and iii.; read 2 Timothy. Just lay aside this volume and look closely into those solemn scriptures, and we feel persuaded you will rise from the study with the deep and thorough conviction that there is nothing whatever before christendom but the unmitigated wrath of Almighty God. Its doom is set forth in that brief but solemn sentence in Romans xi., "Thou also shalt be cut off."

Yes; such is the language of Scripture.—"Cut off"—"spued out." The professing church has utterly failed as Christ's witness on the earth. As with Israel, so with the Church, the very truth which she was responsible to maintain and confess, she had faithlessly surrendered. Hardly had the canon of New-Testament scripture closed, hardly had the first set of laborers left the field, ere gross darkness set in, and settled down upon the whole professing body. Turn where you will, range through the ponderous tomes of "the fathers," as they are called, and you will not find a trace of those grand characteristic truths of our glorious Christianity. All, all was shamefully abandoned. As Israel in Canaan abandoned Jehovah for Baal and Ashtaroth, so the Church abandoned the pure and precious truth of God for puerile fables and deadly errors. The rapid departure is perfectly astounding; but it was just as the apostle Paul forewarned the elders of Ephesus.—"Take heed therefore unto yourselves, and to all the flock, over the which the Holy Ghost hath made you overseers, to feed the Church of God, which He hath purchased with His own blood. For I know this, that after my departing shall grievous wolves enter in among you, not sparing the flock. Also from among your own selves shall men arise, speaking perverse things, to draw away disciples after them." (Acts xx.)

How truly deplorable! The holy apostles of our Lord and Saviour Jesus Christ almost immediately succeeded by "grievous wolves" and teachers of perverse things; the whole Church plunged into thick darkness; the lamp of divine revelation almost hidden from view; ecclesiastical corruption in every form; priestly domination with all its terrible accompaniments. In short, the history of the Church—the history of christendom is the most appalling record ever penned.

True it is, thanks be to God, He left not Himself without a witness. Here and there, from time to time, just as in Israel of old, He raised up one and another to speak for Him. Even amid the deepest gloom of the middle ages, an occasional star appears upon the horizon. The Waldenses and others were enabled, by the grace of God, to hold fast His Word and to confess the name of Jesus in the face of Rome's dark and terrible tyranny, and diabolical cruelty.

Then came that gracious season, in the sixteenth century, when God raised up Luther and his beloved and honored fellow-laborers to preach the great truth of justification by faith, and to give the precious volume of God to the people, in their own tongue wherein they were born. It is not within the compass of human language to set forth the blessing of that memorable time. Thousands heard the glad tidings of salvation—heard, believed, and were saved. Thousands, who had long groaned beneath the intolerable weight of Romish superstition, hailed, with profound thankfulness, the heavenly message. Thousands flocked, with intense delight, to draw water from those wells of inspiration which had been stopped for ages by papal ignorance and intolerance. The blessed lamp of divine revelation, so long hidden by the enemy's hand, was permitted to cast its rays athwart the gloom, and thousands rejoiced in its heavenly light.

But while we heartily bless God for all the glorious results of what is commonly called the reformation, in the sixteenth century, we should make a very grave mistake indeed were we to imagine that it was any thing approaching to a restoration of the Church to its original condition. Far—very far from it. Luther and his companions, if we are to judge from their writings—precious writings, many of them—never grasped the divine idea of the Church as the body of Christ. They did not understand the unity of the body; the presence of the Holy Ghost in the assembly, as well as His indwelling in the individual believer; they never reached the grand truth of ministry in the Church, "its nature, source, power, and responsibility;" they never got beyond the idea of human authority as the basis of ministry; they were silent as to the specific hope of the Church, namely, the coming of Christ for His people—the bright and morning Star; they failed to seize the proper scope of prophecy, and proved themselves incompetent rightly to divide the word of truth.

Let us not be misunderstood. We love the memory of the reformers. Their names are familiar household words amongst us. They were dear, devoted, earnest, blessed servants of Christ. Would that we had their like amongst us in this day of revived popery and rampant infidelity. We would yield to none in our love and esteem for Luther, Melanchthon, Farel, Latimer, and Knox. They were truly bright and shining lights in their day; and thousands—yea, millions will thank God throughout eternity that they ever lived and preached and wrote. And not only so, but, looked at in their private life and public ministry, they put to shame many of those who have been favored with a range of truth for which we look in vain in the voluminous writings of the reformers.

But, admitting all this, as we most freely and gratefully do, we are nevertheless convinced that those beloved and honored servants of Christ failed to seize, and therefore failed to preach and teach, many of the special and characteristic truths of Christianity; at least, we have failed to find these truths in their writings. They preached the precious truth of justification by faith; they gave the holy Scriptures to the people; they trampled under foot much of the rubbish of Romish superstition.

All this they did, by the grace of God, and for all this we bow our heads in deep thankfulness and praise to the Father of mercies. But Protestantism is not Christianity; nor are the so-called churches of the reformation, whether national or dissenting, the Church of God. Far from it. We look back over the course of eighteen centuries, and spite of the occasional revivals, spite of the brilliant lights which at various times have shone upon the Church's horizon—lights which appeared all the brighter in contrast with the deep gloom that surrounded them—spite of the many gracious visitations of God's Spirit, both in Europe and America, during the past and present century—spite of all these things, for which we most heartily bless God, we return with decision to the statement already advanced, that the professing church is a hopeless wreck; that christendom is rapidly hastening down the inclined plane, to the blackness of darkness forever; that those highly favored lands, where much evangelical truth has been preached, where Bibles have been circulated in millions, and gospel tracts in billions, shall yet be covered with thick darkness—given over to strong delusion to believe a lie.

And then?—ah, what then? *A converted world?* Nay, but a *judged church.* The true saints of God, scattered throughout christendom—all the true members of the body of Christ, will be caught up to meet their coming Lord—the dead saints raised, the living changed, in a moment, and all taken up together to be forever with the Lord. Then the mystery will rise to a head in the person of the man of sin—the lawless one, the Antichrist. The Lord Jesus shall come, and all His saints with Him, to execute judgment on the beast, or revived Roman empire, and the false prophet, or Antichrist—the former in the west, the latter in the east.

This will be a summary act of direct warrior judgment, without any judicial process whatever, inasmuch as both the beast and false prophet shall be found in open rebellion and blasphemous opposition to God and the Lamb. Then comes the sessional judgment of the living nations, as recorded in Matthew xxv. 31-46.

Thus, all evil having been put down, Christ shall reign, in righteousness and peace, for a thousand years. A bright and blessed time! the true Sabbath for Israel and the whole earth—a period marked by the grand facts, Satan bound and Christ reigning. Glorious facts! The very reference to them causes the heart to overflow in praise and thanksgiving. What will the reality be?

But Satan shall be loosed from his thousand years' captivity, and allowed to make one more effort against God and His Christ.—"And when the thousand years are expired, Satan shall be loosed out of his prison, and shall go out to deceive the nations which are in the four quarters of the earth, Gog and Magog, to gather them together to battle, the number of whom is as the sand of the sea.[24] And they went up on the breadth of the earth, and compassed the camp of the saints about, and the beloved city; and fire came down from God out of heaven, and devoured them. And the devil that deceived them was cast into the lake of fire and brimstone, where the beast and the false prophet are, and shall be tormented day and night forever and ever." (Rev. xx. 7-10.)

This will be Satan's last effort, issuing in his eternal perdition. Then we have the judgment of the dead, "small and great"—the sessional judgment of all those who shall have died in their sins, from the days of Cain down to the last apostate from millennial glory. Tremendous scene! No heart can conceive, no tongue—no pen set forth, its awful solemnity.

Finally, we have unfolded to the vision of our souls the everlasting state—the new heaven and the new earth wherein righteousness shall dwell, throughout the golden ages of eternity.

Such is the order of events as set forth, with all possible clearness, on the page of inspiration. We have given a brief summary of them in connection with the line of truth on which we have been dwelling—a line, as we are fully aware, by no means popular; but we dare not withhold it on that account. Our business is to declare the whole counsel of God, not to seek popularity. We do not expect the truth of God to be popular in christendom; so far from this, we have been seeking to prove that just as Israel abandoned the truth which they were responsible to maintain, so the professing church has let slip all those great truths which characterize the Christianity of the New Testament. And we may assure the reader that our one object in pursuing this line of argument is to arouse the hearts of all true Christians to a sense of the value of those truths, and of their responsibility, not only to receive them, but to seek a fuller realization and a bolder confession of them. We long to see a band of men raised up, in these closing hours of the Church's earthly history, who shall go forth, in true spiritual power, and proclaim, with unction and energy, the long-forgotten truths of the gospel of God. May God, in His great mercy to His people, raise up such and send them forth. May the Lord Jesus knock louder and louder at the door, so that many may hear and open to Him, according to the desire of His loving heart, and taste the blessedness of deep personal communion with Himself, while waiting for His coming.

Blessed be God, there is no limit whatever to the blessing of the individual soul who hears Christ's voice and opens the door; and what is true of one is true of hundreds or thousands. Only let us be real and simple and true, feeling and owning our utter feebleness and nothingness, laying aside all assumption and empty pretension, not seeking to be any thing or to set up any thing, but holding fast Christ's word and not denying His name, finding our happy place at His feet, our satisfying portion in Himself, and our real delight in serving Him in any little way. Thus we shall get on harmoniously, lovingly, and happily together, finding our common centre in Christ, and our common object in seeking to further His cause and promote His glory. O that it were thus with all the Lord's beloved people in this our day! we should then have a very different tale to tell, and present a very different aspect to the world around. May the Lord revive His work.

It may perhaps seem to the reader that we have wandered a long way from the sixth chapter of Deuteronomy; but we must remind him, once for all, that it is not merely what each chapter *contains* that demands our attention, but also what it *suggests*. And further, we may add that, in sitting down to write, from time to time, it is our one desire to be led by God's Spirit into the very line of truth which may be suited to the need of all our readers. If only the beloved flock of Christ be fed, instructed, and comforted, we care not whether it be by well-connected notes or broken fragments.

We shall now proceed with our chapter.

Moses having laid down the grand foundation-truth contained in the fourth verse—"Hear, O Israel; the Lord our God is one Lord," proceeds to press upon the congregation their sacred duty in respect to this blessed

One. It was not merely that there was *a* God, but He was *their* God. He had deigned to link Himself with them, in covenant-relationship. He had redeemed them, borne them on eagles' wings, and brought them unto Himself, in order that they might be to Him a people, and that He might be their God.

Blessed fact! Blessed relationship! But Israel had to be reminded of the conduct suited to such a relationship—conduct which could only flow from a loving heart. "Thou shalt love the Lord *thy* God with *all* thy *heart*, and with *all* thy soul, and with *all* thy might." Here lies the secret of all true practical religion. Without this, all is valueless to God. "My son, give me thine heart." Where the heart is given, all will be right. The heart may be compared to the regulator of a watch, which acts on the hair-spring, and the hair-spring acts on the main-spring, and the main-spring acts on the hands, as they move around the dial. If your watch goes wrong, it will not do merely to alter the hands, you must touch the regulator. God looks for real heart-work, blessed be His name! His word to us is, "My little children, let us not love in word, neither in tongue; but in deed and in truth."

How we ought to bless Him for such touching words! they do so reveal His own loving heart to us. Assuredly, He loved us in deed and in truth, and He cannot be satisfied with any thing else, whether in our ways with Him or our ways one with another: all must flow straight from the heart.

"And these words which I command thee this day, shall be *in thine heart*"—at the very source of all the issues of life. This is peculiarly precious. Whatever is in the heart comes out through the lips and in the life. How important, then, to have the heart full of the Word of God—so full, that we shall have no room for the vanities and follies of this present evil world. Thus shall our conversation be always with grace, seasoned with salt. "Out of the abundance of the heart the mouth speaketh." Hence we can judge of what is in the heart by what cometh out of the mouth. The tongue is the organ of the heart—the organ of the man. "A good man out of the good treasure of the heart bringeth forth good things; and an evil man out of the evil treasure bringeth forth evil things." When the heart is really governed by the Word of God, the whole character reveals the blessed result. It must be so, inasmuch as the heart is the main-spring of our entire moral condition; it lies at the centre of all those moral influences which govern our personal history and shape our practical career.

In every part of the divine volume, we see how much importance God attaches to the attitude and state of the heart, with respect to Him or to His Word, which is one and the same thing. When the heart is true to Him, all is sure to come right; but on the other hand, we shall find that where the heart grows cold and careless as to God and His truth, there will, sooner or later, be open departure from the path of truth and righteousness. There is, therefore, much force and value in the exhortation addressed by Barnabas to the converts at Antioch—"He exhorted them all, that with *purpose of heart* they would cleave unto the Lord."

How needful then, now, always! This "purpose of heart" is most precious to God. It is what we may venture to call the grand moral regulator. It imparts a lovely earnestness to the Christian character which is greatly to be coveted by all of us. It is a divine antidote against coldness, deadness, and formality, all of which are so hateful to God. The outward life may be very correct, and the creed may be very orthodox; but if the earnest purpose of heart be lacking—the affectionate cleaving of the whole moral being to God and His Christ, all is utterly worthless.

It is through the heart that the Holy Ghost instructs us. Hence, the apostle prayed for the saints at Ephesus, that "the eyes of their *heart* [καρδίας not διανοίας] might be enlightened;" and again, "That Christ may dwell in your *heart* by faith."

Thus we see how all Scripture is in perfect harmony with the exhortation recorded in our chapter, "And these words which I command thee this day, shall be in thine heart." How near this would have kept them to their covenant-God! How safe, too, from all evil, and specially from the abominable evil of idolatry—their national sin, their terrible besetment! If Jehovah's precious words had only found their right place in the heart, there would have been little fear of Baal, Chemosh, or Ashtaroth. In a word, all the idols of the heathen would have found their right place, and been estimated at their true value, if only the word of Jehovah had been allowed to dwell in Israel's heart.

And be it specially noted here how beautifully characteristic all this is of the book of Deuteronomy. It is not so much a question of keeping up a certain order of religious observances, the offering of sacrifices, or attention to rites and ceremonies. All these things, no doubt, had their place, but they are by no means the prominent or paramount thing in Deuteronomy. No; the Word is the all-important matter here. It is *Jehovah's word* in *Israel's heart*.

The reader must seize this fact if he really desires to possess the key to the lovely book of Deuteronomy. It is not a book of ceremonial; it is a book of moral and affectionate obedience. It teaches, in almost every section, that invaluable lesson, that the heart that loves, prizes, and honors the Word of God is ready for every act of obedience, whether it be the offering of a sacrifice or the observance of a day. It might so happen that an Israelite would find himself in a place and under circumstances in which a rigid adherence to rites and ceremonies would be impossible; but he never could be in a place or in circumstances in which he could not love, reverence, and obey the Word of God. Let him go where he would—let him be carried, as a captive exile, to the ends of the earth, nothing could rob him of the high privilege of uttering and acting on those blessed words, "Thy Word have I hid in mine heart, that I might not sin against Thee."

Precious words! They contain, in their brief compass, the great principle of the book of Deuteronomy, and, we may add, the great principle of the divine life, at all times and in all places. It can never lose its moral force and value: it always holds good. It was true in the days of the patriarchs, true for Israel in the land, true for Israel scattered to the ends of the earth, true for the Church as a whole, true for each individual believer amid the Church's hopeless ruins. In a word, obedience is always the creature's holy duty and exalted privilege—simple, unhesitating, unqualified obedience to the Word of the Lord. This is an unspeakable mercy for which we may well praise our God, day and night. He has given us His Word, blessed be His name, and He exhorts us to let that Word dwell in us richly—dwell in our hearts, and assert its holy sway over our entire course and character.

"And these words, which I command thee this day, shall be in thine heart: and thou shalt teach them diligently unto thy children, and shalt talk of them when thou sittest in thine house, and when thou walkest by the way, and when thou liest down, and when thou risest up. And thou shalt bind them for a sign upon thine hand, and they shall be as frontlets between thine eyes. And thou shalt write them upon the posts of thy house, and on thy gates."

All this is perfectly beautiful. The Word of God hidden in the heart; flowing out in loving instruction to the children, and in holy conversation in the bosom of the family; shining out in all the activities of daily life, so that all who came inside the gates or entered the house might see that the Word of God was the standard for each, for all, and in every thing.

Thus it was to be with Israel of old, and surely thus it ought to be with Christians now. But is it so? Are our children thus taught? Is it our constant aim to present the Word of God, in all its heavenly attractiveness, to their young hearts? Do they see it shining out in our daily life? do they see its influence upon our habits, our temper, our family intercourse, our business transactions? This is what we understand by binding the Word as a sign upon the hands, having it as a frontlet between the eyes, writing it upon the door-posts and upon the gates.

Reader, is it thus with us? It is of little use attempting to teach our children the Word of God if our lives are not governed by that Word. We do not believe in making the blessed Word of God a mere school-book for our children; to do so is to turn a delightful privilege into a wearisome drudgery. Our children should see that we live in the very atmosphere of Scripture; that it forms the material of our conversation when we sit in the bosom of the family, in our moments of relaxation.

Alas! how little is this the case! Have we not to be deeply humbled in the presence of God when we reflect upon the general character and tone of our conversation at table, and in the family circle? How little there is of Deuteronomy vi. 7! How much of "foolish talking and jesting, which are not convenient"! How much evil-speaking of our brethren, our neighbors, our fellow-laborers! How much idle gossip! How much worthless small talk!

And from what does all this proceed? Simply from the state of the heart. The Word of God, the commandments and sayings of our Lord and Saviour Jesus Christ, are not dwelling in our hearts; and hence they are not welling up and flowing out in living streams of grace and edification.

Will any one say that Christians do not need to consider these things? If so, let him ponder the following wholesome words: "Let no corrupt communication proceed out of your mouth, but that which is good to the use of edifying, that it may minister grace unto the hearers." And again, "Be filled with the Spirit; speaking to yourselves in psalms and hymns and spiritual songs, singing and making melody in your heart to the Lord; giving thanks always for all things unto God and the Father in the name of our Lord Jesus Christ." (Eph. iv. 29; v. 18-20.)

These words were addressed to the saints at Ephesus; and, most assuredly, we should apply our hearts diligently to them. We are little aware, perhaps, of how deeply and constantly we fail in maintaining the habit of spiritual conversation. It is specially in the bosom of the family, and in our ordinary intercourse, that this failure is most manifest. Hence our need of those words of exhortation which we have just penned. It is evident the Holy Spirit foresaw the need, and graciously anticipated it. Hear what He says "to the saints and faithful brethren in Christ at Colosse," — "Let the peace of Christ rule in your hearts, to the which also ye are called in one body; and be ye thankful. Let the word of Christ dwell in you richly in all wisdom; teaching and admonishing one another in psalms and hymns and spiritual songs, singing with grace in your hearts to the Lord." (Col. iii.)

Lovely picture of ordinary Christian life! It is but a fuller and higher development of what we have in our chapter, where the Israelite is seen in the midst of his family, with the Word of God flowing forth from his heart in loving instruction to his children — seen in his daily life, in all his intercourse at home and abroad, under the hallowed influence of Jehovah's words.

Beloved Christian reader, do we not long to see more of all this in our midst? Is it not, at times, very sorrowful and very humbling to mark the style of conversation that obtains in the midst of our family circles? Should we not sometimes blush if we could see our conversation reproduced in print? What is the remedy? Here it is—a heart filled with the peace of Christ, the word of Christ, Christ Himself: nothing else will do. We must begin with the heart, and where that is thoroughly preoccupied with heavenly things, we shall make very short work with all attempts at evil-speaking, foolish talking, and jesting.

"And it shall be, when the Lord thy God shall have brought thee into the land which He sware unto thy fathers, to Abraham, to Isaac, and to Jacob, to give thee great and goodly cities which thou buildedst not, and houses full of all good things which thou filledst not, and wells digged which thou diggedst not, and vineyards and olive-trees which thou plantedst not; when thou shalt have eaten and be full; then beware lest thou forget the Lord, which brought thee forth out of the land of Egypt, from the house of bondage." (Ver. 10-12.)

Amid all the blessings, the mercies, and the privileges of the land of Canaan, they were to remember that gracious and faithful One who had redeemed them out of the land of bondage. They were to remember, too, that all these things were His free gift. The land, with all that it contained, was bestowed upon them in virtue of His promises to Abraham, Isaac, and Jacob. Cities built and houses furnished, flowing wells, fruitful vineyards and olive-yards, all ready to their hand, the free gift of sovereign grace and covenant mercy. All they had to do was to take possession, in simple faith, and to keep ever in the remembrance of the thoughts of their hearts the bounteous Giver of it all. They were to think of Him, and find in His redeeming love the true motive-spring of a life of loving obedience. Wherever they turned their eyes, they beheld the tokens of His great goodness—the rich fruit of His marvelous love. Every city, every house, every well, every vine, olive and fig-tree, spoke to their hearts of Jehovah's abounding grace, and furnished a substantial proof of His infallible faithfulness to His promise.

"Thou shalt fear the Lord thy God, and serve Him, and shalt swear by His name. Ye shall not go after other gods, of the gods of the people which are round about you; (for the Lord thy God is a jealous God among you) lest the anger of the Lord thy God be kindled against thee, and destroy thee from off the face of the earth."

There are two great motives set before the congregation, in our chapter, namely, "love," in verse 5, and "fear," in verse 13. These are found all through Scripture; and their importance in guiding the life and forming the character cannot possibly be too highly estimated. "The fear of the Lord is the beginning of wisdom." We are exhorted to be "in the fear of the Lord all the day." It is a grand moral safeguard against all evil. "Unto man He said, 'Behold, the fear of the Lord, that is wisdom; and to depart from evil is understanding.'"

The blessed Book abounds in passages setting forth, in every possible form, the immense importance of the fear of God. "How," says Joseph, "can I do this great wickedness, and sin against God?" The man who walks habitually in the fear of God is preserved from every form of moral pravity. The abiding realization of the divine presence must prove an effectual shelter from every temptation. How often do we find the presence of some very holy and spiritual person a wholesome check upon levity and folly; and if such be the moral influence of a fellow-mortal, how much more powerful would be the realized presence of God!

Christian reader, let us give our serious attention to this weighty matter. Let us seek to live in the consciousness that we are in the immediate presence of God. Thus shall we be preserved from a thousand forms of evil, to which we are exposed from day to day, and to which, alas! we are predisposed. The remembrance that the eye of God rests upon us would exert a far more powerful influence upon our life and conversation than the presence of all the saints upon earth and all the angels in heaven. We could not speak falsely, we could not utter with our lips what we do not feel in the heart, we could not talk folly, we could not speak evil of our brother or our neighbor, we could not speak unkindly of any one, if only we felt ourselves in the presence of God. In a word, the holy fear of the Lord, of which Scripture speaks so much, would act as a most blessed restraint upon evil thoughts, evil words, evil ways, evil in every shape and form.

Moreover, it would tend to make us very real and genuine in all our sayings and doings. There is a sad amount of sham and nonsense about us. We frequently say a great deal more than we feel. We are not honest; we do not speak, every man, truth with our neighbor; we give expressions to sentiments which are not the genuine utterance of the heart; we act the hypocrite one with another.

All these things afford melancholy proof of how little we live, move, and have our being in the presence of God. If we could only bear in mind that God hears us and sees us—hears our every word and sees our every thought, our every way, how differently we should carry ourselves! What holy watchfulness we should maintain over our thoughts, our tempers, and our tongues! What purity of heart and mind! What truth and uprightness in all our intercourse with our fellows! What reality and simplicity in our deportment! What happy freedom from all affectation, assumption, and pretension! What deliverance from every form of self-occupation! O, to live ever in the deep sense of the divine presence! to walk in the fear of the Lord all the day long!

And then to prove the "vast constraining influence" of His love! To be led out in all the holy activities which that love would ever suggest! To find our delight in doing good! To taste the spiritual luxury of making hearts glad! To be continually meditating plans of usefulness! To live close by the fountain of divine love, so that we must be streams of refreshing in the midst of this thirsty scene—rays of light amid the moral gloom around us! "The love of Christ," says the blessed apostle, "constraineth us; because we thus judge, that if one died for all, then were all dead; and that He died for all, that they which live should not henceforth live unto themselves, but unto Him which died for them, and rose again."

How morally lovely is all this! "Would that it were more fully realized and faithfully exhibited amongst us! May the fear and love of God be continually in our hearts, in all their blessed power and formative influence, that thus our daily life may shine to His praise and the real profit, comfort, and blessing of all who come in contact with us, whether in private or in public. God, in His infinite mercy, grant it, for Christ's sake!

The sixteenth verse of our chapter demands our special attention.—"Ye shall not tempt the Lord your God, as ye tempted Him in Massah." These words were quoted by our blessed Lord when tempted by Satan to cast Himself from the pinnacle of the temple.—"Then the devil taketh Him up into the holy city, and setteth Him on a pinnacle of the temple, and saith unto Him, 'If Thou be the Son of God, cast Thyself down; for it is written, He shall give His angels charge concerning Thee; and in their hands they shall bear Thee up, lest at any time Thou dash Thy foot against a stone.'"

This is a very remarkable passage. It proves how Satan can quote Scripture when it suits his purpose. But he omits a most important clause— "To keep Thee in all Thy ways." Now, it formed no part of the ways of Christ to cast Himself from the pinnacle of the temple. It was not the path of duty. He had no command from God to do any such thing, and hence He refused to do it. He had no need to tempt God—to put Him to the test. He had, as a man, the most perfect confidence in God—the fullest assurance of His protection.

Moreover, He was not going to abandon the path of duty in order to prove God's care of Him; and herein He teaches us a most valuable lesson. We can always count on God's protecting hand when we are treading the path of duty; but if we are walking in a self-chosen path—if we are seeking our own pleasure or our own interest, our own ends or objects, then to talk of counting on God would be simply wicked presumption.

No doubt, our God is very merciful, very gracious, and His tender mercy is over us, even when we wander off the path of duty; but this is another thing altogether, and it leaves wholly untouched the statement that we can only count on divine protection when our feet are in the pathway of duty, if a Christian goes out boating for his amusement, or if he goes clambering over the Alps merely for sight-seeing, has he any right to believe that God will take care of him? Let conscience give the answer. If God calls us to cross a stormy lake to preach the gospel, if He summons us to cross the Alps on some special service for Him, then, assuredly, we can commit ourselves to His mighty hand to protect us from all evil. The grand point for all of us is, to be found in the holy path of duty. It may be narrow, rough, and lonely; but it is a path overshadowed by the wings of the Almighty and illumined by the light of His approving countenance.

Ere turning from the subject suggested by verse 16, we would briefly notice the very interesting and instructive fact that our Lord, in His reply to Satan, takes no notice whatever of his misquotation of psalm xci. 11. Let us carefully note this fact and seek to bear it in mind. In place of saying to the enemy, You have left out a most important clause of the passage which you undertake to quote, He simply quotes another passage, as authority for His own conduct. Thus He vanquished the tempter, and thus He left us a blessed example.

It is worthy of our special notice that the Lord Jesus Christ did not overcome Satan in virtue of His divine power. Had He done so, it could not be an example for us. But when we see Him as a man using the Word as His only weapon, and thus gaining a glorious victory, our hearts are encouraged and comforted; and not only so, but we learn a most precious lesson as to how we, in our sphere and measure, are to stand in the conflict. The Man Christ Jesus overcame by simple dependence upon God and obedience to His Word.

Blessed fact! A fact full of comfort and consolation for us. Satan could do nothing with one who would only act by divine authority, and by the power of the Spirit. Jesus never did His own will, though, as we know, (blessed be His holy name!) His will was absolutely perfect. He came down from heaven, as He Himself tells us, in John vi, not to do His own will, but the will of the Father that sent Him. He was a perfect servant, from first to last. His rule of action was the Word of God; His power of action, the Holy Ghost; His only motive for action, the will of God; hence the prince of this world had nothing in Him. Satan could not, by all his subtle wiles, draw Him out of the path of obedience, or out of the place of dependence.

Christian reader, let us consider these things; let us deeply ponder them; let us remember that our blessed Lord and Master left us an example that we should follow His steps. Oh, may we follow them diligently during the little while that yet remains. May we, by the gracious ministry of the Holy Ghost, enter more fully into the great fact that we are called to walk even as Jesus walked. He is our great Exemplar in all things. Let us study Him more profoundly, so that we may reproduce Him more faithfully.

We shall now close this lengthened section by quoting for the reader the last paragraph of the chapter on which we have been dwelling; it is a passage of singular fullness, depth, and power, and strikingly characteristic of the entire book of Deuteronomy.

"Ye shall *diligently* keep the commandments of the Lord your God, and His testimonies, and His statutes, which He hath commanded thee. And thou shalt do that which is right and good in the sight of the Lord; that it may be well with thee, and that thou mayest go in and possess the good land which the Lord sware unto thy fathers; to cast out all thine enemies from before thee, as the Lord hath spoken. And when thy son asketh thee in time to come, saying, What mean the testimonies and the statutes and the judgments which the Lord our God hath commanded you? Then thou shalt say unto thy son, We were Pharaoh's bondmen in Egypt; and the Lord brought us out of Egypt with a mighty hand; and the Lord showed signs and wonders, great and sore, upon Egypt, upon Pharaoh, and upon all his household, before our eyes; and He brought us out from thence, that He might bring us in, to give us the land which He sware unto our fathers. And the Lord commanded us to do all these statutes, to fear the Lord our God, for our good always, that He might preserve us alive, as it is at this day. And it shall be our righteousness, if we observe to do all these commandments before the Lord our God, as He hath commanded us."

How prominently is the Word of God kept before the soul, in every page and every paragraph of this book! It is the one great subject on the heart and in all the discourses of the revered lawgiver. It is his one aim to exalt the Word of God, in all its aspects, whether in the form of testimonies, commandments, statutes, or judgments; and to set forth the moral importance, yea, the urgent necessity of whole-hearted, earnest, diligent obedience, on the part of the people. "Ye shall *diligently* keep the commandments of the Lord your God." And again, "Thou shalt do that which is *right* and *good* in the sight of the Lord."

All this is morally lovely. We have here unfolded before our eyes those eternal principles which no change of dispensation, no change of scene, place, or circumstances can ever touch. "That which is right and good" must ever be of universal and abiding application. It reminds us of the words of the apostle John to his beloved friend Gaius—"Beloved, follow not that which is evil, but that which is good." The assembly might be in a very low condition; there might be very much to try the heart and depress the spirit of Gaius; Diotrephes might be carrying himself most unbecomingly and unwarrantably toward the beloved and venerable apostle and others; all this might be true, and much more—yea, the whole professing body might go wrong. What then? What remained for Gaius to do? Simply to follow that which was right and good; to open his heart and his hand and his house to every one who brought *the truth*; to seek to help on the cause of Christ in every right way.

This was the business of Gaius in his day, and this is the business of every true lover of Christ at all times, in all places, and under all circumstances. We may not have many to join us; we may perhaps find ourselves, at times, almost alone; but we are still to follow what is good, cost what it may. We are to *depart* from iniquity—*purge* ourselves from dishonorable vessels—*flee* youthful lusts—*turn away* from powerless professors. And what then? "Follow righteousness, faith, love, peace"—How? In isolation? Nay. I may find myself alone in any given place for a time, but there can be no such thing as isolation so long as the body of Christ is on earth, and that will be till He comes for us. Hence we never expect to see the day in which we cannot find a few that call on the Lord out of a pure heart; whoever they are and wherever they are, it is our bounden duty to find them, and, having found them, to walk with them in holy fellowship "until the end."

P.S.—We must reserve the remaining chapters of Deuteronomy for another volume. May the Lord be graciously pleased to grant His rich blessing upon our meditations thus far. May He clothe these pages with the power of the Holy Ghost, and make them to be a direct message from Himself to the hearts of His people throughout the whole world. May He also grant spiritual power to unfold the truth contained in the remaining sections of this most profound, comprehensive, and suggestive book.

We earnestly beseech the Christian reader to join us in prayer as to all this, remembering those most precious words, "If two of you shall *agree* on earth as touching any thing that they shall ask, it shall be done for them by My Father which is in heaven."

C. H. M.

FOOTNOTES

[2] In referring to infidel writers, we should bear in mind that by far the most dangerous of such are those calling themselves Christians. In our young days, whenever we heard the word "infidel," we at once thought of a Tom Paine or a Voltaire; now, alas! we have to think of so-called bishops and doctors of the professing church. Tremendous fact!

[3] The journey of Israel from Horeb to Kadesh-barnea illustrates but too forcibly the history of many souls in the matter of finding peace. Many of the Lord's beloved people go on for years, doubting and fearing, never knowing the blessedness of the liberty wherewith Christ makes His people free. It is most distressing, to any one who really cares for souls, to see the sad condition in which some are kept all their days, through legality, bad teaching, false manuals of devotion, and such like. It is a rare thing now-a-days to find in christendom a soul fully established in the peace of the gospel. It is considered a good thing—a sign of humility—to be always doubting. Confidence is looked upon as presumption. In short, things are turned completely upside down. The gospel is not known: souls are under law instead of under grace,—they are kept at a distance instead of being taught to draw nigh. Much of the religion of the day is a deplorable mixture of Christ and self, law and grace, faith and works. Souls are kept in a perfect muddle all their days.

Surely these things demand the grave consideration of all who occupy the responsible place of teachers and preachers in the professing church. There is a solemn day approaching, when all such will be called to render an account of their ministry.

[4] "Lectures Introductory to the Pentateuch," by W. Kelly.

[5] With regard to the solemn subject of eternal punishment, we here offer a few remarks, seeing that so very many, both in England and America, are troubled with difficulties respecting it.

There are three considerations, which, if duly weighed, will, we think, settle every Christian on the doctrine.

I. The first is this: There are seventy passages in the New Testament where the word "everlasting," or "eternal," (αἰώνιος) occurs. It is applied to the "life" which believers possess, to the "mansions" into which they are to be received, to the "glory" which they are to enjoy; it is applied to God (Rom. xvi. 26.), to the "salvation" of which our Lord Jesus Christ is the Author, to the "redemption" which He has obtained for us, and to the "Spirit."

Then, out of the seventy passages referred to above, which the reader can verify in a few moments by a glance at a Greek Concordance, there are seven in which the self-same word is applied to the "punishment" of the wicked, to the "judgment" which is to overtake them, to the "fire" which is to consume them.

Now, the question is, Upon what principle, or by what authority, can any one mark off these seven passages and say that in them the word αἰώνιος does not mean "everlasting," while in the other sixty-three it does? We consider the statement utterly baseless, and unworthy the attention of any sober mind. We fully admit that, had the Holy Spirit thought proper, when speaking of the judgment of the wicked, to make use of a different word from that used in the other passages, reason would that we should weigh the fact. But no; He uses the same word invariably, so that if we deny eternal punishment, we must deny eternal life, eternal glory, an eternal Spirit, an eternal God, an eternal any thing. In short, if punishment be not eternal, nothing is eternal, so far as this argument is concerned. To meddle with this stone in the archway of divine revelation, is to reduce the whole to a mass of ruin around us. And this is just what the devil is aiming at. We are fully persuaded that to deny the truth of eternal punishment is to take the first step on that inclined plane which leads down to the dark abyss of universal skepticism.

II. Our second consideration is drawn from the great truth of the immortality of the soul. We read in the second chapter of Genesis that "the Lord God formed man of the dust of the ground, and breathed into his nostrils the breath of life; and man became a living soul." Upon this one passage, as upon an immovable rock, even if we had not another, we build the great truth of the immortality of the human soul. The fall of man made no difference as to this. Fallen or unfallen, innocent or guilty, converted or unconverted, the soul must live forever.

The tremendous question is, Where is it to live? God cannot allow sin into His presence. "He is of purer eyes than to behold evil, and cannot look upon iniquity." Hence, if a man dies in his sins—dies unrepentant, unwashed, unpardoned, then, most assuredly, where God is he never can come; indeed, it is the very last place to which he would like to come. There is nothing for him but an endless eternity in the lake that burneth with fire and brimstone.

III. And lastly, we believe that the truth of eternal punishment stands intimately connected with the infinite nature of the atonement of our Lord and Saviour Jesus Christ. If nothing short of an infinite sacrifice could deliver us from the consequences of sin, those consequences must be eternal. This consideration may not, perhaps, in the judgment of some, carry much weight with it; but to us its force is absolutely irresistible. We must measure sin and its consequences as we measure divine love and its results—not by the standard of human sentiment or reason, but only by the standard of the cross of Christ.

[6] We must distinguish between all true science and "science falsely so called." And further, we must distinguish between the *facts* of science, and the *conclusions* of scientific men. The facts are what God has done and is doing; but when men set about drawing their conclusions from these facts, they make the most serious mistakes.

However, it is a real relief to the heart to think that there are many philosophers and men of science who give God His right place, and who love our Lord Jesus Christ in sincerity.

[7] To apply the solemn address of Christ to the church of Laodicea, as we sometimes find it done in modern evangelical preaching, to the case of the sinner, is a great mistake. No doubt, what the preacher means is right enough, but it is not presented here. It is not Christ knocking at the door of a sinner's heart, but knocking at the door of the professing church. What a fact is this! How full of deep and awful solemnity as regards the church! What an end to come to!—Christ outside! But what grace, as regards Christ, for He is knocking! He wants to come in; He is still lingering, in patient grace and changeless love, ready to come in to any faithful individual heart that will only open to Him. "If any man"—even one! In Sardis, He could speak *positively* of "*a few;*" in Laodicea, He can only speak *doubtfully* as to finding *one*. But should there be even one, He will come in to him, and sup with him. Precious Saviour! Faithful Lover of our souls! "Jesus Christ, the same yesterday, to-day, and forever."

Reader, need we wonder that the enemy should seek to mutilate and misapply the solemn and searching address to the church of Laodicea—the professing body in the last dreary stage of its history? We have no hesitation in saying that to apply it *merely* to the case of an unconverted soul is to deprive the professing church of one of the most pertinent, pungent, and powerful appeals within the covers of the New Testament.

[8] There is an interesting difference between the Lord's "commandments" and "sayings." The former set forth, distinctly and definitely, what we ought to do; the latter are the expression of His mind. If I give my child a command, it is the statement of his duty; and if he loves me, he will delight to do it. But if he has heard me *say* I like to see such a thing done, although I have not actually told him to do it, it will touch my heart much more deeply to see him go and do that thing in order to gratify me, than if I had given him a positive command. Now, ought we not to try and please the heart of Christ? Should we not "labor to be agreeable to Him"? He has made us accepted; surely we ought to seek, in every possible way, to be acceptable to Him. He delights in a loving obedience; it was what He Himself rendered to the Father.—"I delight to do Thy will; yea, *Thy law* is within *My heart*." "If ye keep My commandments, ye shall abide in My love; even as I have kept My Father's commandments, and abide in His love." Oh, that we may drink more deeply into the spirit of Jesus, walk in His blessed footsteps, and render Him a more loving, devoted, and whole-hearted obedience in all things! Let us earnestly seek after these things, beloved Christian reader, that His heart may be gratified, and His name glorified in us, and in our entire practical career from day to day.

[9] The rendering of Romans vii. 6 in our authorized version is manifestly erroneous, inasmuch as it teaches that the law is dead, which is not true. "The law is good, if a man use it lawfully." (1 Tim. i.) And again, "The law is holy." (Rom. vii.) Scripture never teaches that the law is dead, but it teaches that the believer is dead to the law—a totally different thing.

But further, ἀποθανοντες cannot possibly apply to the law, as any well-taught school-boy can see at a glance; it applies to us—believers. Were it the law, the word would be ἀποθανοντος.

[10] It may be that the reader feels a little jealous of any interference with our excellent English Bible. He may, like many others, feel disposed to say, "How is an uneducated man to know what is Scripture and what is not? Must he depend upon scholars and critics to give him certainty on so grave and important a question? If so, is it not the same old story of

looking to human authority to confirm the Word of God?" By no means. It is a totally different thing. We all know that all copies and translations must be, in some points, imperfect, as being human; but we believe that the same grace which gave the Word in the original Hebrew and Greek languages, has most marvelously watched over our English translation, so that a poor man, at the back of a mountain, may rest assured that he possesses in his common English Bible the revelation of the mind of God. It is wonderful, after all the labors of scholars and critics, how few passages, comparatively, have had to be touched; and not one affecting any foundation-doctrine of Christianity. God, who graciously gave us the holy Scriptures at the first, has watched over them and preserved them to His Church in a most wonderful manner. Moreover, He has seen fit to make use of the labors of scholars and critics, from age to age, to clear the sacred text of errors which, through the infirmity attaching to all human agency, had crept into it. Should these corrections shake our confidence in the integrity of Scripture as a whole? or lead us to doubt that we possess, in very deed, the Word of God? Nay, rather should they lead us to bless God for His goodness in watching over His Word in order to preserve it in its integrity for His Church.

[11] Jonah, of course, is an exception; his mission was to Nineveh. He is the only prophet whose commission had exclusive reference to the Gentiles.

[12] The reader must seize the difference between "the fullness of the Gentiles" in Romans xi, and "the times of the Gentiles" in Luke xxi. The former refers to those who are now being gathered into the Church: the latter, on the contrary, refers to the times of Gentile supremacy which began with Nebuchadnezzar, and runs on to the time when "the stone cut out without hands" shall fall, in crushing power, upon the great image of Daniel ii.

[13] We must accurately distinguish between "*nature*" and "*flesh.*" The former is recognized in Scripture; the latter is condemned and set aside. "Doth not even nature itself teach you?" says the apostle. (1 Cor. xi. 14.) Jesus beholding the young ruler in Mark x, "loved him" although there was nothing but nature. To be without natural affection is one of the marks of the apostasy. Scripture teaches that we are dead to sin, not to nature, else what becomes of our natural relationships?

[14] The reader will do well to ponder the fact that there is no such thing in the New Testament as human appointment to preach the gospel, teach in the assembly of God, or feed the flock of Christ. Elders and deacons were ordained by the apostles or their delegates, Timothy and Titus;

but evangelists, pastors, and teachers were never so ordained. We must distinguish between gift and local charge. Elders and deacons might possess a special gift or not; it had nothing to do with their local charge. If the reader would understand the subject of ministry, let him study 1 Corinthians xii.-xiv. and Ephesians iv. 8-13. In the former we have, first, the *basis* of all true ministry in the Church of God, namely, *divine appointment*—"God hath set the members," etc.; secondly, *the motive-spring*—"love;" thirdly, *the object*—"that the Church may receive edifying." In Ephesians iv. we have the *source* of all ministry—a risen and ascended Lord; the *design*—"to perfect the saints for the work of the ministry;" the *duration*—"till we all come unto a perfect man, unto the measure of the stature of the fullness of Christ."

In a word, ministry, in all its departments, is *entirely* a divine institution. It is not of man or by man, but of God. The Master must, in every case, fit, fill, and appoint the vessel. There is no authority in Scripture for the notion that every man has a right to minister in the Church of God. Liberty for men is radicalism and not Scripture. Liberty for the Holy Ghost to minister by whom He will is what we are taught in the New Testament. May we learn it.

[15] The reader may perhaps feel disposed to inquire, On what ground will the Gentile be judged if he is not under the law? Romans i. 20 teaches us distinctly that the testimony of *creation* leaves him without excuse. Then, in chapter ii. 15, he is taken up on the ground of *conscience.*—"*For when the Gentiles, which have not the law, do by nature the things contained in the law, these, having not the law, are a law unto themselves; which show the work of the law written in their hearts, their conscience also bearing witness,*" etc. Finally, as regards those nations that have become professedly Christian, they will be judged on the ground of their profession.

[16] The omission of the article adds immensely to the force, fullness, and clearness of the passage. It is διὰ νόμου νόμῳ ἀπέθανον. A wonderful clause, surely. Would that it were better understood! It demolishes a vast mass of human theology. It leaves the law in its own proper sphere; but takes the believer completely from under its power, and out of its range, by death. "Wherefore, my brethren, ye also are become dead to the law by the body of Christ; that ye should be married to another, even to Him who is raised from the dead, that we should bring forth fruit unto God" (which we never could do if under the law). "For when we were in the flesh"—a correlative term with being under the law—"the motions of sins, which were by the law, did work in our members to bring forth fruit unto death."

Mark the melancholy combination—"under the law"—"in the flesh"—"motions of sins"—"fruit unto death"! Can any thing be more strongly marked? But there is another side, thank God, to this question—His own bright and blessed side. Here it is: "But now *we are delivered from the law.*" How? Is it by another's having fulfilled it for us? Nay; but, "*Having died to that* [ἀποθανόντες ἐν ᾧ] wherein we were held; that we should serve in newness of spirit, and not in the oldness of the letter." How perfect and how lovely is the harmony of Romans vii. and Galatians ii.! "I through law am dead to law, that I might live unto God."

[17] It is needful to bear in mind that although the Gentile was never, by the dispensational dealings of God, put under the law, yet, in point of fact, all baptized professors take that ground. Hence there is a vast difference between christendom and the heathen in reference to the question of the law. Thousands of unconverted people, every week, ask God to incline their hearts to keep the law. Surely, such persons stand on very different ground from the heathen who never heard of the law, and never heard of the Bible.

[18] Some are of opinion that the expression, "on the Lord's day" ought to be rendered, "on the day of the Lord," meaning that the apostle was in the spirit of that day when our Lord Christ shall take to Himself His great power and reign. But to this view there are two grave objections. In the first place, the words τῇ κυριακῇ ἡμέρᾳ, rendered, in Revelation i. 10, "The Lord's day," are quite distinct from ἡ ἡμέρα κυρίου, in 1 Thessalonians v. 2; 2 Thessalonians ii. 2; 2 Peter iii. 10, properly rendered, "The day of the Lord."

This we consider a very weighty objection, and one quite sufficient to settle the question. But in addition to this, we have the argument based on the fact that by far the greater portion of the book of Revelation is occupied, not with "the day of the Lord," but with events prior thereto.

Hence, therefore, we feel persuaded that "the Lord's day" and "the first day of the week" are identical; and this we deem a very important fact, as proving that that day has a very special place in the Word of God—a place which every intelligent Christian will thankfully own.

[19] We would commend to the reader's attention psalm lxvii. It is one of a large class of passages which prove that the blessing of the nations is consequent upon Israel's restoration. "God be merciful unto us [Israel], and bless us; and cause His face to shine upon us, that Thy way may be known upon earth, Thy saving health among *all nations.*... God shall bless us; and

all the ends of the earth shall fear Him." There could not be a more lovely or forcible proof of the fact that it is Israel, and not the Church, that will be used for the blessing of the nations.

[20] The application of John xvi. 8-11 to the Spirit's work in the individual is, in our judgment, a serious mistake. It refers to the effect of His presence on earth, in reference to the world as a whole. His work in the soul is a precious truth, we need hardly say, but it is not the truth taught in this passage.

[21] The word ἐρευνᾶτε maybe either imperative or indicative; but the context, we judge, demands the latter. They had the Scriptures; they were read in their synagogues every Sabbath day; they professed to believe that in them they had eternal life; they testified of Him; and yet they would not come to Him. Here was the flagrant inconsistency. Now, if ἐρευνᾶτε be taken as a command, the whole force of the passage is lost.

Need we remind the reader that there are plenty of arguments and inducements leading us to search the Scriptures, without appealing to what we believe to be an inaccurate rendering of John v. 39?

[22] The expression, "Cutting off the members of Christ's body" is generally applied in cases of discipline; but it is quite a misapplication. The discipline of the assembly can never touch the unity of the body. A member of the body may so fail in morals or err in doctrine as to call for the action of the assembly in putting him away from the table, but that has nothing to do with his place in the body. The two things are perfectly distinct.

[23] The unity of the Church may be compared to a chain thrown across a river; we see it at each side, but it dips in the middle. But though it dips, it is not broken; though we do not *see* the union in the middle, we *believe* it is there all the same. The Church was seen in its unity on the day of Pentecost, and it will be seen in its unity in the glory; and although we do not see it now, we nevertheless believe it most surely.

And be it remembered that the unity of the body is a great practical, formative truth; and one very weighty practical deduction from it is that the state and walk of each member affect the whole body. "If one member suffer, all the members suffer with it." A member of what? Some local assembly? Nay; but a member of the body. We must not make the body of Christ a matter of geography.

But, we may be asked, are we affected by what we do not see or know? Assuredly. Are we to limit the grand truth of the unity of the body, with all its practical consequences, to the measure of our personal knowledge and experience? Far be the thought. It is the presence of the Holy Ghost that unites the members of the body to the Head and to one another; and hence it is that the walk and ways of each affect all. Even in Israel's case, where it was not a corporate but a national unity, when Achan sinned, it was said, "Israel hath sinned;" and the whole congregation suffered a humiliating defeat on account of a sin of which they were ignorant.

It is perfectly marvelous how little the Lord's people seem to understand the glorious truth of the unity of the body, and the practical consequences flowing from it.

[24] The reader must distinguish between the Gog and Magog of Revelation xx. and those of Ezekiel xxxviii. and xxxix. The former are post-millennial; the latter, pre-millennial.